More Deaths than One

A Coroner at the turn of the Millennium

More Deaths than One

A Coroner at the turn of the Millennium

IAN SMITH

HM Senior Coroner for South and East Cumbria, retired

With a Foreword by Gina Campbell QSO

HAYLOFT PUBLISHING LTD

First published by Hayloft Publishing Ltd., 2021

A CIP catalogue record for this book is available from the British Library

ISBN 978-1-910237-64-9

Designed, printed and bound in the UK

Hayloft policy is to use papers that are natural, renewable and recyclable products and made from wood grown in sustainable forests. The logging and manufacturing processes are expected to conform to the environmental regulations of the country of origin.

Hayloft Publishing Ltd,
Cairndoon Farm, Whithorn, Newton Stewart,
Dumfries & Galloway, DG8 8NF

For every new book published, Hayloft commits to plant a tree, chosen by the author, in a new 'Wood of Words'. For this book the author has chosen an oak tree which was planted in early 2021. The woodland will capture carbon throughout its life and help to replace that used in the production and printing process.

Email: books@hayloft.eu
Tel: 01988 501100 or 07971 352473
www.hayloft.eu

For Marian

Contents

CONTENTS

Figure 1: Gina Campbell, QSO.

Foreword

"An inquest will take place shortly to determine the cause of death." However many times one has seen, read or heard this quote through varying media channels when it has seemed perfectly obvious when you examine the story what the cause of death had been. Either knocked down by a motor car, shot, stabbed or even fallen down stairs, so the cause of death is blatantly obvious. But when you read Ian Smith's stories surrounding some of his more "interesting" cases the facts behind an inquest become almost intriguing in a macabre way.

None more so than the very well recorded and dramatic way my late father Donald Campbell died on Coniston Water on 4 January 1967 whilst attempting to break the world water speed record in his very famous iconic boat called *Bluebird*. The world and his wife saw on the newsreels what happened that day as *Bluebird* almost majestically rose off the water surface at over 300mph did an enormous backward flip and the crashed back into the water in a cloud of spray taking my father with her, not to be seen again until 2001.

So when *Bluebird* was recovered along with my father's remains I was more than surprised when Ian Smith, who was the coroner covering Coniston contacted me regarding an inquest. I was surprised because I thought the cause of death was blatantly obvious. But Ian being the man he is explained in detail his duty in law; what a lovely man who treated me and my family with the utmost respect, dignity and care.

Do read this book as you will have the privilege of reading what effort and research of great interest goes into every case where "An inquest will be held shortly".

So thank you Ian, over the period we were in close contact you became not only someone I respected enormously but became a friend as well.

Gina Campbell QSO, January 2019

ONE

The Coroner's World

1 INTRODUCTION

Coroners deal with death. Day in and day out. Death comes in many forms – sudden and unexpected, harrowing and tragic, or perfectly natural and peaceful. Though never actually funny it can have its ludicrous aspects. You might expect a coroner to be morose and introverted but the truth is different. Coroners quickly become aware just how tenuous anyone's grasp on life is and spend every working day dealing with grieving families. A way of dealing with this is to appreciate the value of living and to take advantage of life while you can. A group of coroners is therefore a happy band of people giving constant subconscious thanks for the fact that they were not killed in a car crash on the way to the meeting nor died of an unanticipated heart attack on the way up the stairs.

Coroners are judges though their role is not the same as a judge in a civil or criminal court as I will explain. They have administrative duties to enable sudden deaths to be registered with the Registrar of Births & Deaths. Registration of every death is legally required and the onus to register usually lies with the deceased person's family. Coroners become judges when they hold inquests which are formal public legal hearings.

Each coroner is appointed to a specific geographical area and becomes its exclusive guardian. My area was South & East Cumbria. From 1990 when I was appointed as coroner I was responsible for the area which was previously part of Lancashire, North of the Sands, consisting of Barrow-in-Furness, Ulverston, Grange-over-Sands, and very significantly as we will see later, Coniston. In 2004 when the Kendal Coroner retired I was given additional responsibility for the area covered by South Lakeland District Council and in 2007 a huge area of the county centred on Penrith which is the Eden District Local Authority area.

You might imagine that nothing sinister or distressing would happen in this lovely rural idyll set with lakes and protected by mountains. The million shades of green in summer turn to the reds, browns, and yellows of autumn and the white of winter frosts and snows but into this land of extraordinary beauty have come events which shock and disturb. This book is the story of some of those events seen from my point of view, and the story of people caught up in those events.

It is my story too.

2 WHAT CORONERS DO

The coroner was the people's judge, the only judge the people had power
to appoint. The office had been specially instituted for the protection of
the people.   Thomas Wakley (Doctor, coroner, MP, reformer) 1795-1862

Each year approximately half a million people die in England and Wales. The numbers have been remarkably consistent for many decades. The law in England and Wales (Scotland is different) requires every death to be registered and the cause of death to be certified. The only people entitled to certify the cause of death are the doctor who attended the deceased in his or her last illness or the coroner. This procedure may change in the future but it was the system I worked under throughout my 25 years as coroner. The deaths that could not be certified by a doctor were referred to the coroner. Some deaths must always be reported to the coroner. This means sudden unexpected deaths, deaths resulting from violence, deaths in police custody or prisons. The proportion of deaths reported to coroners increased consistently over the years as care of patients became more fragmented, the use of locum doctors increased and doctors became fearful of committing themselves after the murderous activities of Harold Shipman became known.

Deaths can be reported to the coroner by anyone but most come from doctors. In many cases the discussion is enough to enable the doctor to certify the cause. In my experience this could be as simple as a doctor enquiring if 'Old-Age' was an acceptable cause of death to enter onto a medical certificate. It is, provided the person was over 80 and slipped away gradually rather than from a specific identifiable illness. As one doctor with a lovely turn of phrase put it once, his patient had "turned her face to the wall". She had indeed died of old age. I put it the other way round when I was giving my talk to trainee doctors. If an 85 year old has dropped dead on the badminton court then he has not died of old age.

The police form (Form 38) notifying me of a death usually recited that the deceased had been confirmed dead by a doctor. The form often recorded that the doctor had "pronounced life extinct". My day was improved every time I read that as I imagined a doctor kneeling respectfully over the corpse and raising his head to the waiting police officer to say "Life is extinct". Doctors do not always fulfil this role now because confirming death is not part of NHS work and doctors are not paid for the task so some refuse to attend and it is then the ambulance crews who are left to do the job. An ambulance is usually called when someone has died, although logically an ambulance is not a lot of use then.

MORE DEATHS THAN ONE

Sometimes in my early years as coroner death would be confirmed by a police surgeon. In Barrow they were local GPs who earned a little extra cash by being on call for the police. I remember one lovely GP, sadly no longer alive, telling me about one incident in the course of his work. He was called out to a probable fatality. This is more or less what he said, expletive semi-deleted: "I got there and he'd cut his wrists and his throat. I was up to my ankles in blood. I stood at the door and said he'd died and the police inspector was a bit young and keen and said he wanted me to take a closer look. I just said 'He's f......g dead' and left him to it". No doubt Form 38 recorded that the doctor had pronounced life extinct.

Registrars of Births and Deaths are the next most likely source of reports to the coroner. They may see a doctor has put that the cause of death is, say 'fractured femur', which may well be accurate but is not a natural cause of death and must therefore be reported to the coroner. Sometimes the relatives talk and facts come out. Registration is not a quick form filling exercise and in twenty or thirty minutes contradictions may emerge. Once I was brought in by the registrar when a family member said something like: "She was never the same after she fell down the stairs". Something needed to be investigated.

If the cause of death remains unknown then in most cases it is ascertained by a post mortem examination. Coroners do not carry out post mortems themselves. Most are lawyers though a few were doctors and some were doctors who also qualified as barristers. Since the law was changed in July 2013 no new appointments of doctors as coroners can be made. Pathologists carry out post mortem examinations and report their findings to the coroner. The result of the post mortem frequently shows that the cause of death was in fact natural and then the death can be registered.

Only a relatively small number of cases result in an inquest. In 2018 there were 541,627 deaths in England and Wales but only 29,094 inquests were opened (under 6%) and only 423 required juries. The majority of all deaths are still not reported to coroners as the cause is certified by the attending doctor. In recent years the percentage of deaths reported to coroners has been fairly consistent at 45% to 47%, though by 2018 the proportion had slipped back to 41%. It is possible that a system of medical examiners will be introduced though this has already been delayed several times. This would result in any death that is not referred to the coroner being looked into by an independent doctor. Currently medical examiners are to be introduced on a non-statutory basis gradually across the country.

Once a cause of death has been established the Registrar of Births and Deaths is informed and it is the registrar who issues the Death Certificate, not the doctor or coroner who reports the facts. The document a doctor issues is called the Medical Certificate of Cause of Death, but this is often referred to as the death certificate. Doctors do it all the time and so do undertakers – so did I. The Medical Certificate is issued in a sealed envelope and is supposed to reach the registrar unopened. Some families were no doubt misled by the sloppy terminology we all used and often the envelope would be open by the time it reached the registrar. It usually turned out that the family had called on their loved one's favourite Building Society en route from the hospital to the registrar in a vain attempt to liberate the deceased person's cash.

Coroners are appointed by the local authority, in my case Cumbria County Council. They are also paid by the county but not employed; they are office holders under the Crown (hence Her Majesty's Coroner). This is an unusual relationship and one which some council staff and elected councillors have to be persuaded to accept. A coroner on appointment takes a judicial oath to "well and truly serve our Sovereign Lady the Queen and her liege people and to do everything appertaining to the office of Coroner to the best of my power for the doing of right and for the good of the inhabitants of the County."

The point is that as an independent judicial officer a coroner must be free to comment on or criticise even the activities of the local authority and so a local authority cannot tell a coroner how to work or impose a budget. The key word is 'independent', and the importance of this cannot be overstated. A coroner must not bow to pressure from government, whether local or central, nor police nor any organisation. Equally, whilst being sympathetic to the family, the coroner must retain a distance from them too and ensure that the facts come out and an appropriate verdict (now called a conclusion) is recorded, even if it is one the family does not agree with. I joked that a coroner should be pleased if the epitaph chiselled on his tombstone was 'He was independent'. I did try to accommodate families. I remember soon after I became responsible for the south eastern part of Cumbria opening an inquest at Kendal on a man who had died at Kirkby Lonsdale, which is some miles away. I asked the widow if it would be helpful to find somewhere in Kirkby Lonsdale to hold the full inquest. "Good God, no. Everyone would come" was her reply. I stuck with Kendal as the venue.

I maintained a harmonious relationship with Cumbria County Council. We met regularly, discussed finances and were the second county to invite tenders from undertakers for the removal of bodies on behalf of the coroner. This has to be done when a person dies and a doctor cannot certify the cause. The body has to be taken into the custody of the coroner and removed to the mortuary as soon as possible. This prevents interference with the body and ensures that it is preserved in the best conditions possible.

The contract between the undertaker and Cumbria County Council was so successful that over a few years it saved the county hundreds of thousands of pounds. I made sure that the contract was between the undertaker and the council, not myself as I did not have the staff to deal with any potential problems. My file on the contract contained a section about an inch thick for 'complaints'. This was not as negative as it sounds – every single complaint was from undertakers who had not been awarded the contract about the undertaker who had. The savings were possible because the old system was for the police to call out each local undertaker in turn and they charged a fixed fee which was quite generous. Once competition was introduced the price was beaten down as the undertaker was likely to retain the work and carry out the funeral for the family.

Coroners were required by law to keep a register of all deaths reported, and this initially took the form of a huge leather bound index about two feet wide and eighteen inches in height. This had columns for the obvious facts – name, age, sex, address, cause of death, verdict (if it was an inquest). In 2003 my office joined the modern age and started using a computer. Our forms were now beautifully printed instead of hand written. We kept the old index as a back-up and found it a useful way of searching for some facts the computer was not designed to reveal. Young people who grew up with computers will find it impossible to understand how we worked without them and what a huge effort of will it took for my generation to adapt to them.

The following chapters are my accounts of some of the cases I was involved in, interspersed with other recollections and thoughts. Sometimes I deliberately leave out a name, even though the name was public knowledge at the time. I may record events or facts that the press did not, but I am not breaking any confidences in relation to deaths. I do however record a few meetings with politicians and Ministry of Justice staff because I found their way of working interesting. None of them ever asked that the meeting should remain confidential.

The purpose of my book is to record the world of coroners around the turn of the millennium. Surprisingly the story of the work that coroners do has not often been told. I do have the memoirs of an Australian coroner Derrick Hand published in 2004 called, perhaps a little unimaginatively, *The Coroner*. In England the Coroner for Central London, S. Ingleby Oddie published his autobiography in 1941 and Peter Hatch published a short account of his time as Coroner for Richmondshire, North Yorkshire in the 1980s under the title *On View of the Body*. This was a phrase used historically in every inquisition to record the fact that the coroner and jury had viewed the corpse. I have the book in front of me but it is devoid of any date. Peter was a little eccentric (a bow tie is often a clue) and complained to the national papers that his book had not been reviewed. At least one took up the challenge and published a review. It was not very favourable, but Peter did sell more books as a consequence thus proving the maxim that there is no such thing as bad publicity. He also persuaded the producer of the Wogan show, which was at the time a very popular TV chat show, to take him as a guest. Peter said that the new suit he felt obliged to buy for the appearance cost more than the fee he was paid-£150 if I remember correctly. He sold nearly 1,000 copies in the few days after the TV appearance. He also told me that Terry Wogan introduced himself before the programme and rather than go through a rehearsal simply said "I'll talk to you downstairs" meaning directly to the camera. That way he would get Peter's story naturally.

When I told people socially what I did I expected one of two opposite reactions: either people said it sounded fascinating or they thought it sounded awful and changed the subject. Mostly it was the first. Death remains the greatest taboo subject in our times. Sex and money are talked about but death is still off the agenda. For quarter of a century and more the main focus of my work was death and as such I was part of the world that includes undertakers and pathologists, mortuaries and post mortems, grief and trauma.

This is not a law book and some of the legal explanations are simplified, but the law referred to throughout this book is the law in force at the time which was the Coroners Act 1988. The law changed on 25 July 2013 and though I refer to the new law on occasions and the reform process that led to it, in the main I am referring to the old law because that was what I worked under. Terminology was altered in 2013 so that verdict became conclusion and a coroner's district became a coroner's area. The reform process began nearly two decades ago and is still not complete.

Quotations from my summings up are verbatim extracts from the case transcripts.

3 CORONERS IN CUMBRIA

We speak for the dead to protect the living
Motto of Ontario Coroners Service

Cumbria was a new county formed on local government reorganisation in 1974. It took in Westmorland, Cumberland, part of Lancashire and even a small part of my native, beloved Yorkshire. Initially there were four coroners who had been in post prior to reorganisation. They told me that they were interviewed by the county councillors who wanted to appoint them on probation for a year initially. This was quite illegal as it meant the coroners could be subject to pressure to act in a certain way to make sure they were reappointed the following year. They stood firm, told the county they could not behave like that and the councillors backed down.

Cyril Prickett retired in 2004 and his district was merged with mine to form Furness and South Cumbria. When Ian Morton retired from the Carlisle based North East district in 2005 his district was split between the other two coroners resulting in South and East Cumbria district and North and West. This was not a happy or straightforward process as we will see much later in the book.

When I retired in 2014 Cumbria became one jurisdiction, a solution favoured by central government after the reforms of the coroners system in 2013. The policy was based on coroners being full time professionals who were not also solicitors in private practice. In fact David Roberts and myself were both fully committed to being coroners and gave up practice even though we continued to be paid as part timers. About a year after I retired Cumbria appointed a full-time Area Coroner to assist and deputise for David Roberts. Cumbria had gone from two part-time coroners to two full-timers so the economies of scale clearly did not apply. Such is progress.

4 Availability

Coroners had to be available to attend to their duties and to deal with reports of deaths at all times meaning exactly what it said; 24 hours a day, 7 days a week. This was written into law in the Coroners Rules 1984. A deputy coroner had to be available if the coroner was ill or on holiday. This seemingly impossible requirement led to me taking phone calls in the car when this was still legal, once whilst the car was in a car wash. I discussed deaths whilst shopping for a new kitchen, whilst watching Test cricket and County cricket and whilst in the middle of the crowded concourse of Euston Station. What I had to do was explain where I was, find somewhere quieter and ring back so we could have a private conversation.

Once my wife had to come to the cricket ground where I was playing and haul me off the pitch as the police needed to talk to me. Fortunately it was a weekend when we were playing at home. Sometimes there was genuine urgency such as when permission was needed to take organs from a body for transplantation but other times there was not. The phone could and did ring in the middle of the night and if it did there was no way of settling down again peacefully. The Australian coroner, Derrick Hand puts it well in his book *The Coroner*:

When the telephone rings in the middle of the night it is usually bad news. When the telephone rings in the middle of the night and you are the State Coroner it is invariably someone else's bad news

But it is still a severe disturbance to you and anyone else in the house. I remember well a Christmas morning phone call which I assumed would be family. It was a police officer apologising for disturbing me but he thought I should know about the two pedestrians run over and killed the previous evening. I do not think we felt able to wish each other Happy Christmas.

I learned about a helicopter crash which killed four men as I was having coffee one Saturday morning with my aunt and my cousin at a lovely hotel overlooking Windermere. On another occasion I was attending a course and stayed in a rather pleasant hotel near Malvern. Dinner was ruined as a police superintendent updated me several times by phone on a young lad who had escaped from an institution where he was detained and stolen a car. When he was spotted he ran off and dived into Ulverston Canal ignoring the fact that he could not swim.

Twice the fact that I was coroner meant that I was not told about the deaths of people I knew, so I missed their funerals. They died from natural causes and the paperwork was dealt with by their doctor. This meant that their deaths were not officially reported to me and so I did not hear about them. As a friend said- you don't need to tell the coroner when someone's died. But if the death has not been reported officially to the coroner then you do.

Sometimes being coroner catches up with you when you least expect it. I went out to bat in a cricket match and found that the wicket keeper was the husband of a lady whose inquest I had conducted. As I was wearing a helmet he may not have recognised me. Or maybe he did, but we both said nothing. On another occasion I went to a concert at Kendal Leisure Centre and it was announced that there would be an extra item in the programme. This was a tribute to a schoolgirl who had died in tragic circumstances and I was to conduct her inquest. The music was composed by Roland Fudge and it was hauntingly beautiful.

Somehow these intrusions into leisure time did not rankle too much but it does emphasise the commitment not only of the coroner but of his or her partner. My wife, Marian not only took calls and suffered the disruption of lost sleep but also acted as therapist, sounding board, and emotional support, all unpaid of course. She also sewed up the green bag in which the Koran could be kept safe from non-Muslim hands. We will hear more of this later.

5 IDENTIFICATION

To me correct identification of the deceased was as fundamental as it got. You simply could not have the wrong name attached to a body. This is not always as easy as it seems. Some coroners accepted that if a person died in hospital then the wrist band was an acceptable proof of identification. I am sure that this is almost always foolproof, but I felt that I had to have visual identification if at all possible. Even this could have its problems. Elsewhere in the country apparently a group of friends, all girls went out together and were involved in a car crash. One died and the police asked the parents of the girl they suspected it was to attend. They confirmed that it was their daughter, who had long hair. Some hours later she walked in at home and wondered why her parents were screaming at her arrival. It was her long haired friend who had died.

You may ask why DNA evidence cannot be used every time to avoid the trauma of visual identification. The problem is cost, which was in the thousands of pounds but a greater problem is the delay in getting a report back from the laboratory which could be several weeks. Sometimes DNA is the only way. Five people died in a light aircraft crash in Tanzania and their bodies were brought back to Cumbria where four of them had lived. The aircraft had burned and the bodies were unrecognisable. In the event DNA positively proved the identity of four of the bodies and the fifth failed to produce sufficient tissue to produce an acceptable DNA chart. Fortunately there was a piece of medical metalwork in the body which matched his records and this was enough to confirm that it was the person we expected it to be. The pilot's body should not have been sent to Cumbria as he was from Canada but I suspect someone just wanted a problem off their hands and shipped all the bodies together. At least we were able to send him to his true home with a firm identification.

Identification from surrounding circumstances is usually correct but it does not always follow that a body on which a wallet is found is necessarily the owner of that wallet. Nor does it automatically follow that a body found in a house or flat is the body of the owner or tenant. I did not want to have a mistaken identity even once in my career so my rule was always to get the best available evidence.

Bodies coming in from abroad had to be identified here. This stemmed from the massacre at Luxor in Egypt in 1997. Six victims were British and when the bodies were returned it was discovered that some had been wrongly identified. Once a body is physically present in a coroner's district all the same rules and procedures apply as they do to someone who died here. The fact that death occurred abroad is not relevant.

If the death required an inquest I wanted the identifier to confirm the identity on oath at the opening of the inquest. Again practice across the country varied and some coroners accepted a written statement as the evidence, others had a police officer give formal evidence that the body had been identified to them. I wanted to achieve a number of things by my procedure. I wanted someone to have confirmed who the deceased was in public and on oath and therefore to be subject to the law of perjury if they were lying. I also wanted to meet some-one from the family, let them see who I was and that I was human and I also explained the reasons we were there, the procedure which would follow and how long it might take.

I invited questions and in that way established that we were in this together, that the law had certain requirements and that they could trust me. Information given by me was always as accurate as possible. I never told anyone something that was not correct just to make them feel better. To do that risks being found out. For example in one traffic inquest the deceased was a youngish man who had not been driving badly. His mother had assumed he died outright but never asked. A witness said he had found the man under a van, not the vehicle he had been driving. The witness said "I asked him how he was, but he couldn't speak, he just kind of waved at me." If someone inexperienced had been asked if the man had died outright the temptation would have been to say yes, and it would have been more of a shock to his mother to find out at that late stage that it was not true.

6 A TYPICAL DAY

Death hath ten thousand several doors for men to take their exits
John Webster: *The Duchess of Malfi* c.1610

There was no such thing as a typical day. That was the great joy of the job. There was some structure however. At 9.30 the coroner's officer (my official point of contact with the police) would come into my office and with my sec-retary we would have an informal exchange of information. By the end of that session we would all know about every death reported to either of us so far, decisions would have been taken on whether to have a post mortem or phone the doctor to see if a certificate could be issued without, and the officer knew what to tell the family. The police had a similar meeting in a different part of the building to exchange information. They called this Morning Prayers.

Around lunchtime seemed to be the time that doctors communicated with the outside world. Junior doctors at the hospital had to be cajoled or threatened by the office staff to ring me about any further deaths. They seemed to think that as the patient had died there was nothing else they could or should do, in-cluding write up a medical certificate or ring the coroner. Sometimes they did not bother to speak to the relatives either.

About the same time the pathologists would fax through the results of their post mortem examinations. From the result I could decide if an inquest was needed or if I could inform the registrar that the death was after all natural and could be registered. This was how most deaths reported to me were resolved. The officer needed to know this too in order to tell the family and make sure they knew what part they had to play in the process. This would be either to turn up at the Town Hall to open an inquest (I did not have a courtroom of my own) or else to make an appointment direct with the Registrar of Births and Deaths to complete the registration. The essence of the job was communication as it must be with many jobs. A failure to do so adequately would inevitably lead to difficulties.

Through the day GPs might ring in about a patient who had died. I was available to speak to them unless I was conducting an inquest but the initial gathering of information was usually done by my secretary. One hospital consultant, a delightful lady, refused to discuss things with anyone but me even to the point of questioning why a deputy coroner was on the other end of the phone. But the point was that she took the trouble to ring personally rather than do what many consultants did which was to get a junior doctor to make the call. I sometimes had to insist on speaking to the consultant because it became apparent that the junior had never even seen the patient.

As for a typical day I did make notes about one day when there was a body in a burned-out car. The police had given it the full works; scenes of crime officers, fire investigator, a request for a Home Office post mortem and the car taken on a low loader to headquarters for further examination. It was almost certainly a suicide. Meanwhile a lady of about 50 was found dead in bed for no obvious reason even after a post mortem and an anonymous call to the stand-in coroner's officer said that the husband was not to be trusted (backed up by specific examples) and the lady had recently inherited money. I called into the CID office to pass on the story and initially the overworked junior detectives made it clear they thought I was playing Inspector Morse. But they did do the investigation. And still the same day a couple in a mobile home, one dead one nearly so and the place fouled with vomit and excrement. A very unpleasant job to deal with but no one had thought about carbon monoxide either for their own safety or as a possible explanation.

Another 'typical' Monday many years later is recorded in my notes. Nine deaths were reported that day, some from the weekend. A young man had died falling from a cliff on the coast. It turned out he had taken drugs. Another young man fell – down the stairs this time – because he, too had taken drugs. A man and woman had died in a fireworks explosion at a wedding. An 80 year old man had been due to have an operation, tried to get his wife into a care home for respite as she had dementia, but had not been able to do so. He suffocated her. Just another Monday in sleepy South Cumbria. To be fair the days I have described were not really typical, but anything could happen on any day of the week and it often did. A retired dentist crashing his plane on his private landing strip. A 'murder' witnessed by two children which proved to be a heart attack in the street.

In the period of almost a quarter of a century that I was coroner I dealt with the deaths of sixteen and a half thousand people and of these nearly three thousand required inquests ie public hearings in court.

7 TAKING THE OATH

A coroner takes an oath at the time of taking office. A jury takes an oath to bring in a true verdict. Both of these are referred to elsewhere. Witnesses also take an oath before they give evidence. To my mind it is a simple and all-embracing formula of words. A witness swears to tell the truth, the whole truth and nothing but the truth. This can be done on a holy book or by a solemn and sincere declaration. There is no difference in importance between an oath and a declaration. In the Shafilea Ahmed case I had read up on the subject and had a Koran in English and a book which I assumed to be a Koran but it was in Arabic. The interpreter, who himself had to take an oath to interpret correctly, confirmed it was, and that this would be preferable to the English translation.

The other matter was that the Arabic version was in a green bag which my wife had sewn. This is to prevent the Koran being handed to the witness by a non-Muslim. However it proved a problem to get the process right. One assistant took the Koran out of the bag and handed it to the witness thus defeating the whole object and after this had been sorted out one witness just took hold of the bag and could not understand that he had to take out the book and swear on it, not on the green bag.

The way witnesses took the oath varied. Some police and some doctors waited for quiet in the courtroom and recited the oath solemnly. This was an effective way to establish a serious intention to tell the truth. Some police and the occasional doctor were so used to giving evidence in many courts that they rattled off the oath in a meaningless fashion. I did once or twice ask them to retake the oath as if they meant it.

The best of them all was Dr Alison Armour the Home Office pathologist. By the time she had taken the oath and then recited her many qualifications you knew that she was an expert at the top of her profession and that you could trust her and her findings and her opinions.

8 THE INQUEST

At the appointed hour arrives the coroner, for whom the jurymen are waiting and who is received with a salute of skittles from the good dry skittle-ground attached to the Sol's Arms. The coroner frequents more public-houses than any man alive. The smell of sawdust, beer, tobacco-smoke and spirits is inseparable in his vocation from death in its most awful shapes.

Bleak House, Chapter 11, Charles Dickens.

Dickens certainly had first-hand experience of coroners' courts as a young reporter. It is true that many inquests were then held in public houses though by the time I was practising it was against the law to hold an inquest on licensed premises. This was usually adhered to in the sense that coroners did not resort to public houses to hold inquests, but many town halls were licensed and this had to be skated over because otherwise the places where an inquest could be held would be more limited than they already were.

As explained inquests are only required in a small minority of cases but these have a disproportionate level of interest from the press and the public and many people may not realise that the majority of deaths reported to the coroner do not go anywhere near a court.

An inquest is required for violent or unnatural deaths, any death in custody and where the cause of death or the identity of the deceased remains unknown. Large sections of textbooks have been written on the need for an inquest so please accept this statement as the barest outline. The inquest takes the form of a formal legal hearing in public in which those with a legitimate interest in the death may participate by asking relevant questions of witnesses.

A legal case beloved of coroners explains the requirements of an inquest and the following is taken from a case we all knew as Jamieson. The words are extracted from the judgement of Lord Justice Bingham, later Lord Bingham who sadly died in 2010. The case was decided in 1995. He said:

1. An inquest is a fact-finding inquiry conducted by a coroner, with or without a jury, to establish reliable answers to four important but limited factual questions. The first of these relates to the identity of the deceased, the second to the place of death, the third to the time of death. In most cases these questions are not hard to answer but in a minority of cases the answer may be problematical. The fourth question, and that to which the evidence and enquiry are most often and most closely directed, relates to how the deceased came by his death.

2. … 'how' is to be understood as meaning 'by what means'. It is noteworthy that the task is not to ascertain how the deceased died, which might raise general and far reaching issues, but 'how the deceased came by his death', a

more limited question directed to the means by which the deceased came by his death…

3. It is not the function of a coroner or his jury to determine or appear to determine any question of criminal or civil liability, to apportion guilt or attribute blame…

14. It is the duty of the coroner as the public official responsible for the conduct of inquests, whether he is sitting with a jury or without, to ensure that the relevant facts are fully, fairly and fearlessly investigated. He is bound to recognize the acute public concern rightly aroused where deaths occur in custody. He must ensure that the relevant facts are exposed to public scrutiny, particularly if there is evidence of foul play, abuse or inhumanity. He fails in his duty if his investigation is superficial, slipshod or perfunctory.

Coroners were glad to have a clear explanation of the responsibilities and also the limitations imposed by law. Families and lawyers with unrealistic expectations of the process could be referred to the legal precedent and those who treated the inquest with less than appropriate seriousness could be told too. Some barristers tried to limit the scope of the inquest if their client did not want his her or its actions examined too closely, but it was then possible to quote back Lord Bingham's words that a coroner had to carry out a full fair and fearless investigation.

In a lecture to the Coroners' Society Lord Thomas the Lord Chief Justice described the essence of the work of a coroner as:

A compassionate, speedy and searching inquisition as to how the deceased came by his death.

He quoted from Lord Bingham in the case of Amin:

The purposes of [an inquest] are clear: to ensure so far as possible that the full facts are brought to light; that culpable and discreditable conduct is exposed and brought to public notice; that suspicion of deliberate wrongdoing (if justified) is allayed; that dangerous practices and procedures are rectified; and that those who have lost their relative may at least have the satisfaction of knowing that lessons learned from his death may save the lives of others.

Coroners do not make court orders at the end of an inquest but the process itself is a useful exercise and most importantly those affected can participate directly. Even in those rare cases which reach the civil or criminal courts the parties have little chance to participate. Usually lawyers conduct the proceedings and the aims of the processes are more circumscribed. The people involved may be witnesses but all they can do is answer questions, not make points.

Someone wins the case, someone loses. In an inquest there is a genuine search for the truth. The inquest is an enquiry. The coroner is an inquisitor rather than an umpire adjudicating between competing parties. In an inquest there are no parties. There are no winners. There are no losers.

Inquests are stand-alone cases. A coroner might well hold a number of inquests together for example where a road accident results in more than one death but a series of deaths in a particular setting like a hospital would result in a series of inquests not in a single hearing. Coroners are not supposed to be looking for patterns and should investigate individual deaths though a little creative thinking can be employed as in the series of baby deaths we will look at later.

Inquests take place in public but many coroners have no courtroom of their own. This is slowly being remedied but many local courts are being closed for economic reasons. I had no court and used Barrow Town Hall, Kendal County Offices and Barrow, Penrith and Kendal Magistrates' Courts. Kendal and Penrith are now both closed. Occasionally I had to hire alternatives including a meeting room accessed through an internet café in Penrith – not a good choice, and rooms on business parks near Kendal and Penrith. The problem with meeting rooms is that witnesses think they are in a meeting, not a court hearing and it is harder to enforce the formality a court must have and ensure that other people do not chip in when a witness is giving evidence. One December I turned up at Barrow Town Hall to hold an inquest. I found the council chamber festooned in Christmas decorations and we had to move hastily to another room and rearrange the furniture.

Police witnesses turned up dressed in formal uniform though on one occasion a detective had no jacket and was roundly told off by my officer afterwards (without being asked to do so by me), and I did ask one PC to remove his high visibility jacket complete with truncheon, taser, and radio. Apparently in Australia the New South Wales Coroner had to negotiate with the police to persuade them not to appear in his court wearing guns.

As in life, so in this book there will be much more about cases which led to inquests than those which did not. Inquests are held in public and they sometimes attract media attention. They can be very important in establishing the truth of how someone died. Sometimes a family would focus entirely on the verdict usually intent on a finding of unlawful killing, and it soon became my habit at the start of an inquest to warn against this and say that the process itself, especially the ability to ask questions in public, was more important. That chance to ask questions would probably not be available at any other time.

9 THE JURY

In 2018 a jury was required in only 423 cases nationally. The law required a jury for a death in prison, in police custody or caused by a police officer in the purported execution of his duty. Deaths reportable to a government department also require a jury. This includes deaths on railways and deaths at work. This is a simplification of the full story but in general terms these requirements applied before and after the reforms of 2013. A jury consists of seven to eleven people, not the 'twelve good men and true' who sit in criminal courts. There are procedures available if they cannot come to an unanimous verdict, but in my experience these were hardly ever needed.

According to the first edition of the coroners' textbook, *Jervis*, published in 1829, if a jury could not agree they should be kept "without meat drink or fire" until at least twelve agreed. In those days juries could be up to 23 men. Part of the coroner's job when there is a jury is to keep reminding them that they can only reach conclusions based on evidence they hear in court. They must not research on the internet or elsewhere, nor discuss the case with third parties, nor even in small groups within the jury. They must only do so when they are all present together in the jury room. In my experience juries always took their job very seriously and often asked very penetrating questions.

10 VERDICTS

One outcome of an inquest is the verdict. Verdicts are traditionally very short classifications of the circumstances of the death given at the end of an inquest by the coroner or by the jury in the rare cases where there is one. The obvious ones are accident, misadventure, natural causes, suicide, dependence on drugs, non-dependent abuse of drugs, unlawful killing. Often these were inadequate to classify what had happened and my generation of coroners compared notes at training sessions and at conferences and later on via the Coroners' Society website. We came up with better descriptions of what had happened. This was recorded on the death certificate and was more important for the future than in the immediate period after the inquest because those affected would know the more detailed events.

The registration service and the Home Office, later the Ministry of Justice were not as keen on these departures from the prescribed list as it made classification more difficult for them and they had to invent a new category of verdict, 'narrative verdict' to cover the longer forms. Some coroners perhaps overdid the exercise and wrote pages, turning a simple classification into a detailed report.

The following are a few examples that I used:

Death due to the undesired and unforeseen consequences of appropriate
   medical treatment.
Natural causes made worse by industrial disease and a hospital acquired
   infection
Died as a consequence of the use of drugs and alcohol
Died as a consequence of his own actions whilst suffering from severe
   mental illness

In the reform of 2013 verdicts were rechristened conclusions. It was said that
the public confused coroners' verdicts with the verdict of guilty or not guilty
in criminal cases. I thought that was a patronising and disrespectful view of
the intelligence of the average citizen.

TWO

The People Coroners Work With

1 MORTUARIES

We know about mortuaries from television. The large drawer pulled out so that a relative can identify a murder victim. That is not accurate. At Furness General Hospital there is a viewing room if someone has to carry out the task of identification. He or she has a choice of viewing through glass or of going in to the deceased. The room is as pleasant as possible, removing the clinical appearance of the area. In the past a relative was sometimes told that the deceased was 'not viewable' because of trauma leading to death. Now we are better trained and ensure that the relative can make a decision based on accurate information. If they want to see a photograph before deciding, then this can be done. Some people want to see the body regardless. What people wish to do after the death of someone close should be their choice based on the best information available to them. No longer is the paternal attitude of protecting people from something unpleasant acceptable.

As a parallel example I was told that the mother of one of the Hillsborough victims wanted the Liverpool kit that her child had been wearing when she died. It was duly returned washed and pressed. It was said that mother was furious as she wanted the kit back unlaundered. Grief affects people in different and unpredictable ways.

A mortuary has a function to deliver which is the storage of bodies in the appropriate ambient temperature before the post mortem examination is carried out by the pathologist. Embalming cannot be done before the post mortem. The capacity of a mortuary is limited. A hospital like Furness General can store more than 30 bodies but over the Christmas period this can be barely enough.

2 PATHOLOGISTS, MORTUARY STAFF AND POST MORTEMS

A pathologist is a doctor who specialises in the study of disease processes often by the observation and investigation of bodily samples in order to identify the disease a patient is suffering from. They are the doctors who carry out post mortems. When I was first a deputy coroner there were pathologists who regarded their prime function to be post mortems on behalf of the coroner. Examining samples from the living was incidental. By the time I retired the mind set was almost completely the opposite and many pathologists opted out of working for the coroner at all. I found that the pathologists who I worked with were highly expert, ready to share their knowledge and glad of direct human contact, as normally they did not see patients directly. One, Dr Vijay Joglekar had a real gift for communicating complex medical findings. At one inquest he was telling the son of someone who had died all about how asbestos caused mesothelioma. Dr Joglekar noticed a reaction from the son and asked "Is something wrong?" to which the son replied, "No, I could sit and listen to you all day."

Work carried out at a NHS hospital for the coroner is not NHS work. A payment is made by the county which appointed the coroner for the services provided. This means the pathologist is paid a fee, though it was not a lot of money for the responsibility involved. A separate fee was paid to the NHS Trust for use of its facilities and a daily charge for storing the body. This was known universally but unofficially as the bed and breakfast charge. Home Office accredited pathologists received substantially more than their colleagues but they were trying to establish whether there had been a murder, and recording extremely detailed findings including direction and depth of knife wounds, injuries to the body which might indicate attempts to defend an attack or alternatively tentative self-harm prior to a fatal self-inflicted wound. They were also liable to have to defend their scientific findings under cross-examination by a barrister acting for a defendant charged with murder. The barrister would have a detailed briefing from a different expert pathologist acting on behalf of the defendant. The Home Office pathologist is the elite of his or her profession.

Post mortem is Latin for 'after death'. It is an internal examination of the body to establish the cause of death and in the majority of cases it is successful in identifying the way in which the body has failed. It was the coroner's officer's job to explain that a post mortem was necessary and to answer any questions the family might ask. Sometimes there was an instinctive objection to the idea of a post mortem. George Cubiss, one of my coroner's officers, was very good at defusing hostility and reluctance to accept the fact that there was going to be a post mortem. He rarely had to tell the family that the coroner could order a post mortem whether they liked it or not, though this is legally correct. He called it an operation after death. One husband was mollified by George's explanation but as he was leaving he blurted out, "They won't cut her will they?" which I think was more deliberate self-deception than a misunderstanding of what was involved.

Carrying out a post mortem examination can be dangerous to the pathologist and the mortuary staff. The fact that the body is dead does not mean that the potential infection is. Known intravenous drug users were tested for Hepatitis B and if the test was positive then the body would be sent to a regional centre where the mortuary suite had a room with extra protection against the risk of infection.

The presence of the HIV virus would be dealt with in the same way. Suspected ebola virus would result in no post mortem being carried out at all so great is the risk. Zika virus would result in flu like symptoms to someone infected but the risk to a person of child bearing age is of passing on catastrophic damage to the development of the brain in a foetus. Tuberculosis is an infectious disease caused by bacteria. It is often in the lungs but can affect other parts of the body. It is less common than it was but cases do occur and sometimes the condition has not been diagnosed in life. This is potentially very dangerous to anyone present when the chest is opened and the presence of the disease revealed.

Pathologists spend their working lives at a distance from their living patients. They study samples and there is always the clinical team between them and the person who is ill. But this does not mean they are protected from the diseases they are investigating.

There are few secrets in the post mortem room. It used to be thought that the coroner's officer should be present while the examination was carried out, a practice I brought to an end. George Cubiss had worked in that way and become almost a mortuary assistant. We used to joke that he drew a second salary from the hospital. He was very close to the mortuary staff and came back one day in a state of high excitement. He could hardly contain himself. "Sir… Sir… He had a penguin tattooed on his penis." Something of a conversation stopper, but George had had some time to think about this and was not going to leave it at that, interesting though the information was. "Sir, do you think… that when he was aroused… it turned into an eagle?" Happily we will never know. There are secrets that even the mortuary does not uncover.

One coroner, in private, was less sympathetic than he was in public. He said he could not understand why people were so averse to post mortems. They provided certainty about the cause of death and might even uncover a medical condition which could affect other family members and which could then be treated. His point was that in a day or two the family was going to dispose of the body by burning it, cremation being the usual way of doing so. That coroner wanted no service or memorial when he died.

Post mortems may lead to second post mortems. When someone is murdered the person accused is given the right to a second, independent post mortem by a pathologist of their choice. This is on the basis that the victim might have died of something other than the stab wound/gunshot/beating that the accused knew he had inflicted. Solicitors acting for the accused felt obliged to apply for legal aid for a second post mortem just in case. It was almost invariably a waste of time and money. Some accused waived their right to a second post mortem and this could be said in their favour when they were sentenced.

Some families were outraged at the double injustice they saw. One put it like this: "You mean he killed her and now he can have her cut up again?" I found the way to keep the anger under control was to say that if they wanted justice for their loved one, and for themselves, then there was no way round this. The concept of justice is deeply rooted in us and I found that using it was a potent way of defusing the powerful sense of injustice that some people felt.

Second post mortems in my experience never showed the cause of death to be different from what the first pathologist had said. The one case where a smokescreen was put up successfully was due to the intervention of a second pathologist (instructed on behalf of a driver) months after the body had been disposed of. The first pathologist thought that the deceased had died because a reversing vehicle had knocked him over. The second suggested that he might have had a heart attack and fallen under the wheels. In a criminal trial the prosecution have to prove guilt beyond any reasonable doubt. The jury has to be sure that the driver was guilty. All the defence have to do is to knock down the level of certainty a little and persuade the jury that the deceased might just possibly have had a heart attack and in this case they apparently did so, resulting in the acquittal of the driver.

3 MY CORONER'S OFFICERS

A coroner needs officers to carry out all manner of tasks. The coroner must stay in touch with families, undertakers, the local authority, witnesses and many others but may have to sit in court one day and make pronouncements about what has happened. The coroner must therefore not get too close and must maintain independence. Coroners' officers therefore do much of the day to day contact with these people. Traditionally the officer was a serving police officer though this began to change in the 1990s. Civilian staff employed by the police authority could be employed on lower wages and then police began to ask why they were the ones paying at all and the cost was passed to the local authority. My own officers were always paid for by the police and the first few were police officers. Without getting too personal they varied considerably.

Two of the best had not been the ideal as uniformed constables. I think the police thought they would hand over what they perceived as a problem to me. In both cases they shed the blue tunic and embraced the fact they were now responsible to one boss who they would see day in and day out. They knew their role was special and they rose to their task. A couple of other officers occasionally thought they were the coroner and another got rather too emotionally involved. Overall though they did a splendid job often working beyond their paid hours and dealing with bereaved families every day. I will not name individuals but I count several as my friends and in their demanding role they showed humanity and empathy, understanding and intelligence and a sense of humour to keep us all sane when the grim reality of death was what we were constantly dealing with.

I had an officer in Barrow and another, part-time, in Kendal. It was useful for me to take advantage of their local knowledge and of course they could visit bereaved people and witnesses. Since my retirement the officers are centralised with the coroner and their contact with families is mainly by telephone.

4 THE POLICE

Any coroner has a daily relationship with the police. They will report many of the deaths to the coroner, especially the ones that have occurred overnight and always the suspicious ones. It is true that many people who think their loved one has died will ring the ambulance service, and indeed many people are confirmed dead by that service but they in turn will contact the police. A coroner's day often starts with a pile of forms notifying the deaths the police have dealt with since the previous day. Nowadays this pile may be electronic.

When I left my legal practice in 1995 I had to find accommodation. I was quickly offered an office in the police station at Barrow. I decided to see what the Home Office thought about this as it was not a normal arrangement. After about six weeks they replied setting out the pros and cons and telling me it was my decision. This was not helpful so I spoke to the secretary of the Coroners' Society, the late John Burton. He said it was a good idea and when I asked his view on apparent lack of independence he said that it was the police who hand over the reports, they investigate, the coroner's officer is a policeman so what is wrong with a base in the station. His practical and speedy advice was what I needed and I was soon installed in the police station at Barrow, with my own direct phone and fax line and a lock on the office door. It was in many ways a happy arrangement and a happy place to work.

Police valued the ability to drop in for a chat about particular investigations and I found them to be committed to their work, committed to achieving justice and willing to work beyond their basic hours without complaining. No conflict of interest happened and I was insulated from the office politics that many legal firms suffer from. In the first few years there was even a canteen though that was shut down as an economy measure later.

I was privileged to work in the police station for nearly twenty years and I found the police service generally to be dedicated and hard working. Many times I saw an officer leave lunch half eaten on the common room table to answer an emergency call. One specific happy memory I have is from 2005 when twenty or more of us stood in the common room watching England v Australia at the Oval. We could not bear to sit as Kevin Pietersen decided the best way to ensure a draw and thus win the Ashes series was to smash the ball to all parts. We alternately groaned and stood in awe as his tactics worked and he scored 158. A shared experience which stays in the memory.

The police usually come into the media spotlight when they are being criticised. The public will not be aware of some of the dreadful sights, smells and situations they deal with. The body found weeks after death; the death of someone who has chosen an express train as the means of death. On one occasion an officer was a few feet away from the deceased as this happened. The call handlers who may have someone on the phone for many minutes before death. Even witnessing the grief of someone who has just lost a loved one can be traumatic. I acknowledge the police service with great humility and respect. We should all be aware of the work they do apart from detecting crime.

5 LAWYERS

Anyone with a genuine interest in a death, most obviously a close relative of the deceased, but also someone who may have caused or contributed to the death may be represented at the inquest by a lawyer. There are others too, as listed in the Coroners and Justice Act 2009. The lawyer may be a barrister or solicitor or a specially qualified legal executive.

Their quality varied so considerably in my experience that it is worth recording. There is a fundamental difference between a civil dispute or a criminal prosecution on the one hand and an inquest on the other. The first two are contests between competing parties who are trying to win. They are adversarial. Inquests are a search for the truth ending with findings of fact. They are inquisitorial. Lawyers spend most of their court time on the first category of case and some find it hard to adjust to the second. Very occasionally a lawyer has announced at the start of the inquest that they want a certain verdict or even "we are only interested in the verdict of…" This is the wrong approach as verdicts only become an issue after the evidence has been heard and as I usually said to families at the start, the most important part of the inquest is the process itself, in which questions can be put to witnesses by the family (and others) directly or through a lawyer.

On one occasion in an inquest in Barrow Town Hall I finished asking my questions of a witness and turned to the two lawyers who were sitting to my left hand side. Martyn Tonge was fast asleep and received a fierce dig in the ribs from his fellow lawyer. He did not have any questions. You may wonder what the client thought and how he dealt with Martyn's bill. The truth is that Martyn was far too good a man to be a solicitor, and probably had no intention of submitting a bill. He seemed to know everyone in Barrow (and several generations back into their ancestry). He once turned up at Barrow Magistrates' Court wearing one brown shoe and one black one. When someone pointed this out he said "Aye, I think I've got another pair like that at home." I went to his funeral and the vicar started with the fact that Martyn had attended more funerals than anyone else he knew and at least he wasn't late for his own funeral. You could not be angry with Martyn, even if he was asleep in an inquest.

Lawyers love writing things down. Sometimes they bring a junior colleague to do this for them. What they do with their pages of notes is unclear, but my guess is that they file them and never look at them again. One barrister asked his questions with a small laptop perched in front of him. After each answer from the witness there was a frantic drumming on the keyboard lasting about three seconds. I had to stop myself from asking him if any judge had ever told him how profoundly irritating this was. Maybe it was just a ploy to gain a few seconds to think of the next question.

Some lawyers clearly came with a list of prepared questions but lacked the mental dexterity to depart from them either to follow up a new line of enquiry prompted by an unexpected answer or to skip over matters that were already clear. One TV interviewer – it was either Terry Wogan or Michael Parkinson, I think – was asked if he had any advice for younger aspirants to his profession. The reply was "Listen to the answers." This is very good advice to lawyers. Those at the top of their profession knew what they wanted to come out in evidence, needed no prescribed rigid list of questions and had a conversation with the witness. Perhaps the best I saw in court was Nicholas Hilliard QC, in the Grayrigg inquest. He never needed to raise his voice or browbeat a witness but always seemed to extract what he wanted. He was simply charming to each witness. My assistant in that inquest, Tony Foy and I looked out for the telltale phrase "Now, Mr…, I wonder if you can help me with this…" The witness had become his friend and was only too eager to tell him anything he wanted to know.

Mr Hilliard was soon afterwards appointed as Common Sergeant of London, an ancient legal post making him the senior judge at the Old Bailey. During the Grayrigg inquest the lawyers went for dinner together. One of them even asked me if I wanted to go with them, an invitation I had to refuse since a coroner or any judge in any case must stand back from those involved. To do otherwise would risk being accused of bias, whether actual or apparent. This was an issue I knew about only too well after accusations by the Ahmed family. But I do wish I could have gone to the dinner. I am sure the conversation would have been sparkling.

In one case at Barrow there were several interested persons and three of them had lawyers. A sociologist would have been interested in the dynamics between them. The names have been changed. To my left was Mr Goodman a dapper 60ish barrister of the old school. Beautifully tailored with silk tie and matching handkerchief in his top pocket. To my right Ms. Cross, much younger, more homely in dress. Fortunately between them sat a young male and, in this context, neutral solicitor. Whether the outer pair had exchanged views outside court I do not know, but they clearly did not like each other from the start. Mr Goodman soon dropped in a comment whilst looking at me pleasantly "Those of us with more experience at inquests..." which roused Ms. Cross to interrupt to tell him not to denigrate her in front of the jury. There really is nothing quite like the theatre of a courtroom.

6 THE PRESS

Though the purpose of an inquest is to establish facts, including how the deceased person came by his/her death it is not always possible to work out what happened. The newspapers love this because they can use the word 'mystery' on the news placards and in the headlines. Examples in my experience include a man whose car had broken down on the M6 northbound at night but who was walking on the southbound carriageway and was hit by at least two vehicles. It could have been accidental or deliberate on his part.

Another man was found with his head and upper body in a drain with the cover removed. Medically he died of asphyxia not head injuries. Work had previously been done on the drain to clear it and the man may have fallen in or may have been trying to see for himself if more clearance needed to be done. Either way it was an accident but the exact circumstances were unclear.

And Jan Jenco. What on earth was he doing driving south on the northbound carriageway of the M6? He travelled six or seven miles and reached speeds of 70 mph. There was evidence he had been emotionally unstable earlier in the day. There was no evidence of alcohol or drugs in his system nor of a diabetic or similar medical problem to make him behave erratically and I said in my summing up that he might have been trying to kill himself (though he swerved out of the path of oncoming vehicles at least twice) or he might have been playing some totally idiotic game. Inevitably I recorded an Open Verdict.

Looking through my cuttings book I see that I am not mistaken. The word 'mystery' does indeed crop up in headlines over and over. Occasionally an imaginative sub-editor uses 'riddle' instead. I got to know the local reporters and found most of them fair and reasonably accurate most of the time. It was usually headlines that were a problem and if I said so the next time I saw the reporter the answer was always that it was not their doing and the headline was written by a sub- editor.

The worst inaccuracy I remember was on local radio. After a car accident in which three people died the BBC reporter got two of the names wrong and said the car had gone over a two metre high wall (it was two feet). She is now an international correspondent on national BBC. Radio Cumbria generally gave a very fair report of any inquest they covered. Martin Lewes, one of their presenters, was a great fan of the inquest process, because it was public and witnesses were liable to be questioned and challenged. It was a female reporter who incensed Charlie Johnson one day by ringing and asking in a very jaunty fashion "Have you got any deaths for us?" He told her that any deaths we were dealing with were not for them. It brought to mind the mediaeval call in plague years of bring out your dead. Charlie was not amused.

By law the media can print or broadcast a fair and accurate report of any legal proceedings. This includes inquests. The problem is that an inquest which lasted say four hours may be reported in a few column inches which can be read in thirty seconds, and even a direct quotation from a witness may be misleading if only part of what he or she said is recorded.

The media could be difficult. They had my office number and would often ask me what I was going to do in a particular inquest. If I had been foolish enough to tell them in advance it would have meant they did not need to travel to listen to the actual inquest and I had to disappoint them. The evidence that comes out is not always what you expect. The regional and national media on occasions seemed affronted when I declined their invitation to be interviewed on camera, something no judge should do.

Coroners and judges answer to courts which are superior to theirs as I did in the Shafilea Ahmed judicial review. We do not answer directly to the media. I remember many years previously a coroner telling a training session how he had taken part in an interview on TV. First there had been an exchange of question and answer but then the interviewer was recorded asking questions alone and these slightly different questions would no doubt be edited into the broadcast version as if they were what the interviewee was answering. The whole slant of the interview can be changed by a clever journalist. The journalist also has complete control over how much of what you say is broadcast. A direct answer to a question may be followed by an explanation or qualification. The broadcaster can edit this out leaving a short straight answer which may not tell the full story as the interviewee intended. For these reasons it is best in my view to avoid direct engagement with the media. If you do speak and start your answer by saying it is off the record then you would expect any journalist to respect that.

I had a number of disagreements with the local newspaper, though overall the relationship between us was good. On one occasion I made an order that the name of a witness under the age of eighteen should not be published. This is very clearly within the coroner's powers under the Children and Young Persons Act 1933. The reporter rang more or less as I got back to my office from the inquest and told me I could not do this. I pointed out the section of the Act of Parliament but she said that I had no such power. In the end we just had to disagree and fortunately she did not test the issue by ignoring me.

I made a similar order in a different case and found the story was the front page lead and that the child had not been named. But also on the front page was a separate story, making no mention of the inquest, in which the minor was named with a photograph. If the second item had appeared on its own in a different issue then I could not have complained, but to me this was a blatant attempt to ignore my order so I reported the case to the Attorney General. Unfortunately they did not act with any sense of urgency and took many weeks before they passed the investigation to the local police, who promptly arrested the editor. Too long had expired, the damage had been done but a point had been made.

Another problem was over the use of quotation marks. The paper published a headline with words in quotation marks attributed to me. They were not words I had actually used and I had the transcript to prove this. The editor did try to talk her way out of the error by saying that it gave the headline more emphasis if quotes were used. This may be true but she knew she was in the wrong and I confirmed in writing that I would not accept anything other than a direct quotation being put in quotation marks. It was an abuse of the basic rules of grammar anyway. It did not happen again.

The press can manipulate what we think and claim a spurious authority for their statements. When they begin "It is thought that…" they do not tell us who was doing the thinking; perhaps the reporter? They also use "a source close to the coroner said…" And there were occasions when a reporter would ring my officer or assistant and have an informal chat then report that "A spokesman for the coroner said…" We learned our lessons and tried to remember to keep everything off the record. Even then it was once reported "The coroner is known privately to be furious about…" I cannot remember now what it was. I think I was mildly annoyed. As for the report, I was privately furious.

THREE

Lady in the Lake

The story of Carol Ann Park and her violent death stretches across many decades. My part in it started on Sunday 10 August 1997 when a few members of the Kendal branch of the British Sub Aqua Club went for a dive off Bailiff Wood on the east side of Coniston Water. John Walsh told me at the inquest that he had dived there perhaps a hundred times but he and his buddy, David Mason, went beyond the underwater cliff edge that they normally stuck to and went further into the lake. At a depth of nearly 25 metres and between 150 and 200 metres from the lake shore they came across a bag with several ropes or cords on it. They tried to loosen them to investigate further but, perhaps fortunately, were unable to do so. The bag was heavy and they could not move it so they carefully noted its position and went back on Wednesday 13 August with lifting equipment and brought the bag to the shore. Mr Walsh described the bag as "a dark coloured canvas type kit bag, tied at one end with a dark cord tied round its middle". He also noticed that there was what appeared to be lead piping hammered flat attached to it by another cord. David Mason cut the drawstring and about twelve inches along the bag, found a second bag – a black plastic bin liner which he also cut through. Very sensibly the next action of these two men was to ring the police.

The contents of the bag were fairly obviously human remains and the police arranged their removal to the mortuary. Such objects do not end up on the bed of Coniston Water by accident so levels of suspicion were high. No time was wasted and a post mortem was carried out the following morning by Dr Edmund Tapp. He is a Home Office accredited forensic pathologist, one of the elite members of his profession. He confirmed that the body was wrapped in a canvas like material. This later proved to be a pinafore dress that had been sewn to turn it into a bag and as well as the black plastic bag there were remains of what had probably been a rucksack. The body was tied by several pieces of rope and string in a foetal position. The body was wearing a nightdress and two labels could still be read: 'Halwin' and 'Nylon is Flammable'.

Dr Tapp noted "A weight which had been separated from the body by PC Baldwin consisted of flattened lead piping which had been folded over several times to form a mass 30cms (a foot) in length and 6,400g (28lbs) in weight. Looped through a fold in the pipe was a three ply blue plastic rope."

Figure 2: Carol Park

Later, in his evidence at the inquest, he said the weight was on the outside of the bundle but attached and not surprisingly he thought its purpose was to weight the body down.

Dr Tapp suggested there was some evidence of bleeding to the inner right side of the skull due to a prominent brown discolouration which was not present on the left side. He said that the facial bones were fractured into several fragments and some of these contained one or more teeth. There was a fresh fracture to the fifth metacarpal bone of the left hand and the hamate bone from the left wrist was also fractured. His initial conclusion was that death was due to facial injuries caused by blows with a heavy sharp object, though in his final report he said that the cause of death should be regarded as unascertained.

He said that the position in which the body had been tied up would require the body to be extremely flexible when this was carried out and therefore the body was tied up very shortly after death during the two to four hours which would normally elapse before rigor mortis set in. He added that it was unlikely the body would have been tied up after rigor mortis had passed off three or four days later, since by that time putrefaction would be well established – instead there had been formation of a substance called adipocere, a chemical reaction particularly prone to developing in moist conditions leading to formation of fatty acids which kill bacteria in the tissue and thus prevent putrefaction.

Dr Tapp referred to extensive shattering of the upper jaw and said "the injuries are the result of several deliberate impacts on the central part of the face. These could be in the form of blows with a heavy blunt object or by kicks, but the appearance of the teeth and the anterior border of the zygoma suggests strongly that the implement also had a sharp edge on it and that the central part of the face was destroyed by at least two blows in a downward direction." The pathologist thought that the two injuries to the left hand and wrist were "totally consistent with them being sustained during a defensive act such as the deceased putting her hands up to her face to ward off blows."

At this time the body had not been identified. The police tried to match descriptions of missing persons with the appearance of the body and it did not take long for a potential match with Carol Park to emerge even though it was more than twenty years since she was last known to be alive. Carol's dental records, fortunately, still existed and the damaged jaw was reconstructed and the two matched. Whilst all this was happening, Gordon Park, who had been Carol's husband but was now remarried, was on holiday in France and on his return to this country he was arrested and on 25 August 1997 charged with the murder of his first wife Carol Ann Park.

At this point it is necessary to explain the process of registering a death when a murder charge is pending. Firstly, I had to open an inquest which was done on the 22 September 1997 at which evidence was given to prove the identity of the body. Subject to the right of the accused person to have a second post mortem, the body is then released for burial or cremation and the Registrar of Births and Deaths is notified so that the death can be registered. The inquest is adjourned indefinitely until the murder trial is over and although there is a discretion to reconvene the inquest this is not often done. The facts emerge in the course of the criminal trial and the law does not allow the inquest to come to any conclusion that conflicts with the outcome of the trial.

Because of the long gap between Carol's disappearance and the finding of her body, I had to be extremely careful about how I worded the information leading to the registration of her death. If I had put that she was a school teacher and that her usual address was the house in Leece where she and Gordon Park had lived together, then that was a potentially prejudicial finding that that was when she was murdered. In theory she could have been living an entirely different life for several years and so I chose to complete the documentation by recording:

Last known occupation – School Teacher.
Last known address – Bluestones, Leece, Ulverston, Cumbria.
Cause of Death – As yet unascertained.
Marital condition – not known.

This was accurate but it did not please the Office for National Statistics who supervise the registration of births, marriages, and deaths. They prefer certainty and wanted me to change the wording so that it would record that Carol was a school teacher and did live at that address. I simply had to stand my ground. There was also the complication that Gordon had gone through a formal process of divorce from Carol. This is what I wrote to the Office of National Statistics by way of explanation:

This certificate was worded with extreme caution and after considerable thought because of the extremely unusual circumstances.

As you are probably now aware the husband of Mrs Park has been charged with her murder and the prosecution case is that he murdered her, disposed of the body and some years later went through a bogus form of divorce when he in fact knew that his wife was already dead.

His case, I understand, is that his wife walked out on him and never contacted him again and that he therefore validly divorced her for that reason.

If on the Coroner's Certificate I were to record that her last address was Leece and that her last occupation was school teacher then that is going to be recorded on a death certificate which is available to anyone in the world, including, of course, the press and will therefore be capable of use by them as showing that Mrs Park did die at the time when her husband says she simply walked out on him and this could also be used by the defence to claim prejudice and say that a fair trial is no longer available to Mr Park.

I am happy to delete the words "as yet" from the cause of death and have done so but because of the unusual circumstances of the case, the pending murder trial and the wish to ensure that no one can read into the death certificate more than is actually intended I do not feel it appropriate to alter the other three items i.e. the two in box 6 (Occupation and Address) and the marital condition of the deceased.

I appreciate that this does not fall in line with your preferred practice but the problems involved if I accept the other alterations you would prefer far outweigh the administrative inconvenience caused by me leaving the rest of the certificate unaltered.

Since I was unwilling to back down, apart from removal of the two words "as yet", the Registrar simply had to accept the way that I had completed my certificate and register the death using my wording.

Having released the body for cremation and enabled the death to be registered, my part in the process appeared to be over. Then on the 6 January 1998 the Crown Prosecution Service filed and served Notice of Discontinuance which means that they had decided not to pursue the charge of murder and so Gordon Park was now a completely free man, discharged from any bail conditions he might have been under.

Much more significantly from my point of view was the fact that since there was now no pending criminal trial I would have to conduct a full inquest and there was a danger that this could turn into a murder trial under a different title. I had to ensure that it did not. I had to learn much more about Carol's history and I have to say that her story is not a very happy one.

Carol was born in 1945 to a married woman whose husband was away on active service abroad. She was immediately given up for adoption and her adoptive parents were Mr and Mrs Price who had two children of their own, one older than Carol and one younger. Carol did sufficiently well at school to be going to college but unfortunately her father died at that time and so instead of going away she took up employment at Barrow-in-Furness Town Hall. During this time, she started a relationship with Gordon Park but went two years later to a Teacher Training College and, upon qualification, she and Gordon married in 1967.

In April 1969 Carol's younger sister Christine was murdered at the tender age of seventeen by her partner, leaving a twelve month old daughter, Vanessa, who in due course was adopted by Carol and Gordon. In other words Carol, herself adopted, was now adopting her dead sister's child. Carol and Gordon had two children, one boy and one girl, and Gordon also changed career and qualified as a teacher.

Carol had an affair with a local man lasting many months and not long after this ended she started another relationship with someone she met at an Open University summer school. This time Carol left Gordon apparently for good and set up home in the North East. A bitter battle was fought over the children, resulting in Gordon being awarded custody. Ultimately, Carol could not bear the loss of her children and she returned to the family home in Leece in July 1975. Gordon also terminated a relationship at this time. The following year cannot have been an easy one.

Carol worked at a school locally and term ended on 16 July 1976. A family trip to Blackpool was planned for the following day. Blackpool was a strange destination because Gordon Park hated the place and what it stood for. In the event, Carol did not go. The children were told that she was ill and when they came home there was no sign of her.

Gordon did not hide the fact that Carol was missing from friends and neigh-bours but did not report her disappearance to the police until the end of the summer holiday, 4 September 1976, and he did so by instructing solicitors on his behalf. At the time the police found no trace of Carol. She had not contacted any friends or family, had not withdrawn money from her bank, all of which I took into account later when I conducted the inquest. Carol had left her rings behind which she had never done in the past when she had left. Gordon went through the process of divorce and five years to the day after Carol's disappear-ance he remarried, though that relationship was short lived and extremely dif-ficult not least to the children involved. Gordon married for the third time in 1993.

Let us now return to the inquest that I was legally obliged to hold in order to provide the answer to four specific questions laid down by statute – who was the deceased and how, when, and where did she come by her death. The identity, though not straightforward, had been established by dental records, together with circumstantial evidence, i.e. the nightie that the body had on when discovered matching a nightie that Carol certainly had and the pinafore dress which had been turned into a bag, matching exactly a pinafore dress which Carol had worn and indeed there were photographs of her wearing it.

As to the question of how she died, I was left in no doubt that she had been killed. The concealment of the body and the injuries to the face which could be seen even 20 years later left little doubt. A pathologist, Dr Lawler, who had been instructed by Gordon Park in connection with the defence suggested she could, in theory, have died from natural causes or suicide, or an accident, and that it was possible the facial injuries had been inflicted after death. He did ac-cept that, on the balance of probabilities, Dr Tapp's interpretation of events might be correct but he would not go that far himself. Dr Tapp had said he could not conceive of the injuries being accidental and he thought it more likely the injuries had occurred shortly prior to death, though even he would not go so far as to say that they were definitely the cause of death. Dr Tapp also said in his report that the condition of the body was consistent with having died in 1976.

Gordon Park gave evidence and did not decline to answer questions. He had a right not to answer "any question tending to incriminate himself". There is no verbatim transcript but he said he had been to Blackpool with the children and Carol was gone when they came home.

In my summing up at the end of the inquest I said that I was totally satisfied beyond any reasonable doubt that Carol Ann Park was unlawfully killed and I said that I was satisfied the fractures seen in her little finger and in her wrist were:

> the result of the attack from which she was forlornly trying to defend herself.

That still left two questions of when and where she was killed and I came to the conclusion that she was killed on or about 17 July 1976 and I said:

> I find it inconceivable that this lady would have gone away, decided to live another life, and just abandoned her children completely. She would have taken money out of her account and so on. I think that the evidence points very firmly to the fact that she died very shortly after she was last seen. I am not saying nor inferring who did that and I don't want anybody to go out of here and say or report that I have inferred who did that because we do not know.

An inquest being a fact finding exercise and most certainly not a trial, it is not allowed to come to any conclusions which appear to determine criminal responsibility or indeed civil liability. I was at pains to ensure that Gordon Park could not say that I had made it so obvious what I thought that everybody knew I was saying he had done it. As for the final question of where Carol Park died, I simply said I did not know because there was no evidence to say where she died. There was no evidence that she died at Bluestones, Leece. After the body was found in 1997 the police had taken possession of the property which had been sold to someone else in the meantime and gone over it forensically and found not a single trace, for example, a blood spot, that might have even suggested that Carol died there.

The murder was always referred to as 'The Lady in the Lake' and indeed I have used that heading for this chapter but at the end of the inquest I said this:

> This case, this killing, has attracted the name throughout the media of 'The Lady in the Lake' and I have to say that gives a certain romanticism almost to what is most certainly not in any sense romantic. This lady was killed, brutally and horribly, her body was to some extent mutilated, thrown into Coniston and I can see why the media have made of it what they have but I ask them not to lose sight of the fact that this was an extremely vicious and an extremely brutal murder of this woman.

At the very end I said something that I had obviously thought of but had not definitely decided to say. I have never written out my summings up word for word in advance but always, with detailed notes and headings in front of me, let the actual words come naturally and this is how I ended the summing up:

> As regards who did it I hope that if that person is still alive, which 20 odd

years later they may not be, if that person is still alive then I hope they have a conscience and I hope that their conscience is troubling them.

People have asked me if when I said that I was staring Gordon Park in the face. I was not. I also note, as I write this 20 years later, that I did not refer to 'he' or 'him' or 'the man' though I think I could easily have done so and explained that this was not something that I thought for one moment a woman could have done.

That closed the inquest but it did not close the case. In January 2004 Gordon Park was once again charged with murdering his wife and a year later he was found guilty, sentenced to life imprisonment with a recommendation that he serve at least fifteen years and his appeal against sentence was rejected.

Figure 3: Gordon Park

On 25 January 2010 Gordon Park was found unconscious in his prison cell and pronounced dead on his 66th birthday. Even then the case was not closed. Some of Gordon's family referred the case to the Criminal Cases Review Commission.

In the course of the discussions they had with me, months after I retired, I formed the view that they thought the decision should be overturned. On 1st May 2020 the Court of Appeal rejected the application and said the conviction was safe. This should end the legal process, nearly 44 years after Carol's disappearance.

The inquest was held in Barrow Town Hall on 7 September 1998. From my office I could look across to the Town Hall and see a battery of TV cameras and newsmen hovering outside and waiting for pictures. I steeled myself and walked with my clerk and good friend Charlie Johnson straight towards them and I think I rather floored them by saying, "Good morning, gentlemen" as I walked past.

Most people who have no wish to be in the media spotlight apparently pretend they are not there. Just as nervous must have been Gordon Park because his solicitor, Barbara Forrester, now a Circuit Judge, told me before the event that she had a way of getting her client into the Town Hall without being filmed or photographed. In the event this was not so. On TV a large car draws up somewhat hastily outside the Town Hall entrance opposite to the one I used,

Figure 4: My colleague and friend, Charlie Johnson (left) and I arrive at the inquest into Carol Park's death at Barrow Town Hall

three men get out – Gordon Park and one 'attendant' on either shoulder and the effect was to make him look extremely guilty. As we shall see, there are many parallels (including this one) with the case of Shafilea Ahmed about whom we will hear more later.

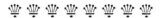

Carol's memory was represented at the inquest by lawyers acting for the children but more directly by her brother Ivor Price who appeared himself and behaved with great dignity and even addressed me (quite properly but rather archaically) as 'Mr Coroner'. I suspect he had his own view of who was responsible but made no accusations. Sadly nearly ten years later I was to conduct an inquest into Ivor Price's death due to his past contact with asbestos. Ivor had two sisters murdered but even more shocking is the thought that Vanessa had two mothers murdered.

Whilst researching for my book I came across a short piece in the *North-West Evening Mail* which records such a tragic coincidence that it should be retold here. Ivor Price says that in 1955 "Donald Campbell came to our house, on the edge of Roose, with the politician Edward du Cann who knew my father. They came to see us on a fleeting visit. I remember Donald Campbell picking up Carol in his arms. It is strange to think that they both died in that lake."

I saw enough of Ivor Price to trust what he said and to know he would not invent something like this for effect. It means that the people in two of my highest profile inquests met and that in each case they were recovered from Coniston and in each case decades elapsed between their death and the finding of the body. I find this truly remarkable and even a little shocking.

FOUR

My Own Story

I wrote the book because we're all gonna die.
Jack Kerouac: *On the Road*

I was born in 1949 in Doncaster, South Yorkshire. My mother was from Rochdale, Lancashire, and my father from Bentley, near Doncaster. They had met on holiday in Blackpool. They married in 1940 when Dad was about to be posted to Egypt as a mechanic in the RAF on Spitfire engines. Mum said "I didn't know if I'd ever see him again." In fact it was three years before she did. After the war Dad became a junior school teacher by emergency post-war training. This was, I think, just over a year of intensive training rather than the three years normally allowed to train a teacher.

Mum was a victim of the discrimination against girls in the twenties and thirties. She had a scholarship to go to Grammar School in Rochdale but had to go to work instead as the family needed the income. When my brother David arrived in 1946 she became a full time mother. I always say that any intelligence I inherited was mainly from my mother. She helped us through school, testing us on French or Latin vocabulary and showing me how to write my first history essay. She once read *Crime and Punishment* for me and provided me with a daily summary.

I was brought up with a strong Methodist work ethic and a liking for sport. At the end of the lower sixth at Percy Jackson Grammar School I was doing well at Latin, French and German, but it dawned on me that I would never be good enough to be a translator at the United Nations and that all you can do with three languages is teach. I had known for years that I did not want to do that so I needed a plan. In those days the only options I recall to start afresh were sociology (which had the same credibility then as media studies has to some people today) or law, which was much more worthy and did interest me.

I talked to a former pupil of Percy Jackson Grammar School, John Lee, who had been to University College London and enjoyed it so I applied there and was accepted. In those days universities put no pressure on students they wanted so all I had to do was get two A Level passes and I was in. For my self-respect I did better than that. The Grammar School opened in 1939 and the pupils were largely from working class families, many of the fathers being miners. Many pupils went on to university or training colleges at a time when this was unusual. Several were accepted by Oxford and Cambridge often on miners' scholarships. It was a highly effective means of social mobility.

University College London, founded in 1826, was a happy choice. It was predominantly Northern, state school and non-conformist as opposed to King's College, which was establishment and Church of England. In the cloisters of University College were the mortal remains of Jeremy Bentham, its spiritual founder. They were dressed in his clothes and securely contained in a glass fronted cabinet. His head was an effigy but the real thing was reputedly in a box within the larger display case. In the early years after his death in 1832 he was solemnly placed into his old seat when meetings of the college governing body were held. The minutes apparently recorded that he was present but not voting.

I had no family connections with the law but I was taken in hand by Bernard Hargrove QC, who lectured us in family law and criminal law. When I told him that I was thinking of becoming a factory inspector he said something like "Bloody hell Ian, we don't want people like you poking around in the back streets of Finchley. Get yourself properly qualified", by which he meant as a barrister or solicitor. He helped me to do so by introducing me to his own solicitor George Pazzi Axworthy at Gamlens in Lincoln's Inn where I completed my articles on £500 a year (which I was surprised to find from my first pay packet meant £9.62 per week not £10 per week). If wages were ever mentioned Mr Axworthy would remind me and my fellow articled clerks how lucky we were. He had had to pay his principal a premium for the privilege of learning legal practice and there was an iniquitous stamp duty on the deed called Articles of Clerkship. I recall he said it was several hundred pounds. I completed my articles in 1973 and stayed with the firm but at their branch office near Heathrow Airport. When I qualified my salary rocketed to £1,500 a year.

By the time I was a coroner the Factory Inspector had become a Health & Safety Inspector and the organisation seemed to be more interested in prosecuting people for breaking regulations. This was particularly evident in the case of David Thompson. He was renovating his own home, had put scaffolding up around it and was unfortunately found dead at the foot of the scaffolding. The Health and Safety Executive were called and attended but as soon as they realised it was Mr Thompson's own property they were much less interested because there was no one to prosecute. They had to prepare a report for me but this was very short and not very helpful.

At the inquest itself, the Inspector gave his evidence and then simply left the court room. The evidence continued and with the help of photographs and witnesses it became apparent what had really happened. At the top of the scaffolding one of the boards was clearly not designed for standing on but was simply a thin piece of wood on which Mr Thompson put his tools. He had obviously stepped on it, forgetfully, and fallen as a consequence. The two halves of the board and the fracture in the middle were clearly visible in one of the photographs but all of this became apparent only after the HSE Inspector had left.

The other strand in my own story is just as important and happened when I was thirteen. My parents handed my brother and me over to my Aunty Hazel and Uncle Bill for a few days. They lived in Lytham St. Annes but took us to the Lake District with our cousin Josephine. We went north in their soft-top Morris Minor, cream with a red roof. Aunty Hazel said that in the back we would have to wrap up warm with the roof down. At thirteen of course you know better than adults and I said I would be warm enough. Within a few minutes and at about thirty miles an hour I was getting as low as I could and pulling the bedspread which Aunty Hazel had brought tight around me. We stayed at what was then the Post Office in Grasmere and visited Tarn Hows, Keswick and Lakeside on Windermere. Apart from being able to spot a number of unfamiliar railway engines, I was obviously smitten with the Lake District and part of me must have decided I was going to live there one day.

In 1975 I applied for a job in Carlisle. The very first thing the partner said to me when I went for interview was, "Look, I'm not sure we've got a job after all." They hadn't. It was a long way to go for that greeting. I then replied to a small advert in the Law Society's *Gazette* for a job "on the fringe of the Lake District." This proved to be Barrow-in-Furness. I turned up there on the Friday night sleeper the week of the Moorgate tube disaster. Wesley Ellison took me to his home, his wife Jean offered me breakfast, he virtually offered me a job and as he was about to take me back to the station said "I suppose you'd better have a look at the office." I was indeed offered a job at £4,000 a year, a huge increase on my London salary.

Wesley was coroner, having inherited the job from John Poole. At that time there were about two hundred coroners' districts in England and Wales and it was not such an onerous job as fewer deaths were reported to coroners and inquests were short. Although the local authority appointed the coroner it was the job of the coroner to appoint a deputy and an assistant deputy though this last position was optional. It was difficult to persuade anyone to be deputy probably because some coroners were reluctant to offer any kind of payment. Things were very different twenty years later when I would receive regular unsolicited CVs often from barristers in Manchester or London trying to persuade me that they would be a highly valuable member of my team if only I would appoint them as one of my deputies.

Back in 1978 the minute I had the necessary five years qualification as a solicitor I was appointed, at twenty-nine years of age, Deputy Coroner for the Furness District of Cumbria. I was a very willing recruit and went to the first ever training course for coroners in 1980 at Wakefield. This was run by the Coroners' Society not by the Home Office. When Wesley retired I was appointed coroner in January 1990, and five years later I left private practice behind.

I was lucky enough to do the job I feel I was made to do. As years went by my area expanded, the number of cases reported to coroners increased and the complications of the work multiplied. But whereas you can only do so many divorces or conveyances without feeling you have seen it all before, I always went to work as coroner wondering what the day would bring.

Inquests were done differently forty and more years ago. The first jury inquest I did as a new deputy was a road traffic death. Juries were required then for road deaths though the law soon changed. I duly called the witnesses, heard their evidence and then summed up to the jury. I told them what the options were for a verdict and sent them out to their room.

Juries then were called at short notice and very informally, and across the country juries consisted of publicans and insurance agents as the police could ring them and they could give up an hour or two in the working day. The same individuals were called time after time. Once the jury had retired I asked the coroner's officer how I had done. "Well," he said "I think they were surprised when you gave them a choice of verdicts, and they were very surprised when you sent them out to think about it."

I did few cases with a jury when I was deputy coroner but I did change one thing. A juror must swear an oath and when I started the practice was for them all to say it together. This was like a school class reciting a poem and seemed to me undignified. Also it was impossible to be sure that each individual had actually said anything at all, let alone the right words. I made each juror take the oath in turn. The oath does bear setting out in full:

I swear by Almighty God (or, I do solemnly and sincerely declare and affirm) that I will diligently enquire on behalf of our Sovereign Lady the Queen into the death of A.B.C. and give a true verdict (conclusion) according to the evidence.

It is a difficult oath to read fluently and nearly everyone stumbled over the word 'diligently'. Having jurors take the oath individually made each of them realise they were taking part in a serious exercise and it also let the family and witnesses know that a formal legal process was starting.

The government made much in the reform process of "putting the family at the centre" of the inquest. Later this became "putting the family at the heart", an even cosier concept. The point however is that the inquest is officially on behalf of the Crown dating back centuries to when the coroner was there to protect the Crown's interests.

Another case from the early days was in some ways informative, but as we will see in other ways it was not. A doctor rang to say his patient had died but he did not know the cause. A post mortem was carried out and the cause of death was confirmed by the pathologist as:

1a) Idiopathic cardio respiratory arrest.

This reassured me, but being young, keen and afraid of looking foolish I looked up the words in the medical dictionary. Cardio respiratory arrest is fairly obvious: the heart and lungs have stopped working. Idiopathic means "the cause of which is not known". This was not quite the explanation for the death I had hoped for but according to the pathologist it was as far as I (or he) was going to get and the death was natural so I had to accept it. People often accuse lawyers like myself of being clever talkers but it seemed to me the doctors had us beaten all ends up at that game.

One of my solicitor partners was unimpressed when I was appointed coroner. He said it was "A licence to make pompous statements of the bleeding obvious" and I admit that I did tell anyone present once that allowing little children access to matches unsupervised was not a good idea and on another occasion that using a very old shotgun as a walking stick was not clever. Not if there was a cartridge in the barrel and the hammer was so defective that it could click against the cartridge. Too late for the elderly gentleman who was shot through the abdomen and too obvious for everyone else. And by the way it was definitely not deliberate.

FIVE

Getting Through the Day

1 CHANCE

The difference between living and dying can often be so fractional that it might seem arbitrary. Some would say that the person who lived was being protected by God; others would put it down to pure luck. Coroners only come across those cases where the person dies, but either of the two following examples could have had a completely different outcome.

In one instance David Robert Shaw was a serving soldier in Afghanistan. As a private in the Duke of Lancaster's Regiment he was known as a Kingsman. He was sheltering in a compound which was under attack from Taliban firing at it from several hundred yards away. Looking at events by reading the file, I would have expected anybody in the armoured refuge to be safe from the attack, but a bullet did just clear the protecting wall and lost enough of its trajectory for it to hit Kingsman Shaw. He was very badly wounded but the medical support both on the spot and at the army hospital was outstanding and Kingsman Shaw was flown home to Birmingham where he died. His family was enormously grateful to have had the chance to be with him. Jurisdiction was passed to me by the Birmingham coroner as David and his family were from my area.

David's Sergeant and other colleagues and the female medic on the spot were excellent witnesses at the inquest. They were the kind of people you would literally trust with your life. At the inquest I asked the female medical attendant who dealt with David if she was a doctor. No she was not. Was she then a nurse? No. She was specifically trained to deal with injuries received in combat such as bullet wounds and blast injuries and she inspired huge respect for her professionalism.

When I had first read the report on what had happened, I could not believe how unlucky David had been. If he had been standing six inches one way from where he actually was the bullet would have missed him and indeed the sergeant himself had been struck by a bullet, possibly a ricochet, in the back against his body armour and he knew just how lucky he himself had been. There was even a moment or two of humour as I asked the sergeant questions. Firstly he explained that when a new recruit joins the regiment he the sergeant becomes the recruit's mother at which point he looked at David's real mother and apologised. Then there was this:

Coroner: I believe you were struck too
Sergeant: Yes
Coroner: You were saved by your body armour
Sergeant: Yes
Coroner: You were a very lucky man
Sergeant: I was fu…… Yes I was very lucky

In death David saved the lives of others as his organs were donated by his parents. This is a difficult decision to make at such a time but the benefits to the recipients can be life-changing in a very positive way.

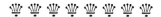

In an entirely different setting a man called Anthony Robinson was also exceedingly unlucky. Dr Adam Padel was the pathologist and had two post mortems to perform. One was on a man who had been found in water after being out looking for his dog. I anticipated there might well be an inquest. Mr Robinson had been working on clearing some scrub land prior to building work, when he simply fell down for no apparent reason and we all assumed he had probably had a heart attack. That would mean no inquest was needed.

I was travelling to London and by chance met Dr Padel on Oxenholme station platform as he was returning to Lancaster. Our conversation was a great surprise to me and proved that you should always keep an open mind. He told me that the man in the water had died from natural heart disease but he had discovered at the post mortem on Mr Robinson that in the base of his brain was the link off a piece of chain. This was embedded to a depth of about four inches. The police had noticed an injury around the neck area and assumed it was caused as Mr Robinson fell. In fact it was an entry wound.

The death we had assumed to be natural was anything but and the one we expected to lead to an inquest was natural. What had happened to Mr Robinson was that someone else on the site was working with a strimmer. The head of the strimmer had been changed so that the two projections that do the cutting were short sections of chain. The end link had come off one of them and flown, hitting Mr Robinson and killing him. It could have gone anywhere and again if he had been standing even a few inches to one side it would have whistled past him and he may never even have known it had happened.

In 2012 a couple were staying in a wooden camping pod. The husband was found dead and a disposable barbecue was found inside. The wife survived and had a vague recollection of going to the toilet block in the night. If she had not, she too would probably have died. The problem was of course carbon monoxide poisoning.

In my own life I have often been in the wrong place but never at the wrong time – the proverbial conjunction that leads to tragedy. I stood on top of the Twin Towers in New York in September 2000. A year later they were demolished in the terror attack with about 3,000 deaths. I still wonder that it wasn't more. As it happens from that viewpoint we watched the P&O liner *Oriana* glide along the Hudson River on a short cruise. We embarked on her a few days later to cross the Atlantic and she was hit by a huge wave and damaged. She had to hove to and running repairs were made. We were ordered at one point to sit on the floor and not move. One lady nearby asked if we were all going to die. No-one did. Wrong place wrong time but the consequences were worrying not fatal. We found out later that it all happened close to where the *Titanic* sank.

In January 2003 my wife Marian and I spent several days at Yala in Sri Lanka. It was idyllic, with the sea breaking gently, a huge rock protecting a natural pool, with palm trees and sun. A few miles inland there were wild elephants, exotic birds and the chance of seeing a leopard. At a conference lecture a couple of years later we heard from someone whose job was to try to identify the victims of the 2004 Boxing Day tsunami. He showed what was left of Yala, which was a lump of concrete. Had we been there at the wrong time we would have died.

On a plane from Vancouver heading to Heathrow overnight I was woken by what sounded like a sack of potatoes being dropped on the floor. In fact it was a gentleman trying to get to his wife who was seated a couple of rows behind him. He was full length in the aisle and my wife, by training and inclination a nurse, went to him and realised he was in a very bad way. The air crew told her to leave him; it happened and he had probably had too much to drink. Marian protested and the crew accepted a doctor was needed and a call was put out. A British doctor was the only one on board, or at least the only one who owned up to being a doctor. For over thirty minutes Marian and the GP attempted resuscitation with a cabin full around them, the wife asking them to keep trying and a German teenager translating between them. The cabin crew seemed to be in shock.

Eventually the dead man had to be manhandled into the galley. When we landed six police came on board – two sergeants – and no-one on board the plane was allowed to leave until statements were taken. Over three hundred passengers were kept on board for over an hour. As we left the plane the whole of the flight and cabin crew were having a de-brief at the front of the plane but we had to rush to catch our shuttle flight to Manchester. We later learned that the man who collapsed had had a burst aneurysm and could not have survived. We also learned that the London coroner responsible for Heathrow had only had five similar occurrences in thirteen years. I would have expected deaths in flight to be much more frequent.

Marian kept in touch with the doctor who was soon rewarded with a business class ticket to anywhere in the world. Marian wasn't; she is a mere nurse though she had spent longer with the man and given him mouth to mouth. The doctor protested and British Airways did the decent thing and gave Marian the same reward. At the risk of this becoming a travel book I will tell you that we went to Mexico. The flights were uneventful, the holiday enjoyable, but on the train journey from London back to Cumbria, at Warrington, someone jumped in front of the train.

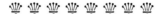

Two men went out on the fells in summer, perhaps rather poorly equipped. This probably would not have been a problem but a mist descended and they could not find their way down. They were literally benighted. Next morning one had survived and one had died of hypothermia, a fact which his family could not come to terms with. Why had their son died when he looked so much fitter and stronger than the one who survived? Twice subsequently, several years later, I received letters from the mother asking why and there was little I could say. Nature is not predictable.

Because I live in the area I was responsible for I usually knew the places where tragedy struck. Sometimes I was not very far away from what happened. One Saturday my wife and I had been to Hawkshead and as we returned we saw fireworks across the lake. This was odd as it was broad daylight and the fireworks were going off haphazardly. As we travelled from Ambleside towards Windermere police were controlling the traffic and I found out later that two people had died. As this was shortly before I retired I did not complete the inquest myself and it remained unclear what had started the fireworks igniting.

2 COINCIDENCES AND CLUSTERS

Coincidences in fiction often seem too contrived to be true but all of the following did happen. I have changed some of the names for privacy.

Two ladies were killed in a car accident in Canada and they lived on Dundas Street in Barrow but their bodies were repatriated and so I had to carry out an inquest. I corresponded with the coroner in Canada to ask for as much information as possible. His address was 80 Dundas Street, London, Ontario.

Within a period of 24 hours, deaths were reported to me of Mary Edwards and Mary Doris Edwards.

In 1996, on one day only two deaths were reported, one of them being at 5 Dorset Crescent, Barrow and the other being at 6 Dorset Crescent. There was no connection whatever between the two deaths and the houses were not opposite each other.

In 2007 two consecutive deaths reported were Arthur Heywood, born 16 March, 1921 and Herbert Heywood, born 16 March, 1920. They were not related.

In an inquest that I did into the death of a man who had fallen off a crag whilst climbing, I called four witnesses. One was a companion who was with him, two were from Mountain Rescue and the fourth was the pathologist who carried out the post mortem. All four had the Christian name Nicholas.

From my home I can see a fell called Pavey Ark, part of the Langdale Pikes. If the light is right or light snow has fallen I can see, or at least imagine that I can see, a diagonal line running across the front of the hill. This is called Jack's Rake and it is officially a rock climb. It is as near to the boundary between fell walking and rock climbing as you can get. It is an airy and beautifully rugged place and on the one occasion that I climbed it I felt a great sense of achievement. During the 25 years I was coroner, four deaths occurred here, three of them by falling and the fourth a bizarre suicide who took the trouble to climb part way up and then off in order to hang himself from a tree, thereby putting people trying to recover the body at great personal risk. The thing is that all these deaths occurred within a short space of time of only a couple of years. Likewise there was a series of deaths on Striding Edge, Helvellyn within a short period of a few weeks then none for several years. In the early part of my time as coroner there were as many as eight deaths at Hodge Close which is a flooded quarry where people got into trouble scuba diving. I am sure people carry on doing this activity but fortunately there were no deaths for many years until the hot summer of 2018, and he was not a scuba diver.

Another cluster related to mental health. Drugs often prescribed to combat depression included Seroxat and Citalopram, from the SSRI family (Selective serotonin re-uptake inhibitors). I dealt with a number of people who died by their own hand either just after they started the drug or after they came off it or if the dosage changed. I reported my observations to the Department of Health though I have to say they took little interest even though similar findings were written up in the medical journals.

3 HUMOUR

Fortunately there are sometimes things that make you smile.

In 2007 a gentleman of the road was found dead in the churchyard of St Mary's, Windermere. His family was traced and were extremely pleasant and helpful. They were also fairly poor and tried for some time to raise the cash to pay for the funeral. Where there is no money to pay for a funeral the responsibility falls on the hospital where death occurred and if it was not in hospital then on the local authority. Ultimately the family phoned in to say they simply couldn't raise the money "so he'll have to have a state funeral".

At the opening of an inquest in 2008 when I was 59 my officer was talking to the family outside and telling them what to expect in court. She told them the coroner was Mr Smith only to be greeted with, "He must be getting on a bit. He did our Dad 15 years ago."

People making statements to the police sometimes contradict themselves. In the following example the names are made up. An elderly gentleman had died and there was nothing sinister or unusual about it but his grandson made a statement just to give some background. This is what he said:

> I am the grandson of the deceased Joe South. I knew Joe South and he had relatively good health. He had suffered a bit of angina. He was a heavy drinker and went out every day and would on average drink about 10 pints of beer a day. He had been in hospital recently because of the angina. He had had both legs amputated but was still active and could get round in his wheelchair. He also had a bad chest and was a heavy smoker, smoking on average 40 cigarettes a day. He had smoked all of his life.

In another case a relatively young man had died in America and his body was flown back to Cumbria. Among the paperwork was a statement from the American friend of the deceased. The main point he was trying to make to the person interviewing him was that the deceased drank a lot and this might explain why he had died. The friend used the words, "He was English – if that tells you anything." Is that really the reputation we really have abroad?

Throughout my career I dealt with funeral directors on an almost daily basis, but they, like me and my staff, must have a sense of humour to get through their day to day routine and I wonder if some of the following are deliberate.

One funeral director lives at Ashland House, another at The Ashes. He assured me it was called that long before he was born, but added that he certainly was not going to change it. In Barrow we had Burns Funeral Service and in Blackpool, Box Brothers.

Even the police sometimes have difficulty in dealing with death. A particular officer may only be called out to a sudden death on rare occasions and sometimes it is clear that they do not know how to react. In one road traffic death a senior experienced officer took a statement from a witness who was not directly involved in the accident but saw it. The statement was about six pages long and detailed everything about the witness from when she got up that day to what she had for breakfast, and described in detail what she did afterwards but did not make a single reference to the actual accident and what happened.

Another officer demonstrated his unease about death by going to the opposite extreme when he attended a flat where there was concern about the occupant. This is what he wrote:

> I entered the flat and noted an overpowering putrid smell. I entered the lounge which was a complete mess with rubbish, papers and shopping lying all over the place. I noticed what I believed to be a male person, apparently asleep on the settee. He appeared purpleish and his skin was peeling away. I went over to him. The smell seemed even stronger and I said to him, "Are you all right mate?" But received no reply.

Part of the procedure when fixing an inquest, is to check with witnesses when they might have prior commitments, particularly holidays. My officer sent out a warning along these lines to one lady who filled in the calendar that we provide and wrote this:

> Dear George,
> As you will see from the calendar I do have swimming and keep fit activities on Monday, Tuesday and Wednesday. Although I enjoy these, they are not above being cancelled for something as important as the Inquest. The only appointment I need to keep is a hair appointment on Monday 18th.
> Cheerio for now.
> See you soon.

After an inquest into a death on the roads the local paper perpetrated an unfortunate misprint. The police investigator was Sgt Jon Skelton but the paper named him Sgt Jon Skeleton.

I will risk two examples of black humour and hope they do not offend.

One Christmas an elderly gentleman was engaged to play Father Christmas at a hotel dinner. He arrived fully kitted out and as he stepped over the threshold collapsed dead of a heart attack. He was taken away in his gear and from there it is a bit more hazy but I imagined his nearest relative being asked to identify him and saying, "No it's not him; he didn't have a long white beard".

The other story came from the mortuary. A man had died in a car fire started deliberately by himself. His remains were sparse. Only when the pathologist started a detailed examination did it emerge that his dog had died in the fire too. When the remains were put back someone put on a label 'Dog and bone'. As soon as the mortuary manager saw this it was removed

4 SUICIDE

Suicide is the deliberate taking of one's own life. To come to this conclusion a coroner had to be satisfied beyond reasonable doubt, which is the criminal standard of proof. In 2018 the High Court decided that coroners and textbooks had been wrong about the law and that the true standard of proof to come to a verdict of suicide was the balance of probabilities. This decision was upheld on appeal. There may be a further appeal to the Supreme Court. This was a major change because throughout my career I and my fellow coroners regarded it as clear and unarguable that suicide could only be recorded when you were sure beyond reasonable doubt.

Coroners used to add the phrase "whilst the balance of his mind was disturbed" to the verdict of suicide, but for me if that was the case then the requirement of a clear intent to die was missing. I evolved a number of verdicts such as "x died as a consequence of his own actions whilst intoxicated by alcohol/drugs/whilst suffering from mental illness". Researchers sometimes complain that the true suicide statistics are skewed. If they look only for the verdict 'suicide' then they will indeed be inaccurate. Although suicide per se is no longer a criminal offence it does still carry a huge stigma, and family members often thanked me for using one of my slightly more imaginative forms of words instead of the stark single word 'suicide'. The purpose of an inquest is not to provide data for researchers anyway. They just need to apply a little lateral thinking when obtaining their raw material.

Men are much more likely to end their own lives than are women. People who take their own life sometimes try to rule those they leave behind from the grave. One man, accused of child abuse, walked up Dow Crag, and left behind a detailed account of his last day, where he had walked, what he had eaten and how hard it was to find somewhere to jump off. He also left detailed instructions to his family about how they should live their lives in the future.

Another man killed himself in his car using the exhaust gases (this is much more difficult now that cars have catalytic converters). He had a wife and a girlfriend and was taking money from his company but still had a lot of debt. He left his girlfriend a two page set of instructions. In the photograph of the inside of the car I noticed that the mileage on the old fashioned odometer was 86669; 666 is, according to Revelations in the Bible, the number of the beast. Though what that means I really have no idea.

Early into this millennium there was a spate of deaths of people in mental health units who were voluntary patients and who just walked out and within a short space of time killed themselves. One lady walked in front of a train. Another chose a heavy lorry. A third, who had threatened to hang herself, walked to a toilet just off the mental health unit within a larger hospital and used the cord from the dressing gown she had foolishly been allowed to wear. One elderly man was discharged from a mental health unit only to kill his wife and then himself.

These deaths are just a few examples and they prompted me to try to find out how often this happened across the country. The Department of Health did not keep statistics for voluntary patients who died by their own hand as opposed to patients detained under the Mental Health Act for whom statistics were kept.

Enquiries among my fellow coroners showed that deaths among voluntary patients were common. I thought that this was a national scandal and I continued to tell the Department of Health about the subject but towards the end of my career there were several more deaths of mental health patients who were receiving treatment but still took their own lives. Patients discharged by the mental health services were also prone to taking their life shortly after discharge. The only hard evidence I could get was in a report of the Cumbria Commissioning Group which identified twenty self killings in a period of nine months. I found this quite shocking and I still feel that the care available for people with mental illness is inadequate across the country.

Motivation for suicide was often found in a note left by the deceased but now a note may be on a computer and not immediately obvious. One should never leap to conclusions. I did once ask the girlfriend of someone who had died about a note that appeared to be clear proof that he meant to end his life. "Oh," she said, "he was always writing those. This one is a few weeks old".

I am not being flippant if I say that some people who leave suicide notes do so in order to have the final word. Indeed the act itself can be the means of having the final word. One thoughtful man wrote a letter for a different reason and posted it to me. It was delivered the next day at the office at lunchtime and I was shocked to read that he was taking his own life and it would be better for the police rather than his family to find his body. When the police arrived they found he had indeed done what he said.

The deaths of two people together may be a genuine suicide pact or a murder/manslaughter followed by a suicide. The first person to come on the scene may be deeply traumatised. One such was an estate agent showing people round a house for sale only to come across the owners both dead by asphyxia, one strangled, one hanging. A more thoughtful couple in a more secluded spot put a notice on the door telling whoever first arrived to stay outside and call the police.

Suicide can be a spur of the moment decision and there are stories of people being pulled alive from gas filled cars who then live for many years and never attempt suicide again. Many years back, one lady killed herself in her car. Her last act was to draw a picture of the scene in front of her. Less than a week later on the day of her funeral her husband drove the same car to the same place and ended his life in the same way.

Money problems can trigger suicide but more often in my experience it is relationship problems. Young men (usually) who fall out with their girlfriend. Men accused of improper behaviour with children. And occasionally there is literally no explanation, no clue in anything which has happened, no money problem, no disagreement, nothing. That must be very difficult indeed for those left behind.

The foot and mouth epidemic in 2001 resulted in several suicides to my certain knowledge. Farmers are prone to suicide as they often work alone and have access to dangerous equipment, quiet places like barns and usually shotguns. Foot and mouth pushed some farmers beyond what they could tolerate. Many suffered the loss of their animals, which were often the product of decades or generations of breeding. Buildings were disinfected and some were destroyed. Several years afterwards a rumour went round that the disease had broken out again and that was enough for another farmer to kill himself. Foot and mouth disease justified the use of the word 'devastating'.

Cumbria felt under siege for weeks. Near Kendal a small tank was placed by the roadside trickling some form of disinfectant across the road. This could not have been very effective as a disinfectant for tyres but was a constant reminder that we were 'unclean'. Footpaths were closed and visitors stopped coming. During a cricket match I played in, a squad arrived in the nearby farm and began shooting the sheep. My wife had to travel across to the North East of the country and from Hartside, a viewpoint across the Eden Valley and to the Lake District, she saw eight separate plumes of smoke – eight funeral pyres – eight farmers burning their stock.

The management of the outbreak from London was appalling. The politicians had no idea of what life in the country was like. People were threatened that their pets would have to be put down. Hauliers were reputedly offered huge sums to transport dead animals on the basis that their trailers would have to be destroyed afterwards. The disease is treatable by injection anyway and is no threat to humans but animals that are not free of foot and mouth cannot be marketed. When it was decided that the outbreak was over Tony Blair announced that "The countryside is open for business". That phrase encapsulates the disconnection between the urbanites who run the country and those of us who live in the rural parts of the country from choice. To me the countryside needs to be open to walk in, to breathe fresh air, to stop and watch the birds and to be aware of the rhythm of the seasons.

5 WALNEY MURDERS

Charlie Johnson was my only assistant in the office for ten years. He had been head of the accounts department at the firm of solicitors where I worked so we were colleagues for over thirty years. He was drawing up manual spreadsheets before most businesses had heard of them and he encouraged us to learn about computers when they began to be available to small businesses. He was also a very good friend and for years we went together to the Headingley Test Match.

He retired from the accounts department aged 65 and came to look after the paperwork in the coroner's office which in the late 1990s was a part-time job as I only had my original area and a few hundred deaths reported each year. He retired from my office aged 75 and sadly died a few years later. Charlie though was never allowed to forget a throw-away remark. He looked up from his papers one morning and said "It's ages since we had a murder."

In the next few months from April 1999 to September 2000 we had five murders on the Island of Walney alone. Walney is a long narrow island protecting Barrow-in-Furness from the worst of the Irish Sea. About 10,000 people live there and many houses were built for workers in the Vickers shipyard. Some streets are named after exotic sounding ships – Euryalus Street and Niobe Street for example. Japanese tourists apparently often come to take their own picture in front of the Mikasa Street name. *Mikasa* was a battleship built at Barrow for the Japanese navy and launched in 1900. After various rescues and restorations she can still be seen at Yokosuka Japan as a museum ship.

There were two double murders and a Chinese restaurant worker took the ultimate revenge on his former employer with one of the tools of his trade, a meat cleaver. He owned up immediately to what he had done and was dealt with by the courts within three months and sentenced to life imprisonment. There was almost a feeling among the police that he had made everything too easy for them.

For that short period Walney's murder rate would have made it, statistically the most dangerous area on the planet. Happily statistics do not always tell the truth. Walney is a pleasant and happy place to live. But it is windy.

SIX

Donald Campbell

Figure 5: Bluebird at speed.

The story of Donald Campbell's life and death is well known and is documented in many films and books. I was seventeen-years-old when the crash which took his life occurred and I saw it on a grainy black and white television set. At the time I was studying for my A Levels at Percy Jackson Grammar School just north of Doncaster and a few weeks later I would be accepted to read law at University College London. I had no idea that 34 years later I would have a central role in the legal process which followed on from Donald Campbell's death.

Bill Smith searched for and found *Bluebird*, Donald Campbell's boat, in nearly 150 feet of water in 2001 and raised her to the surface early in March in front of the world's press.

The search for Donald Campbell's body continued until towards the end of May with rather less publicity. I was told that on Bank Holiday Monday,

28 May, his remains were likely to be brought ashore. The police were told and because I had a good relationship with them and occupied a room in Barrow Police Station as my office, Inspector Bob Clegg arranged for a police presence at Coniston but he agreed not to put anything on the police computer to try to keep privacy and keep the press away. This plan was successful. I confess that I had no need to be there but this was something historic and I went to the pier at the north end of Coniston with my wife Marian.

There I met Gina Campbell, Donald's daughter, and explained to her the legal processes that would follow. After some waiting Bill Smith's launch appeared and a makeshift coffin draped in a Union Jack was brought onshore and set down on the grass. Gina placed three deep purple tulips on the coffin and spent a little time alone there. Pier Cottage is where *Bluebird* was put into the water each time so it was appropriate for Donald Campbell's remains to return there. The tulips came from my garden, thoughtfully picked and taken along by Marian.

The law requires that any human remains must be examined and identified and for this reason the remains had to be taken to the nearest mortuary which was at Furness General Hospital in Barrow. There was a lack of communication between the police and the funeral director because we had to wait about an hour and a half for the hearse to turn up to take the coffin away. The press camped out at Furness General Hospital for a while and the medical director at the time was about to issue a statement to them. Fortunately I was asked to agree the wording and said that the arrangement between the hospital and the coroner was outside the NHS and any comments would be issued by me.

Identification should never be assumed but should be proved by the best evidence available and although there was circumstantial evidence to suggest that this was indeed Donald Campbell, there was a method of proving that it was him which was DNA profiling. Over the following days samples were taken from Gina, from Donald's sister and nephew, and samples from the remains on the lakebed were sent to a laboratory in Wetherby. At the first attempt the laboratory was unable to obtain any DNA from the sample provided but thankfully at the second attempt they were successful and the various samples were compared and matched confirming that, without any doubt, the remains of Donald Campbell had been discovered. The cost of the scientific tests was over £4,000 paid for by Cumbria County Council. They are under legal obligation to pay for expenses properly incurred via the coroner.

An inquest was opened so that Donald Campbell's remains could be released and a funeral take place. This took place at Barrow Town Hall and as is required by law it was held in public. The interest of the media can be gauged from the picture which shows the media scrum, Gina Campbell and two figures in the background walking back to the police station. They are my officer George Cubiss and me.

Figure 6: Gina Campbell and media scrum.

Gina Campbell organised her father's funeral and invited me to attend which I did. The service was held at the Parish Church of St Andrew, Coniston on 12 September 2001. It was a celebration of his life not a mourning of his death. It was one of those days when Coniston produces a kind of rain that I have not experienced anywhere else. It rains gently with tiny drops just beyond a mist and it soaks you completely to the skin. The coffin had been brought to the church via the lake in a glass sided hearse pulled by two magnificent black horses and as the procession came in Gershwin's *Rhapsody in Blue* was played and those of us mercifully waiting in the dry were immediately uplifted. There were rousing old fashioned hymns and I was honoured to be there. Some of my colleagues might say that getting in any way personally involved like this is unacceptable because it can blur the fact that you have to come to a dispassionate and disinterested (as opposed to uninterested) view of events and facts and come to a conclusion that is objective and not swayed in any way by personal involvement. I accept all that but this was a very unusual inquest in that it was conducted decades after the events in question when the rawness of bereavement had passed and at a time when Gina was older than her father had been when he died.

The law requires that if a coroner is notified that a body is lying within his or her jurisdiction then an inquest must be held unless it is shown that the death was natural and a medical certificate of cause of death can be issued by a doctor. Plainly that was not the case here and as I was the coroner for the area I was required to conduct an inquest. The fact that events had occurred 34 years earlier was irrelevant. The police were not keen to spend money on a special investigation into something that had happened so long ago and where no apparent crime was involved but they provided enough cover to support me by means of a liaison officer PC Ian Scales and my own coroner's officer George Cubiss who was happy to remain involved in the investigation.

In one sense it was extremely obvious what had happened because I had seen it happening on television and no doubt seen it replayed in documentaries subsequently but equally despite the many theories there was no definitive answer to how and why *Bluebird* had left the water and somersaulted with such catastrophic consequences.

The pathologist, Dr Wendy Blundell, confirmed that the skeletal parts present had undergone extensive trauma consistent with the well documented high speed accident. The consultant radiologist, Dr Crawshaw, confirmed this and said that the right-sided bones had suffered most damage.

I decided to do some first hand investigation. I went to see Ken Norris, one of the two brothers who designed the boat. He was in his 80s and he took me to his office at Hurn Airport near Bournemouth in his large blue Jaguar. He was a charming, slim, upright gentleman with a military bearing and a military moustache and he explained and confirmed a number of facts which I will deal with later when explaining how the accident happened. He told me he thought Donald was keen to get the record and go on to the Boat Show in London where he was promoting a jet boat (i.e. one powered by a jet of water), and that he may have therefore gone for the record in conditions that were slightly less than ideal.

I also went to South Shields to Bill Smith's premises where *Bluebird* was stored for renovation. The boat from the cockpit backwards was in a remarkable state of preservation. The trademark blue of all the Campbell boats and cars was intact and the metal much better preserved than I could have imagined, remembering it had been under water for 34 years. With me was Tony Foy, a police officer, whose job was to investigate road traffic collisions and work out how they had happened and an expert who was to review all the available information and prepare a report on the accident and in due course he would be the main witness at the inquest. The expert was Dr Julian Happian-Smith who I had come across previously in a road traffic accident involving a trailer loaded with a car. He was a consultant engineer with a background in crash dynamics and mathematical modelling of vehicle impact dynamics, crash testing and vehicle crash worthiness. He is a large man with a real scientist's beard.

I obtained from the archives a copy of the papers that had been filed in 1967 and among them were copies of statements from witnesses some of whom had since died. No inquest could be held at that time because there was no body discovered but the statements were read out at the inquest which I subsequently held. I record the following statements in full as they are now historic documents and the people who made them are well known. Interest in Donald Campbell remains. His story is that of the quintessential English hero and his legacy has been loyally preserved by his daughter Gina, herself a record holder.

Leo Villa was the chief engineer on the *Bluebird* project. He died in 1979 and this is his statement from 1967. 'Plus 47' means 297mph. Robbie is Anthony Robinson from the Sun Inn, Coniston.

I was a chief engineer on the *Bluebird* World Speed Record attempt. I am 67 years of age and reside at Reigate, Surrey.

About 7.20 am on Wednesday, 4th January, 1967, I went to *Bluebird* boathouse on Lake Coniston to prepare for a record run. In the semi-darkness the lake appeared fairly smooth and sometime later I approached Mr Campbell and pointed out that the lake could possibly be suitable for a run. Mr Campbell advised me not to waste time and to go to my station. I then went by car to the northern kilometre post where the boat I was using was moored. I had been on board some time when Mr Campbell spoke to me by radio from the boathouse and enquired the conditions of water and weather. My reply was that the water was reasonably good. Mr Campbell's reply was that he intended to make a run and to stand-by. Some minutes later Mr Campbell said over the radio that *Bluebird* had left the jetty and had started a run. After a short interval, Mr Campbell explained that his engine had cut out and this information was quickly followed by him stating that the nose had lifted and *Bluebird* was on the way.

A very short time after this Mr Campbell came into view and passed my launch at very high speed and appeared to be rising very steadily at the correct planing angle. Mr Campbell was describing the run but mechanical noises prevented me from hearing him distinctly over the radio. Mr Campbell appeared to be alright at the south end and I next heard him enquiring over the radio what speed he had attained. After a short interval the replay from the timekeeper was plus 47.

After a further interval of a few minutes, the next thing I was aware of was that Mr Campbell had started his return run. I saw *Bluebird* into the southern kilometre and realised the craft was going very fast indeed. After covering approximately two thirds of this distance, the bow of *Bluebird* suddenly and very rapidly started to lift. I realised something was amiss and turned quickly to Robbie and shouted, "Let's get going".

By the time I had turned round *Bluebird* had disappeared in a huge cloud of spray and by the time we reached the scene where she had disappeared, there was nothing but the two front main floats and other debris floating about. I asked Robbie to drive very slowly in case Mr Campbell should surface. We picked up his crash helmet, the inside of the helmet with earphones attached, then one boot with a sock inside, then I found his Mae West which had not been inflated, and the other boot and sock. Drifting further away was his air bottle and one glove.

We continued to search hoping Mr Campbell would surface for approximately one and a half hours during which time we picked up several bits of debris from the surface.

By this time, two skin-divers had arrived from Barrow and they endeavoured to locate *Bluebird* under the surface of the water, but it was found that the water was too dark and they abandoned the attempt.

Bluebird was in 100% mechanical condition.

I have known Donald Campbell all his life and have been employed by him and his father before him. He was a perfectly healthy man and suffered no ill effects from his previous accident in the United States in 1962.

Norman Buckley was present at the record attempt as an observer for the Royal Yachting Association. He held several water speed records and like me was a solicitor. He died in 1974. The certificates of his records were on display at the Langdale Chase Hotel near Ambleside but when I was last there I was told they had been given to the Windermere Steamboat Museum which was to open soon afterwards. He made a fairly short statement which is as follows:

I am a solicitor, aged 58 years and reside at 'Cragwood', Windermere.

I am the official Observer for the Royal Yachting Association.

About 8.45 am on Wednesday, 4th January, 1967, I was at the north timing post at the east side of Lake Coniston when the boat *Bluebird* piloted by Donald Campbell made a run on the lake from north to south in a time of 7.525 seconds which is equal to a speed of 297 miles per hour. This speed was radioed to Mr Campbell. He turned and made a return run. His speed was estimated to be in excess of 300 mph and the boat was about 150 yards from the northern end of the measured kilometre when it became airborne, crashed into the water and disintegrated. Rescue boats went to the scene within two minutes.

The lake surface was in perfect condition. There was nothing anyone could do to help Mr Campbell.

Another statement from 1967 was made by Keith Harrison who was still alive at the time of the inquest and indeed contacted me subsequently and he said:

I am a journalist, aged 38 years, and reside in Huddersfield.

About 8.45 am on Wednesday, 4th January 1967, I was aboard a motor launch at the south end of the measured kilometre on Lake Coniston. I saw *Bluebird* travel from north to south of the lake at a fast speed, then turn and commence to make the return run. I saw *Bluebird* enter the kilometre travelling very fast. I heard Donald Campbell say over the radio, "The water is not good." About this time the starboard sponson of *Bluebird* lifted out of the water and the boat travelled for a distance in this position. It then resumed an even keel and I thought it was alright, but *Bluebird* immediately lifted out of the water and the crash occurred. I went at once to the scene and was dispatched to base by Mr Leo Villa for assistance. Visibility was good and although there was a slight swell on the water, it was suitable for a run in my opinion.

A statement by PC Sherdley included this:

… a team of naval frogmen from the Naval Base at Rosyth, Scotland arrived at Coniston and commenced diving on the morning of Thursday 5th January 1967. Small pieces of wreckage were found and during the afternoon the main wreckage consisting of the hull of *Bluebird* which had been severed from the cockpit and nose-piece was located and marked with a marker buoy. Included in the wreckage brought to the surface by the divers were the remains of the steering wheel and the safety harness worn by Donald Campbell.

Diving operations continued each day until Sunday, 15th January 1967 when the officer-in-charge decided to call off the search. A dawn to dusk search of the lake by motor launch was commenced by myself and other police officers on Thursday, 12th January 1967 but so far without success. Patrolling the lake will continue in case the body should rise to the surface.

Because of the difficulties with identification and the time spent in investigating the events of 1967, it was some time before the inquest could be held. This took place on 25 October 2002 at John Ruskin School, Coniston. The venue was for sentimental reasons and to maintain the close links between the Campbell family and Coniston Village and its people and as it happens it coincided with records week which was then held on Windermere. Records Week is, as its name suggests, a meeting of powered boats of many classes attempting to break the speed record for that particular class. I was taken to the court by PC Tony Foy in a police car. We got there before the press arrived. The school had put up good signs and controlled the press and the Campbell enthusiasts well. The school canteen did a good trade in hot drinks and cakes but hardly anyone paid the parking fee.

I heard evidence from Bill Smith and Dr Julian Happian-Smith, and Tony Foy had set up a display screen so that as witnesses referred to illustrations they were visible to the public and the press and of course Gina Campbell who was clearly emotionally affected by the pictures on the screen in front of her though doubtless she had seen them many times over the intervening years. The use of graphics on a screen visible to everyone in the courtroom was a novel but successful innovation. Before this the lawyers, the witness and I would have numbered photographs in front of us but no one else could see what we were talking about. This was particularly annoying for the press who felt they should have full access. The same idea was used later in the Grayrigg train crash inquest.

An inquest must answer and record the answers to four questions, namely, who was the deceased and how, when, and where did he come by his death. The formal outcome of the inquest was recorded as follows:

Donald Malcolm Campbell born on 23rd March 1921 died on 4th January 1967 at approximately 8.50 am when he was attempting to break the Water Speed Record in his boat *Bluebird*. The boat became airborne during the second (northbound) run on Coniston Water, crashed, and the deceased was killed.

The verdict was: "Donald Malcolm Campbell died as the result of an accident."

I did, however, say quite a lot more. The conclusions that a coroner comes to have to be based on evidence heard in court. This is most often verbal evidence but can be written documents, photographs, or more unusually film but of course all of those things were available here. I recorded the fact that *Bluebird* had achieved 297 miles per hour on the first run and that on the return run it achieved 328 miles per hour. I said:

Bluebird was designed by Norris Brothers Limited in 1954, and had its first trial in February 1955, nearly twelve years prior to the events we are talking about. Originally it had a Beryl Jet Engine and in 1965 that was replaced with a higher powered Orpheus Engine and in 1966 by a second Orpheus Engine and we are of course talking here about effectively jet aeroplane engines harnessed to a boat.

In 1967 the design and the boat itself was not a new boat. It was twelve years old and it seems to me extremely significant that it was designed to have three points of contact with the water and that when it was travelling as it was designed to at 300mph it would raise onto the planing shoes and there would be fourteen square inches of contact between the boat and the water. If you cut a sheet of A4 paper into six you get very roughly fourteen square inches. The whole of the boat is sitting on that and it goes to a depth in the water of one tenth of an inch so in effect, although it's a boat, it's very nearly an air-craft.

A number of theories had been put forward to explain what happened. This is how I dealt with them.

The first one is that possibly *Bluebird* hit a submerged object, a log, anything really, that might have been floating. Now there is not one scrap of positive evidence to that effect, nobody saw an object, no object was recovered later and in any event I have evidence from Dr Happian-Smith which I accept, that if *Bluebird* had hit a submerged object then it would have had precious little effect on it anyway so I am happy to dismiss that theory completely as being a non starter.

Another theory that's been put forward is that *Bluebird* ran out of fuel and this is sometimes backed up by the fact that Donald Campbell did not stop after the first run to refuel before making the second run. Again Dr Happian-Smith has said, well, the boat had a 48 gallon tank and he's done detailed cal-culations and he thinks that at the point where it lifted off there were probably still at least seventeen gallons of fuel left on board and again I am happy to accept that evidence and say that there is no evidence available to me to sug-gest that *Bluebird* did run out of fuel. I don't think it did. If we just deal briefly with the fact that Mr Campbell did not stop to refuel. Firstly, as I have said, he had no need to, he had enough fuel to do both runs. He'd done it before about six times so I am told and having done 297 mph southwards there are a number of things that might have happened. One; he might have thought the sooner I get this over with the better, I'll take advantage of the conditions while I can, they are OK, I'll get going. Two; he might have showed the extremely human emotion of fear. He might have thought, I really do want this over with as quickly as possible; I'm not hanging around to refuel. If he did, that just shows to me what a very human human being he was but, as I said, there was no need for him to stop anyway, he could carry on, do the second run without stopping, wasting a few minutes in refuelling and possibly losing the conditions, a wind could have come across at a moment's notice and just stopped him being able to take the second run so for whatever reasons he did the second run straight away without interruption and I read nothing significant into that, as I say I don't think that he ran out of fuel.

There was also mention of the fact that you can be starved of fuel, an engine can be starved of fuel without actually running out if there is foaming, if aeration gets into the fuel, you can get an air bubble and effectively that stops the supply of fuel. I have heard that this would be a theoretical problem in aeroplanes and that as a consequence kerosene, which is the type of fuel being used, has an additive to prevent foaming and I accept that that was done. I accept that foaming did not occur, foaming was not the reason that all this happened.

Further there is reference to a phenomenon called "inlet tract icing" whereby the front of the engine, because of prevailing conditions, ices, forms a frost shield if you like. There was no reference to that ever having happened in respect of *Bluebird*, there is no mention of it by Mr Campbell on what he was talking about and the evidence therefore simply does not exist to support the theory that the inlet tract did get iced up and that caused the lack of forward momentum from the engine and that in turn led to the accident.

We also have to look at the possibility of an engine mount failure. Dr Happian-Smith told me that there clearly was an engine mount failure, he saw that, but what is not clear is how and when that mount did fail. If it had failed during the run then the boat would not have continued in the way that it did on the surface of the water, there would have been, if I can put it this way, all hell let loose I am sure behind Mr Campbell, he would have known there was something desperately wrong and he would have had to abort the run so I don't think that the engine mount failed at an early point and as we know there were tremendous forces applied to the boat in the course of what happened to it, particularly the cart wheeling phase, and I think that the most likely explanation for that failed engine mount is that it happened during the after effects, i.e. it was not the cause.

What I come to next is the fact that *Bluebird* had a safety margin of six degrees when travelling in ideal conditions at 300 mph which meant that if the front moved six degrees off level that it is likely to become airborne. A number of factors come into the equation that tell me that this is where we are getting to the crux of what did happen to *Bluebird*. Firstly there is no doubt that *Bluebird* got up to well over 320 mph, probably 328, that may not be precisely to the exact mile, but well over 320 anyway so it was getting not far short of 10% above it's designed speed, the 300 mph at which there is a six degree margin of safety so it was over that. Extra speed means extra lift, the boat is going at the fastest speed it has ever gone at and the other conditions that do come into play in my view are these.

Firstly the lake was not an absolute smooth mirror surface. It's been said, well, it never is and you can sympathise with that, it's true that its very rare indeed to be totally flat but nonetheless any slight ripple, however caused, whether it's by the wind or by any other cause, is going to have some, albeit minor, effect on the overall stability of the boat.

The second factor that came into play was the wake from the southern run because as we have said *Bluebird* turned around straight away and went back. The refuelling process might have, well it would have allowed the wake to die down to an even greater extent. I am not suggesting that the wake was creating big waves or anything like that but it's another factor that goes into the equation and as we have heard the brake was used on the southern run and the brake would, I think, create its own wake which again would be affecting the lake surface so we have a number of factors that are making the lake surface slightly less than ideal and it was demonstrated very clearly on the video in particular, which was evidence, and I have been shown a photograph which is technically not evidence before the court but nonetheless I have seen it showing that very shortly before *Bluebird* took off one of the sponsons had lifted a very significant, a very noticeable degree off the water, probably as much as a foot and that is clearly a serious thing to happen.

Now I come back to the three points of contact which I said I thought was very significant and the significance is this, that with a four point of contact boat if it rolls to the side it retains some degree of stability, the movement is in a sideways motion only. With three points of contact if there is a roll to one side it also is a slight pitch of the boat backwards or forwards and so any movement off an absolute level will create more than just the one effect of as I say going left or right. It will also induce a slight forward/backward motion as well. That's 'tramping' and 'tramping' I think is the big factor that if you like is the final thing that causes *Bluebird* to take off.

We discussed at some length the possibility that the final factor was Mr Campbell backing off the throttle and that became a little bit complicated but the outcome of that seems to me to be that it was a deliberate policy to back off the throttle going into the measured kilometre and I accept that that was done for reasons of safety at the end, i.e. deceleration reasons. I entirely accept that there is no evidence whatsoever, although I had thought so earlier on, that Mr Campbell ever said "I am having to pull back" or words to that effect. As I said, what I have to go on is evidence before this Court. The phrase comes from a book. It was picked up by Dr Happian-Smith. He assumed that because Mr Norris had been involved in that part of the book that it might be right but then I took evidence from Mr Evans and from Mr Smith and indeed I think from Mr Robinson which none of them could remember that phrase being used and so, as I say, there is no evidence it was used therefore I accept that it was not.

The throttle was however clearly after the event in an off position and it seems to me that what happened is that almost as an instinctive reaction at the point where Mr Campbell knew the boat was going airborne he took his foot off the throttle, that's why it's found in that way afterwards also the brake, the water brake, was deployed and I think again there would be an instinctive reaction to try to use that to brake the speed of the boat and keep things safe and it was just too late. That's not a criticism of Mr Campbell. As we know, if he had deployed that brake at any point the record attempt was off. He would have come to a halt and most certainly not have gone through the measured kilometre at anything above the speed record let alone 300 mph so, yes the throttle was off, yes the brake was deployed and probably they were the instinctive reactions of somebody who knew the boat, just doing that almost without thinking, and that's why they were found in that way. The brake is a two inch rod and as I say the clear evidence discovered after the boat was brought back up to the surface of the lake was that it had been extended.

I want to deal briefly with the perspex cover. That was shattered, it had sharp edges and although it's probably a difficult issue to discuss it is a possibility that one of those sharp edges literally decapitated Mr Campbell. It is equally possible that the forces involved acting upon Mr Campbell alone caused his head to come off. The forces are absolutely tremendous. The head is an unstable part of the body attached by fairly breakable items and so it is possible that decapitation occurred simply as a consequence of the forces involved.

I also want to mention the harness. People may say well, he should have had a five point harness not just the four point harness that he was wearing I have got to say that whatever he was wearing it would have made not one jot of difference because of what was involved. It is not the fact that he may have submarined through the harness that had anything to do with his death, it is the forces that were involved on him so whatever harness is being used it would have made no difference.

What we have to remember throughout this is firstly that we are looking at what happened in 1967 and not 2002. This was an attempt on a world record. The boat was not designed for safety and safety alone and in saying that I am not saying that safety was ignored, it clearly was not ignored, but what we are looking at is a boat at the absolute cutting edge of technology, of record breaking attempts where speed is the overriding factor and so by saying that speed is of the essence of this boat I am not criticising either the project as a whole or indeed any individual who may have designed it, certainly not. I think we should just retain a sense of reality. It was an attempt to go faster on water than anybody in the history of the world had ever gone. It is an inherently dangerous activity. Mr Campbell himself must have known that, the whole team must have known that and as we have seen the quality of the engineering that went into the boat is borne out by the fact firstly that it endured this absolutely horrendous crash, hitting water at about 185 mph and cartwheeling and then spending 34 years immersed in water on the bed of the lake and despite that we have all seen either the original or else photos of what it looked like 34 years later when it was brought up and I think that says that the engineering that was used on *Bluebird* was of an extremely high quality indeed. Can I also just remind us that *Bluebird* was designed and built by human beings without the benefit of computers and, as I say, nothing I say is intended as a criticism of its design or build, quite the reverse.

I also dealt in the summing up with what I called 'the suicide theory'. I did so because there were some rumours and whispers that Donald Campbell had somehow deliberately engineered his own death. I said:

> There is not one shred of evidence before me today, or indeed in anything else I have ever seen, read or heard, that persuades me that there was any motive for suicide, any intention of suicide or that Mr Campbell had any kind of unusual state of mind at the time. As I say I wouldn't even have discussed this but for the whispers and the rumours that have gone on.
>
> As we have heard Mr Campbell very nearly did gain the world water speed record. He had done 297 mph on the southern run. He had reached 328 or thereabouts on the run back north and he would have been an absolute publicist's dream. He was good looking, he was charming, he would have been able to cash in, if that's the right way to put it, on his good looks and on the fact that he had achieved the record and he was worth far more in that state than ever he would have been committing some kind of so called heroic suicide so I have no doubt whatsoever this was not suicide. I hope that puts an end to that myth once and for all.
>
> This was what it looks like – it was a courageous, it was a very inherently dangerous attempt as any attempt must be on a world speed record and so my verdict is that this was an accidental death. It was an unexpected, and unintended event that arose like most accidents do from a combination of several factors that all happened to occur at the same time and those factors, I have gone through them already, but just to recap, they are that the lake was not absolutely calm, whether from the wake of the first run, the water brake, a passing breeze whatever, it was not absolutely calm, the boat was 'tramping' and the speed was well in excess of 300 mph which is greater than anything *Bluebird* had done before.

Having come to the formal end of the inquest I perhaps went a little further than some of my colleagues might have done and I could be accused of playing to the gallery but I said:

> I have felt enormously honoured and privileged to have had any part in this inquest at all. I was seventeen years old when it happened and I saw the crash on a black and white grainy television set. At that time Donald Campbell was a hero to me, by which I mean a person that you can genuinely look up to and

respect. My more recent involvement in his story has just enhanced my feelings towards his status. I very much like the story, I hope it's not just a story, that on Christmas Day 1966 Donald Campbell took out *Bluebird* for a run on the lake with a few of his friends helping him, no time keepers, no official team, and he got up to 250 mph. If that's true it's wonderful. He was not one of these persons who I might describe as an automaton who just pressed on for glory without thinking of risks. He was not reckless and foolhardy. He knew that he was taking a risk as anybody involved in that kind of venture must do. He made his calculations and his judgements at huge speeds literally under enormous pressure and with very little margin for error. As I say I feel he was a very human human being. He matches up to any definition of courage that you might like to give and to me he was and he remains a true hero.

As I stopped speaking I saw three people (one of them was Bill Smith) make as if to applaud and then realised that being in a court they should not do so. In the middle of my summing up there was a torrential downpour which was so loud drumming on the roof that I had to stop for a short time. I still today feel enormously privileged that I was the coroner in post when Donald Campbell was found and therefore the one to conduct the inquest.

♛ ♛ ♛ ♛ ♛ ♛ ♛ ♛

When I obtained the 1967 Coroner's file from archives I found something very strange.

When someone dies and the body is not recovered it can cause endless difficulties in registering the death and dealing with the person's property. No inquest could be held in 1967 and no medical certificate of cause of death could be issued because the body had not been recovered. There was a procedure that could be used. The coroner could write to the Home Office and the Home Secretary could authorise the coroner to proceed with an inquest even in the absence of a body. This is a rare example of a government minister being able to dictate the actions of a judicial officer.

John Poole, the coroner at the time, duly wrote to the Home Office but was refused permission to hold an inquest. The thought processes I discern from the exchange of letters are that everyone in the world with a television set had seen what happened and there was no suggestion of negligence so what was the point of an inquest. However also on the file the Home Office told John Poole that they and the Registrar General's Office had discussed the circumstances of the case and the Registrar General was prepared, on the evidence available, to authorise the local registrar to register the death if someone went to the Registrar's office for that purpose. So Donald Campbell's death was

Figure 7: Donald Campbell with his daughter Gina on Bluebird.
Clear evidence of a strong bond which endures.

registered a couple of weeks after his death in what I regard as a rather questionable procedure. The cause of death was recorded then as: "Killed when the speedboat *Bluebird* which he was piloting crashed"

That is not really a cause of death at all but very like a coroner's narrative verdict even though the coroner had been denied jurisdiction. The informant – the person who went to the registrar at Coniston to register the death – was the dutiful PC Sherdley part of whose statement was recorded earlier in this chapter. I hope no one builds a conspiracy theory on this. It was a different era. People were willing to accept what they saw at face value and did not need to dig for a hidden story. There was no suppression of the inquest. It was simply that neither the coroner nor the Home Office saw any pressing need to hold one and the problem of registering the death was solved with extreme practicality.

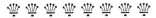

Shortly after the discovery of Donald Campbell's remains I received a call from a man who said that his uncle had gone missing in a boating accident on Coniston in 1969 and every time a body was discovered in Coniston (and over the years there have been a few) he wondered whether it was his uncle whose body had never been found.

After the inquest and the inevitable worldwide publicity, a number of people contacted me. Keith Harrison who supplied one of the 1967 statements read at the inquest told me he thought the cause of the accident was pure speed and that *Bluebird* was not going to be used after the record attempt but was to be at the Boat Show the day after the accident and then taken to the Science Museum for permanent display.

A man rang to say that the engineers at Imperial College's wind tunnel had said the boat was inherently unsafe. I also received a 'green ink' letter, though to be fair it was not written in green and it was signed. It read "Mr Donald Campbell commit suicide to go at that speed. He didn't want to live is our point of view, the speed was to (sic) great."

With Donald Campbell's body were several artefacts of historic interest. The most important was the blue overalls but there was also a glove and a belt. The police were told that as they had been in water for 34 years they should stay in the same medium or they would disintegrate on drying out. Carl Langhorn a scenes of crime officer with Cumbria Police went to Coniston to collect enough water and found it very difficult to do without feeling observed. When he did eventually collect what he needed it was so heavy that he slipped and fell in the lake. The objects stayed in a waterproof plastic box stored in the police station loft space for some time. I did check them myself after a while and found the water was evaporating. This would explain why any passing tourist might have seen a bald office worker in a suit and tie one morning with a plastic bucket on a rope trying to collect water from Coniston. This was me and collecting water like that is not at all easy, though I managed to get enough to keep the overalls covered. I was happy to hand the problem over to Bill Smith soon after.

SEVEN

How People Deal with Death

1 REACTIONS TO DEATH AND GRIEF

Calpurnia:

> *When beggars die there are no comets seen*
> *The heavens themselves blaze forth the death of princes.*

Caesar:

> *Cowards die many times before their deaths;*
> *The valiant never taste of death but once.*
> *Of all the wonders that I yet have heard,*
> *It seems to me most strange that men should fear;*
> *Seeing that death, a necessary end,*
> *Will come when it will come.*

Julius Caesar, William Shakespeare

Sudden and unexpected loss of your partner or anyone else close to you can result in collapse or anger, certainly disbelief and denial. I met thousands of people within a few days of the loss of someone very close to them. Most people kept their emotions well in control at the opening of the inquest which is when I first met them, but as coroner I had to be prepared for any kind of response and not to betray any surprise myself.

On one occasion a man whose wife had died came in with a blanket over his shoulder, patting it and saying, "There, there, don't worry, it'll be alright." If it helped him then that was fine so long as I did not react in a negative or shocked way, and by the time he attended the full inquest a few weeks later he had moved on and was coming to terms with his grief.

In my early days as coroner I opened an inquest in my solicitor's office. Again it was a man who had lost his wife. We went through the formal legal process and I explained what the procedure would be in the coming weeks all of which he accepted calmly and sensibly. Then I asked him if he had any questions. "Yes" he said, pointing over my shoulder "who painted that picture?" (The answer in case you want to know was W. Heaton Cooper and it was of Scafell Pike.)

I had to make sure whoever was in front of me regarded me as reliable and unemotional at a time when they had lost their grounding in normality and stability.

On another occasion a group of three people came into a room at the Kendal Police Station to open an inquest – the widow and two friends. It was one of the friends who, while still walking in asked very angrily "And who are these people?" (Answer, two plain clothes police officers). It would have been easy to respond with anger or sarcasm but it would not have been helpful so I simply asked him to take a seat and said I would explain everything and answer any questions.

These three all happened when I was opening the inquest in an informal setting, possibly because no court room was available. Looking back now I wonder if that altered the dynamics to allow a different response because in a court room there really is no mistake as to who is in charge since the coroner sits elevated above the court's floor level. Sitting round a table is different. These days inquests are not opened in the same way and identification is usually accepted from a written statement. Family members do not often attend. I feel this is an opportunity wasted. I found that the opening was a chance to introduce myself to the family, to explain the process and to let them ask any questions. Answers were always truthful. Often I would be asked when the inquest would be held. Sometimes, when I said it could be two or three months, or in the case of a road traffic accident eight or nine, my reply was greeted with disbelief. I found it better to be accurate than unrealistically hopeful. If I had said the inquest would be finished in a few weeks I would inevitably have a disappointed family and I would have lost their trust.

A much more immediate reaction to grief happened one Sunday afternoon. A lady took her elderly mother out for a drive to the Lake District. Mother went quiet; worryingly quiet. Somehow the daughter found where the doctor lived in Coniston and he confirmed that mother was indeed beyond any help. At that point the daughter had her course of action clear though it was not what the textbook would have said. Instead of waiting for the doctor to ring the police, the body to be taken to Furness General Hospital and the inevitable waiting, explanation and probable post mortem the lady drove her mother all the way back to Blackpool and sorted out the process there. When all this was relayed to me on Monday morning it was impossible to have the police tell her off for a gross breach of procedure or even to have a quiet word along the lines of "If this happens again…"

Behaviour at inquests was usually responsible and emotions were usually under control during the process but might be released at the end. I recall one lady being rather insensitive. Her husband had killed himself, and his family blamed her for going off with another man. She turned up at the inquest with her new partner and since inquests are open to anyone he could not be denied admission. In a different inquest an eighteen-year-old man had to give evidence. His father gave him a round of applause when he finished.

One doctor walked into an inquest a few minutes late, sat down and drained a can of Coca Cola. Drinks were a potential problem. There was always water and a glass available at inquests but it became the fashion for some people to clutch a bottle of water wherever they went. There is a difference between someone taking a drink out of an upturned bottle rather than sipping demurely from a glass so bottles were not allowed. There was also the question of what was in the bottle. I always had one advantage over other judges if someone behaved badly. I did not have to say they were being disrespectful to me, I could say they were being disrespectful to the deceased.

Most people turned up reasonably dressed though fewer and fewer men came in suit and tie as the years went by. My officers were under instruction to make witnesses and others aware of some rules. Mobile phones were to be switched off. No hats were to be worn in court (fairly obvious to most people but not always to baseball cap wearers). No chewing was allowed when the witness was giving evidence. I sometimes wondered how bereaved family members would react if they came into court and found me in a polo shirt or, like one witness at an inquest opening, three-quarter length shorts. So it was always suit and tie for me and I did have one superstition. On the first day of any inquest scheduled to last more than a day I wore the same tie. It was black yellow and blue with a single small white rose motif. This is one of several Yorkshire County Cricket Club ties that I possess.

Sometimes grief can turn to anger and not always against the right person. One lady lost her son. He was assaulted and survived long enough for the assailants to be convicted and sentenced for causing actual bodily harm. Then he died. Mother blamed the doctor and I had to summon him to court anyway because he failed to write the report I had asked for. At the lunch adjournment I left the Council Chamber and walked right by the family having a shouting match with mother apparently in a minority of one. The family had already made it clear in court they did not condone the way the mother was questioning the doctor. The police were already on the way and after lunch I just told them all to behave which they did. The death was clearly down to the assailants not the doctor, but mother felt, understandably denied full justice because the guilty parties could not be charged with murder or manslaughter. They had already been dealt with by the criminal court while the victim was still alive.

Someone else had a bone to pick with a doctor and achieved his goal in a very controlled but effective way. A man had lost his wife and though the doctor had not caused her death the husband thought he could improve the doctor's manner. He did not tell me the details in advance but insisted he had questions he wanted the doctor to answer. I thought that as the doctor could also help me understand what had happened I would call him as a witness. I asked my questions and gave the husband his turn. I cannot claim this is verbatim but it is close.

Husband: Do you remember coming to see my wife before her operation?

Doctor: Yes

H: Do you remember me being there?

D: Yes

H: Do you remember marking which leg you were to operate on?

D: Yes

H: And do you remember that you didn't say a single word to either of us in the time you were there?

The doctor accepted that his communication skills needed improvement and the husband had made his point. Many lawyers could learn from that exchange too. Quiet pursuit of the answer you want and no histrionics when you get it. If I had known in advance what exactly the husband wanted to ask I should, on a strict reading of the rules, have refused because the question had no bearing on the lady's death. But I know that the exchange was very important to the bereaved husband and to have denied him would have been morally wrong. Inquests can sometimes achieve more than the strictly limited findings required by law. It may even be that the doctor learned a lesson and improved his bedside manner. I do hope so.

Sometimes after a post mortem it was necessary to send an organ, often the heart, away for examination by a specialist. This gave the family a problem, because the funeral could go ahead but without the heart or other organ, or they could wait until the body was complete which might mean a delay of several weeks. They usually chose to go ahead and the organ would ultimately be cremated or buried in the same plot as the body. The information gathered could be extremely significant, for example identifying a defect which might be inherited and about which living members of the family should therefore take medical advice.

The real problem was however with blood and even urine samples when the opinion of the Human Tissue Authority was that the family should be asked about the ultimate disposal of these rather less emotive samples. Invariably the family asked that the sample be destroyed. I would have preferred not to have to ask at all.

Sometimes the property of the deceased became a problem. I was told this story from a time before I was coroner. A man hanged himself using, rather unusually, a garden hosepipe. Some weeks after the funeral and the inquest a relative turned up at the police station asking for the hose. The stand-in coroner's officer said it would take some time to get it out of storage so suggested the relative come back later. This gave the officer time to go home, retrieve the hose and hand it over as promised. I do not know if he had to explain that it had been in a damp bit of the store.

Altogether different motives came out when a different coroner's officer dealt with the death of a man who seemed to have few friends apart from his cat, Billy. She gave the cat a good home for several years rather than send him to the uncertain fate of a rescue society.

2 MEMORIALS

Many people are laid to rest in earth with an elaborate memorial stone. Others say in advance that they want no such thing. A previous secretary of the Coroners' Society, Dr John Burton, directed that there be no service or memorial of any kind after his death.

I went deliberately to one memorial, the National Memorial Arboretum which I found to be a dignified and respectful place and somewhere bereaved relatives could go in memory of the one they had lost.

Others I came across by accident. By Horse Guards Parade in London is a memorial to police who lost their life on duty. On the day I was there the book of remembrance was open at the name of PC Bill Barker a Cumbrian policeman who died in 2009 when a bridge collapsed after prolonged rain leading to devastating floods. On the embankment on the south side of the Thames in London near to St Thomas' Hospital is a simple plaque remembering the victims of Human BSE (vCJD), i.e. Creutzfeld-Jakob disease. I will tell the story of one victim later.

On Oxenholme Station is a plaque to remind us of the death of PC George Russell who was shot there in 1965 pursuing an armed criminal. In Wigan Parish Church is a memorial to two cousins Ralph Thickness, nineteen, and Thomas Woodcock, twenty, who died on Windermere on 13 September 1863.

Memorials can go wrong. This one is from 1831 and the worthy sentiments usually attributed to the Victorians were already in fashion. Engraved on a headstone at Woolwich, the facts and the homily clash.

Sacred to the memory of Major James Brush who was killed by the accidental discharge of a pistol by his orderly, 14th April 1831
Well done thou good and faithful servant

We are all familiar with bunches of flowers left by the roadside or in front of a building. Sometimes the flowers are renewed for months or even years on end. I had to issue a public warning about this once. The press gladly picked up my words as it gave them a new angle on the sad story of three young people killed in a car crash.

It was on the A590 at Greenodd and people were parking just off the main road and walking along to the point where the car had left the road. There were the usual flowers and teddy bears and strangest of all an iced cake. Getting to that point however was extremely dangerous as the road has no path and very little verge. It also bends both ways and visibility ahead for vehicles on the road is limited. It is a place where apart from this you would never see a pedestrian. Whether it was because people listened to what I said or whether from pure good fortune, there were no further injuries or deaths.

My officer George Cubiss visited one lady whose husband or partner had died when his car went into some trees off the road. Flowers were placed at that spot for years after. What George told me was that the lady had a coffee table and its base was a wheel from the car.

Figure 8: Plaque by the Thames, south bank.

3 DEATHS WHICH HAPPEN ABROAD

Coroners sometimes have to investigate deaths which have occurred abroad. This happens when a body is repatriated to this country. A coroner has legal jurisdiction and a legal obligation to investigate when a body is lying within that coroner's district. Military deaths in recent conflicts resulted in inquests in England and Wales because current practice is to return the body rather than bury it where the deceased fell. Those who died in the First and Second World Wars were buried in France, Singapore or wherever they died as can be seen from the war graves in many countries around the world. The deaths of those people would not have resulted in an inquest in England or Wales.

I dealt with a variety of deaths abroad. A road traffic case in Canada. A man who fell from a block of flats in Hong Kong. A man indulging in a risky solitary sex act in China. Many deaths were quite natural – simply people having heart attacks whilst on holiday. One thing worth noting though is that our European partners tended to be the least co-operative in supplying information. France and Spain were the worst, with officials frequently failing to respond to simple requests for facts.

In 1998 Clive Allison drowned in the river Soane at Lyon in France. His parents, Jim and Pat were not helped by the French authorities either at the time Clive went missing or afterwards when they needed information and the results of any investigation the French police had undertaken. Nor did the local British Consul offer any useful help. Mr and Mrs Allison enlisted the help of their local MP Tim Collins. There was even a short adjournment debate in the House of Commons. I saw the debate and it was sobering to hear a letter I had written to Mr Collins about the shortcomings of our European partners read out in such an august place. Some limited information did come through. It was in French and though I could understand the sense of what was there I had to have the documentation translated so that the inquest could be completed. The toll on Clive's parents must have been considerable at a time when they needed support and Jim was kind enough to write to the local paper, the *Evening Mail* in support of the local coroner service some time later when possible reforms might have removed the service from the hands of local people.

In 1996 I dealt with the death of an English worker on a German building site. He had been unfortunate enough to be underneath a crane load of girders which came adrift and fell on him. The German investigation was hopeless and I was told off the record that was often the case – the labour force might be unofficial and after something like this everyone would disappear and there would be no investigation such as our Health & Safety Executive would do. The German Public Prosecutor did inform me that there was to be no prosecution. The police report I received was very short of detail about what had happened and failed to identify a single witness. I tried to highlight this problem in the summing up in the hope that the newspapers would pass on my warnings about working on building sites in Germany.

On the other hand I remember a very helpful report from police in Zimbabwe (many years ago before the country got into its present state) and a very detailed police report and post mortem report from China translated into excellent English. The mortuary staff said the stitching on the corpse was the best they had ever seen. One body returned from the USA had been given so much post mortem make up that the family could not immediately recognise their loved one.

4 BORDER REIVERS

In the Middle Ages the area north and south of the England/Scotland border was a dangerous place to live and to farm. A large tract of territory was referred to as The Debatable Lands. Border reivers were raiders, cattle rustlers and not particularly interested whether you were English or Scottish. Many farms still have a building which is solid and fortress-like, because it was exactly that – a defence within which people and cattle could be secured from the marauders in the hope that they would give up and move on to someone else's land for easier pickings. Not only were they responsible for rape and pillage, loot and plunder but they also broke that rule we learned in school, i before e except after c. The point of recounting this however is to explain that people who had lost a close relative at the hands of the reivers were be-reived or as we now spell it bereaved. The story is told in full in Rory Stewart's excellent book *The Marches*.

5 HOW DOES ENGLISH LAW DEAL WITH DEATH?

Because death is unavoidable and inevitable it might be expected that parliament would have legislated on the subject, defined what death is and when it happens and kept the law up to date. In fact there is no statutory definition of death in English law. Laymen may assume that death is an event whose time can be fixed with accuracy if observed and with reasonable certainty if not, but from a medical point of view death is a process not an event. Different organs cease to function at different times rather than all at once. Determining the time of death is essential to the plots of many detective novels but it is something pathologists often refuse to speculate on.

I remember asking one senior pathologist for his estimate of a time of death. He asked for more information about the finding of the body and the deceased's known movements. I told him, let us say, that he had been seen putting out some rubbish by a neighbour on Thursday night, and was found dead at the bottom of the stairs on Saturday morning. The pathologist responded by telling me that the time of death could accurately be stated as sometime between Thursday night and Saturday morning. I did not know whether to laugh at the expert's effrontery or angrily tell him he would never do another post mortem for me. I did neither and just accepted the lack of help.

Legally speaking there are many reasons why the time or date of death may be important. Only after death can someone's financial affairs be resolved by applying for letters of administration or probate. A policy of insurance may either have lapsed or still be valid, depending on the date of death. Distribution of property may be affected by when a person dies. This is seen most dramatically when husband and wife die in an accident. The law assumes that the older person died first but if there is evidence that one person did survive the other then the actual order of death applies. This can have an almost arbitrary effect on who inherits the couple's assets assuming there are no joint children. Inheritance tax can also be greater or lesser depending on how long someone has survived after giving property away.

It is also important to family members to know as accurately as possible when a loved one died. Could a person have been saved if they had been visited or telephoned at a certain time? Was the deceased conscious or unconscious, dead or alive for hours after a fall?

Because parliament has not legislated on death it is the job of the courts to rule on specific cases which become precedents and result in a degree of certainty as to when death does occur. This also has the effect of allowing the courts to evolve the law as medical science advances. Death can be defined as the absence of vital functions but that is not helpful. The absence of breathing and heart beat was a previous refinement but the current benchmark is the absence of brain stem function. There are detailed protocols for confirming this. The law can use the brain stem test without the need for legislation as there was no legislation for the previous test.

Organs may only be taken from a person who has died (obviously this does not apply to transplants from living donors such as a single kidney or bone marrow). If it were otherwise the cause of death would be the removal of the organ and this would make the medical team guilty of murder and conspiracy to murder with all the inevitable criminal and professional consequences, as well as civil liability for compensation to the deceased's estate and dependents. To be as effective as possible the donor's circulation must be working to keep the organ in optimum condition. A definition of death based on absence of circulation would not be helpful but a test of brain stem death means that all concerned, namely the medical staff and the family can proceed on the basis that the donor is dead, even though the heart and lungs are kept working artificially.

Murder is not defined by statute. Again this allows the courts to deal with specific problems in specific cases and a concept and definition of murder emerges at common law, i.e. the law as enunciated by the courts. In one case it was argued that a victim had died because the doctors switched off life support rather than as a consequence of the violence inflicted on him by the accused. The judge was able to dismiss this unworthy argument and said it was: "Somewhat bizarre to suggest that where a doctor tries his conscientious best to save the life of the patient... skilfully using sophisticated methods, drugs and machinery to do so, but fails in the attempt and therefore discontinues treatment, he can be said to have caused the death of the patient." Putting it another way, the patient died despite what the doctors did, not because of their efforts.

From the thirteenth century it was part of the common law that for offences involving death, an act or omission was conclusively presumed not to have caused the death if more than a year and a day elapsed before the victim died. This was at least a partial definition relating an event (assault) to a consequence (death). The rule, which sounds as quaintly English as it sounds arbitrary, was abolished by the Law Reform (Year and a Day Rule) Act 1996 following a Law Commission Report and a campaign by Alan Milburn MP on behalf of a constituent affected by the rule. It was so specific and so entrenched over centuries that legislation was thought necessary to repeal it.

Tony Bland was a victim of the football disaster at Hillsborough. He was left in a persistent vegetative state, where the conscious activity of the brain had ceased but the brain stem was not dead. The hospital trust where he was being cared for applied to court and the case came ultimately to the House of Lords (now the Supreme Court) where it was decided that all life-sustaining support could be discontinued including ventilation, nutrition and hydration. The justification for this was that it was in his best interests, that the principle of sanctity of life was not absolute and was not violated by ceasing to give treatment to which he had not consented and which conferred no benefit on him. Tony Bland had left no advance directive as to how he should be treated in these circumstances.

This case was heard before the Human Rights Act 1998 came into force. The European Convention on Human Rights and Fundamental Freedoms grants in Article 2 a right to life which has been much discussed interpreted and (some would say) extended by courts at home and in Europe. Other cases similar to Tony Bland have been to the courts since and with the same result.

HOW PEOPLE DEAL WITH DEATH

The consequence of the rulings is that all intervention is withdrawn. Feeding and hydration is stopped and death may take many days. Pure logic would say that it would be more humane to administer a lethal injection to end life quickly. The owner of a suffering animal is liable to prosecution for allowing it to suffer a slow death rather than have it humanely destroyed. In relation to humans however the law keeps steadfastly to the position that a person may in some circumstances be permitted to die, but may not ever be killed.

One of the judges acknowledged the moral dilemma but could not solve it. Lord Browne-Wilkinson said:

> How can it be lawful to allow a patient to die slowly though painlessly over a period of weeks from a lack of food but unlawful to produce his immediate death by a lethal injection? I find it difficult to find a moral answer to that question. But it is undoubtedly the law and nothing I have said casts doubt on the proposition that the doing of a positive act with the intention of ending life is and remains murder.

I pose another dilemma. If an application were made to court to withdraw all support including feeding and hydration from an elderly demented incontinent person on the grounds that it was in their best interests, how would the court react? I am sure the application would be rejected as there are tens of thousands of people in that sad state across the country. To allow many of them to starve to death would simply not be socially acceptable. But if you asked healthy people how they would like to be sustained if they fell into that state then I suspect many would want to be allowed to die. Indeed many would want the lethal injection which is not permitted in law. There are no simple answers but it is at least now open to us all to leave advance notice of how we wish to be dealt with if certain conditions overcome us.

The answer to the question at the head of this section is for me that parliament keeps well clear of the thorny questions posed by death and lets the courts deal with them. This reflects what happens to ordinary people in their lives. Death is not a topic of conversation. Even a person on their death bed who wants to talk about what will happen is likely to be met with "Oh, don't talk like that."

The courts in turn adopt a pragmatic approach and try to do justice in the particular case rather than apply precedent strictly. Attempts have been made in parliament to legislate on euthanasia, always by Private Members Bills and always without success. Governments have not thought it wise to express a firm policy on the subject as it evokes such strong feelings and whatever view was put forward it would alienate a large section of society. Other problems surrounding death are so varied and specific that it would be impossible to legislate for all eventualities so it is probably best that parliament stands back and leaves the courts to provide answers in individual cases. English law therefore deals with death on an ad hoc basis, confronting it only when it must; with dignity, practicality and stoicism – which is the English way.

I sense a slow change in attitudes to death. People do fly to Switzerland to end their life at the Dignitas clinic. Family members who accompany them risk prosecution for aiding and abetting suicide but no prosecutions have actually followed. There is debate in the correspondence columns of the papers and several people have applied to the courts to seek some kind of assurance that if their loved one does assist the death when they can no longer carry out the act then they will not be prosecuted. These applications never succeed and cannot do so under the present law. They do however keep the debate in the public consciousness. Doctors are divided. Some would happily help a patient to avoid suffering whilst others do not wish to be put in a position where they might be pressured into ending a life. There is no likelihood of an early resolution to the problem.

EIGHT

Modes of Dying

1 DRUGS

In the mid 1990s I noticed a dramatic increase in the number of people dying from the abuse of drugs, up from two or three a year to double figures. A recurring theme was people taking a multitude of drugs in a short space of time, their effects often being contradictory, and amongst these frequently the drug methadone appeared. Methadone is supposedly a heroin substitute and used in therapy for people addicted to heroin. Heroin itself was surprisingly uncommon in the lists of drugs that people who died had been abusing. It emerged that people who were prescribed methadone were selling it on and with the help of the local MP, John Hutton, subsequently Lord Hutton, we were able to persuade the health authorities to institute a regime in which patients prescribed methadone had to take it in the physical presence of the pharmacist dispensing it. This did lead to a marked decline in the number of deaths from drugs and especially those involving methadone. One professional told me that the younger generation was now shunning methadone as a drug of abuse following all the adverse publicity. Sadly they were still experimenting with other drugs and in the many cases where a death followed multiple drug use, alcohol was the most common.

Coroners voluntarily report drugs deaths to St George's Hospital Medical School in London and in 2003 I noticed considerable discrepancies between the numbers that were recorded in their annual report. They were considerably higher than the actual numbers of cases I had reported to them. I pressed them about the discrepancy and ultimately, after more than a year, was told that there had been 'a coding error'. Unfortunately it was too late to rectify the effect locally which had been the local newspaper reporting that Barrow was the drugs death capital of England based on unfortunately incorrect statistics. The St George's Hospital reports were not Government funded but obviously were taken at face value to the great detriment of Barrow-in-Furness's image.

I compiled annual figures of drug deaths showing the drugs used including alcohol, and the age groups and sent the report to anyone I could think of who might be interested including the press. Coroners have no power to make anyone do anything, and are not expected to identify trends or gather information together in this way. Nothing however prevented me from doing so and I hope that highlighting the problem made the medical profession more aware of the problem. I remember one GP being horrified when she discovered in an inquest that it was one of her trusted patients who was suppling the person who had died. The GP thought that he had been genuinely trying to give up drugs.

For a while I was asked to attend the local Drug Action Team meetings which I did with a senior detective Ian McBride. We found ourselves among a group of social workers and medical professionals who dealt with drug users. From my perspective the main problem at the time was the fact that methadone was killing far more people than heroin, i.e. the cure was more dangerous than the addiction. I remember asking in one meeting "why not give users heroin on prescription?" and being aware of a stunned silence lasting several seconds, until one person suggested "They live less chaotic lives on methadone". I also managed to silence the meeting once by asking "Shouldn't we have a drug user at these meetings", though the suggestion was acted on and a reformed drug user was asked to attend and did have useful information to offer.

In the world of the drug user reality is sometimes absent. In the inquest into the death of a man called Ronnie (I leave out his second name deliberately) a strange story emerged. Ronnie and his friends had an evening in and drank a lot and took a lot of drugs. The next day a friend (let's call him Jim) got up and found Ronnie slumped in a chair and asked him if he wanted a brew or if he would prefer a can of lager. When he got no reply he casually shook Ronnie whose head fell back lifeless against the chair back.

So what did Jim do? Ring the police? Ring for an ambulance? No. Jim smoked a couple of joints then had a walk into Barrow town centre, bought a bun, drank a can of lager and went to sit in the park. When he had done this he thought he had best go home and see what he could do for Ronnie. As you might expect, not very much.

Statements in drugs cases had recurring themes. There were always lots of people in the house. They usually did not know each other's real names but did know the strange nicknames they had. Two I remember were 'Slinks' and 'Dull'. The deceased person had often been snoring loudly not long before being found to be dead. And no-one who made a statement ever saw the deceased actually taking anything.

Towards the end of my time as coroner, I became aware that the problem was beginning to recur. A new generation of doctors and pharmacists needed to learn the lessons of history because prescribing had slowly reverted to the patient being able to take the methadone away with them so that once again it could be sold on the black market or stored up to be taken in one go as a binge which might well prove fatal. Barrow was also seen as a soft target by gangs from the big cities and there were many drugs deaths around 2018.

S. Ingleby Oddie was coroner for Central London from 1912 to 1939. In his 1941 autobiography he relates the story of an actress called Billie Carleton. She was starring in the West End at the Haymarket Theatre and aged 22. She was a user of heroin and cocaine and on 28 November 1918 after appearing on the stage twice the previous day and then celebrating victory in the Great War late into the night she was found dead at 4.30pm. She had been heard snoring loudly some time before. Mr Oddie explains that the strength of cocaine varies from one supplier to another and so it is easy to take more than you are accustomed to and overdose fatally. We assume this to be a relatively recent problem but clearly it is not. Mr Oddie also describes "excessive post-war drinking and drug taking amongst young people." The hippies of the 1960s thought they invented free love and free use of drugs but like most human behaviour it had all been done before.

Drugs became relevant in a different manner in the case of a sad young ten year old who was found hanged. He had had fourteen different homes and four schools. He was diagnosed with depression and Attention Deficit Hyperactivity Disorder and prescribed fluoxetine for the first condition and ritalin for the second. In the summing up I said this:

> We as a society quite rightly try to stop children dabbling in drugs by which I am referring to street drugs; we try to stop them experimenting with drugs, we denigrate it when they do experiment and we tell them they are messing with their own minds and yet a child with this label of Attention Deficit Hyperactivity Disorder is prescribed by doctors, under supervision of course and controlled, mind altering drugs of a very powerful nature – the full consequences of which I do not believe are still fully understood – and that's borne out by some remarks in the forensic science report and indeed the pathologist's report.
>
> Dr Witkowski who did the post mortem says it is very difficult to speculate how the two drugs fluoxetine and ritalin could affect Harry's mental state, however the influence cannot be excluded. And in the forensic reports they are saying that it is actually very difficult to measure the levels of these drugs in children so it seems very much to me as though these drugs and their effects and their levels and the measurement of their levels is still very much a work in progress from the point of view of medical science.

I could not accept that at ten years old he had proper insight into what his actions meant. He had told someone he wanted to kill himself and when asked why he said "Because it would be funny". I recorded a verdict that he died as a result of his own actions without understanding the true consequences. I found this one of the saddest referrals I dealt with. He was so young, bullied, medicated, misunderstood.

2 WATER

Water has perhaps played a disproportionate role in deaths locally, but then we do have lakes, rivers and the sea. At various times, people have fallen or jumped from boats in the Irish Sea, to be washed up on the coast. One person was found in a stream one New Year's Day having fallen in and been unable to get out. Twice people on boats on Coniston died when a sudden violent squall blew up on a previously clear day, and overwhelmed the boat. In one case the husband's last act was to hand his life jacket to his wife who survived. Another man drowned in a stream after his 'friends' gave him a cake laced with cannabis and he wandered off from the cottage where they were staying.

Councillor Les Burns was drowned trying to walk across the sands from Piel Island, near to Barrow-in-Furness, overcome by the tide. I decided it was accidental and ruled out suicide. I remember someone stopping me in the street in Barrow after the inquest and telling me that my decision had been very popular. Being popular is not part of a coroner's role. I was however glad to have been able to put an end to the rumours that had apparently been circulating that Councillor Burns had committed suicide.

Another death in the Barrow area was very sad in more ways than one. A toddler wandered into someone's house then out again but the occupants did nothing. Later he was found in the ornamental pond of another house. The person who found him did not pull him out but went off to get help. The ambulance crew had problems getting to the scene because a group of neighbours was gathered round and in the way. The child was lying face down on grass with his airways partially blocked. Whose windows were later smashed? The parents? The neighbours who saw the child but did nothing? No, the owner of the house with the pond.

A young man called Darrell Teal died at Devil's Bridge, Kirkby Lonsdale, where the motorbikers gather. He and his friends tried tombstoning which is aptly named. They jumped off the parapet into the River Lune ignoring the signs saying that this activity is both dangerous and against a local byelaw. Darrell hit the water, failed to surface and was swept along by the current unconscious and unable to do anything to try to save himself.

Satvir Singh, Harvinder Singh and Tajinder Singh died in an awful tragedy in Ullswater on 29 September 2006. One person who could not swim suddenly got out of his depth and quickly others got involved trying to help. As well as other Sikhs, two members of the public Mark Waters and Zak Radcliffe each pulled one person out and saved their lives. They all acted very bravely. The families of those who died accepted it stoically and with dignity. They said God had chosen that time and that beautiful place to take their sons back. They suggested warning signs that the lake shelves suddenly from paddling depth to very deep but if you put up one sign, when do you stop?

Deaths happened from time to time especially in hot summers. Someone would go for a swim not realising the water stays cold even in hot weather and get too far from the shore and safety. I recall one death where two children tried in vain to keep their father afloat when he got into trouble. In another a group of Scouts were being properly led by an adult and there was also an adult 'tail end Charlie'. Unfortunately it was the last man who got into difficulties and no one noticed as he stopped swimming and drowned.

Water was central to the death of Kathleen Mary Johnson but in a quite different manner. Her own mother had drowned and she suffered from mental health problems. She had been seen by a river and the worry was that she might drown herself. Whilst a resident on a mental health ward in Kendal she was allowed to have a bath unsupervised and put her head under the water for long enough to cause damage from which she died a few days later. Another sad lack of lateral thinking by those looking after her.

Water comes into most of the stories I tell at length, Donald Campbell and Carol Park and Coniston. Shafilea by the River Kent and the vapour which spread Legionnaires Disease. Water is essential to life but is often a factor in death.

3 Asbestos

The economy of Barrow-in-Furness is built on shipbuilding, a result of nearby haematite (iron ore) deposits and a sheltered position thanks to Walney Island and Barrow Island. There was also a steel works which had just closed when I moved to the area in 1975. The relevance to my position as coroner was that these heavy industries had used asbestos. It was particularly attractive in shipbuilding because of its fireproof qualities. A fire on a ship at sea is likely to be disastrous. It was used in sheets and as a paste and sprayed onto pipes as lagging. This was also done in the old hospital in Barrow and no doubt in many other buildings. Asbestos is a problem when it is disturbed, cut or broken and tiny fragments become airborne. When inhaled it can cause various lung ailments some of which may occur many years later.

I heard the same tales from workers both when I was a solicitor putting in claims for clients and as coroner. No-one told the men it was dangerous. There were no masks. Asbestos was screwed into 'snowballs' and thrown around and at each other. I saw a letter written by a factory inspector shortly after the Second World War to Vickers telling them asbestos was potentially dangerous but it was years before the risks were fully appreciated.

The consequence for me and other coroners in areas of heavy industry was that men and women dying of lung disease had to be subjected to a post mortem and a detailed examination of their lung tissue under the microscope. This usually showed if the disease was industrial in origin or natural and this in turn often conflicted with what the deceased person and his or her family had been told by the doctor. Some doctors would assume that because their patient worked in the shipyard then any lung disease was caused by the conditions there. The biopsy sample that can be taken from a live patient is very small and as compensation and state benefits were at stake the tendency was to err on the patient's side. After death a larger sample could lead to a more definite diagnosis. I found myself often in the position of having to tell a family that their loved one had died from a natural illness, not an industrial one or conversely that death was industrial not natural.

My verdict was not always appreciated, and though no compensation was claimed back by insurance companies so far as I know, the evidence of the pathologist might stop a claim succeeding if it had not been settled at the time of the death. Women were not immune from asbestos. Many women worked in the shipyard and especially in the war covered jobs that men traditionally did. Others were bogie girls, who drove around little trucks ferrying material and components from one part of the works to another. The most common story that I heard was of wives washing their husbands' overalls, and giving them a good shake-out in the back yard beforehand. In these various ways women might inhale asbestos. I was told that the specific disease of mesothelioma is caused not by a long and heavy exposure to asbestos but by a single fibre which decades later initiates cancer in this aggressive form.

Other areas of the country had their own specific industrial diseases. The area I come from, Doncaster in South Yorkshire, had a legacy of pneumoconiosis, lung disease suffered by coal miners. As a schoolboy in the sixth form I was part of an outing to see life at the coalface. Three miles underground at Brodsworth Pit as I recall it. It took weeks to get the dust out of our ears and we came away with a very different opinion of the men who spent every working day in that environment.

4 ROADS

I have said in inquests that roads are not inherently dangerous but the activities of human beings on roads can be. It is true that statistically some places have a disproportionate number of accidents. However, it is still human activity that causes things to happen. Excessive speed can cause accidents. A driver or pedestrian who has used alcohol or drugs increases the chances of an accident, but sometimes the causes are different.

One such was in 1999 on the M6 when a car went out of control because one of the tyres deflated suddenly. The police always investigate fatal accidents in considerable detail and have officers who are trained to a high level of expertise and who do the job full time. The road is shut for several hours and the investigator carries out a minute examination of the area looking for debris, marks on and near the road and they use the information collected together with witness statements to produce a report on how the accident happened. On this occasion they discovered that the tyre in question was thirteen years old and was the original tyre on the car from new and had done 84,000 miles. It is not that the tyre had no tread left, nor had maintenance on the vehicle been neglected, but the tyre had simply outlived its useful lifetime and disintegrated. Tyres are just not meant to last that long.

One tragic death of a young man from Durham was eminently preventable. He had what I called in the summing up:

> not really a motorbike at all, but a moped with a 49cc engine and a very low horsepower – we don't know exactly what it was but maximum would be about six horsepower.

Unfortunately he decided to take out the moped engine and replace it with a motorbike engine with approximately 60 horsepower. He cut the frame to accommodate the bigger engine, welded it back together and inserted no additional strengthening. He even put his alterations on the internet for all to see and received lots of feedback from far more experienced people telling him it was not a good idea, it was dangerous and one even used the words 'death trap'. Sadly the young man went ahead in defiance of all this advice, took his bike out on the road, and at about 50mph the bike became uncontrollable and crashed.

The Mitsubishi Delica was intended for use in urban Tokyo at quite low speeds and was only ever imported to the UK on the grey market i.e. privately. It had the disturbing ability, if travelling fast and braked hard, to rear up on its front wheels and so become uncontrollable. This happened on the M6 and two women died. This story was used by the media and one Delica owner wrote asking me what to do with his vehicle. I could not give him an answer. All I could do was what I had done, which was to investigate via my police experts and make the facts public in the inquest.

One man died when a Reliant Robin was being towed with a standard tow rope. The rope went slack, the three-wheeler caught up and 'skipped the rope' which went round the single front wheel causing the car to become unstable and overturn. Reliant said towing should only be done with a rigid cradle.

In a period of about eighteen months, around 2005, I dealt with half a dozen road traffic accidents with remarkable similarities. In each case there was an elderly couple, always with the man driving and in each case he made an error of judgement and it was almost always the wife who died. The common theme was misjudging the speed and distance of an approaching car on the main road as the elderly driver pulled out on to it.

The Crown Prosecution Service had a policy of not prosecuting someone who causes the death of their 'nearest and dearest'. This meant the driver was not brought before the Magistrates' Court or Crown Court on a charge of driving without due care and attention or dangerous driving or causing death by dangerous driving and so the opportunity for a court to remove his licence never arose. A driver could voluntarily give up his licence but then there was nothing to stop him re-applying for it later. The police told me about one driver who gave up his licence but then received a letter from the DVLC asking if he would like it reinstated and not surprisingly when a government agency tells you that your licence can be returned he duly said yes and started driving again.

A coroner has no power to ban someone from driving so after one of the inquests I approached the driver, a retired doctor aged 84, who was with his son, and suggested that he might stop driving. He was very annoyed indeed, despite his son agreeing with me, and said that anyone can make a mistake and he was perfectly all right to carry on driving.

Other accidents have a touch of inevitability about them. One man, banned from driving in the UK following a fatal accident, died on holiday in Crete riding a motor cycle, twice over the UK drink driving limit and not wearing a helmet.

I dealt with many motorbike deaths. A mistake on a motorbike is more likely to lead to serious consequences than a mistake in a car. This is simply because of the difference between two wheels and four and the inherent instability of a motorbike. Once it falls over the rider can go anywhere. You might assume the victims would be young tearaways and indeed some were young but far more deaths were older men, sometimes referred to as born-again bikers. These were middle aged men, usually doing well in employment or running their own business. They could buy modern high powered machines some being capable of 150 mph or more. The first good weekend of spring was often a bad time. Widows left behind perhaps with children reacted in different ways ranging from saying that at least he died doing something he loved to what a selfish … for not thinking about his family and what his death would do to them.

Most men on bikes do not get into difficulty and enjoy what must be a thrilling and sociable pastime. They always wear helmets and are conscious that not all motorists pay as much attention as they should and so they leave a margin for error (i.e. error by car drivers).

As for helmets they do undoubtedly save lives though I remember one unfortunate man who had a low speed accident in Barrow many years ago. He had a helmet and he was wearing it but had not bothered to fasten the strap under his chin. When he came off the bike the helmet went one way, he went another and he suffered fatal head injuries. This problem reminds me of a similar one in a different pastime. Horse riders used to wear hard hats but these were loose and often came off in a fall. Now they have straps connected to the helmet at three points and this means they are unlikely to come off.

I regularly stop at the sandwich wagon on Devil's Bridge at Kirkby Lonsdale where bikers gather. My counterpart in North Yorkshire Geoff Fell once suggested that he and I should do some preventative work. I think it was black humour but he suggested we go to Devil's Bridge dressed as the Grim Reaper complete with scythes and engage a few bikers in conversation. Just as a reminder of what could happen. Needless to say we never did it.

In a short period two young men died separately just by lying down in the road at night and being run over. The father of one asked why I referred to his son's drinking. He did not see what that had to do with it. At a blood alcohol level of 337mg/100ml I had to disagree. That is not far short of a potentially fatal alcohol poisoning level and four times over the legal limit for driving.

Sometimes what you learn from an inquest or investigation is not relevant to what happened. One lad gave evidence about the accident he was involved in. He was driving a farm tractor and trailer, and anticipated that a car coming the other way had not got room to pass and was not going to stop. He steered as far the opposite way as possible but the car did not stop in time and the driver was killed. What came out of the investigation was that the lad worked six and a half days a week, starting at 5.30am and finishing when his work was done. After the accident he was in severe shock but the boss pestered him to finish his day's work. This was 2007 not 150 years earlier.

Large farm vehicles are an example of the problems caused by incompatible road users. In most cases that I was involved with the error lay with the car or motorcycle rider making no allowance for vehicles which inevitably travel more slowly and take up a lot of space on the carriageway and take much longer to turn off.

As my area was so large I spent a lot of time on the road and had a closer contact with some events than anyone needs. It was not uncommon to find my way home on the A590 blocked by an accident. Friday afternoon was a common time. One morning I saw traffic slowing ahead and a cloud of smoke. I was able to make a detour but later in the day I learned that a man had died in what had happened. One Monday I had to go to Carlisle and took the scenic route through the Lake District rather than the faster M6. On this occasion it was a good decision as the motorway became blocked by a car transporter going through the central reservation again with fatal consequences. Even then on my return journey at a roundabout a trailer pulled by a tractor had overturned. Happily this time there were no casualties.

The A590 is the main road into Barrow-in-Furness from the east which is where almost all traffic comes from. The comedian Mike Harding described it as the longest cul de sac in the country. In an inquest I described it as a road littered with tragedy along its length. The road changes from dual carriageway to single several times and there are many places where there is no margin for error by which I mean when a driver makes a mistake there is no room to escape a collision. I dealt with dozens of deaths on this road over the years. In one inquest I mentioned the fact that when I drove along the A590, as I did frequently, I was conscious of each place where a fatal accident had happened. *The Evening Mail* managed to report this by saying I was 'haunted' by the road.

One place was the scene of many accidents. Greenodd was the mid-point of the railway line which ran from Lakeside, at the southern end of Windermere to Ulverston. This branch line was closed after the Beeching cuts though the section from Haverthwaite to Lakeside still exists as a working steam railway for tourists. The track at Greenodd was removed and a dual carriageway installed to bypass Greenodd village. It is amazing that the main road ran (more often crawled) through here until the 1980s. A junction with the A5092 was created which had a very wide central reservation. Cars emerging often misjudged the speed of traffic on the main road or simply failed to notice it and pulled out with dire consequences.

One such was a family from Malaysia in 1995. The lady in the centre of the rear seat died though all the other occupants were virtually unscathed. My officer at the time was George Cubiss. I talked to George and got it out of him that he had taken the family to his own home given them a meal and gone well beyond the call of duty. The family said he would be welcome at their home in Malaysia any time and I myself received a very heartfelt Christmas card from them even though it was plain in my summing up that their car had pulled directly into the path of the one on the A590. Coroners are not allowed to 'apportion blame' but often the facts speak for themselves as they did here.

Strangely enough it was more often local people than tourists who got into trouble at this junction. Perhaps they were less cautious because they felt they knew the problems of the road or perhaps tourists who had never seen the junction before were extra cautious in working out how to negotiate it. I did report what was happening to the Highway Authority. The police had given evidence of ten minor collisions four serious and two fatal in a period of about eight years. The road markings had already been altered to try to slow down the traffic on the main road.

Coroners can draw attention to facts which might result in further fatalities but have no legal powers to force anyone to take any action. In 2014 the junction was completely remodelled and is now a roundabout.

Another notorious black spot was High and Low Newton. There was little leeway if you made a mistake here, and vehicles often came into contact with those coming the opposite way. Two deaths happened within a week of each other and perhaps as little as twenty yards apart. The way the two accidents happened was not the same however. One was a vehicle which wandered inadvertently across the centre line, the other a car turning deliberately across oncoming traffic into a property. Campaigns were launched and the local MP at the time, Tim Collins, had a constructive meeting with me in which I told him that most accidents I had dealt with, i.e. the fatal ones, were a result of driver error and that the problem was the lack of margin for error. There was no verge and little distance between the two opposing lanes of traffic.

In 2008 a bypass was opened with very limited access points to minimise the risk of accidents. It is dual carriageway and so far appears to have been very successful from a safety point of view. It also has a bridge across the road which forms a perfect frame for the Coniston fells especially when the sun is setting, and there is a mysterious contraption of wires across the road. Its purpose is to help pipistrelle bats to negotiate the road safely. I cannot say if this has been successful.

Another bypass which did result in less accidents is the Dalton bypass opened in 1993. There are only three access points but the road is not dualled. In twenty years there were two fatalities in one incident. A motor cycle going very fast went out of control and collided with one of two girls walking along the road. Very few people do walk on this road. The police tell me that there are frequent minor collisions at the roundabouts but overall safety has improved. The bypass takes most traffic away from the infamous Ruskinville Bridge on the Barrow side of Dalton. This was once painted with the sign 'This bridge kills' because several motor bike riders lost control as they negotiated its left then right turns. There was a theory, never proved, that diesel exhausts from the trains passing under the bridge left deposits on the road surface making it slippery. It is just as likely that a left curve followed by a right curve was a temptation for motorcyclists and some simply got it wrong.

Motorways are said to be the safest roads and this is because the opposing lanes are rigidly separated from each other and although there is a mixture of cars, motorbikes and lorries there are no pedestrians or bicycles. There is a very strong bicycle lobby, especially in London, and cyclists are often killed and injured sometimes by large lorries when the driver fails to see the cyclist. Whilst each incident is different it does seem to me that motorised traffic is fundamentally incompatible with cycles just as it is with pedestrians. The only solution of different routes for the different forms of transport is impractical and so the problem will continue.

NINE

Dr Richard Frederick Stevens

Richard Frederick Stevens was a highly professional and well respected doctor – a Consultant Paediatric Haematologist and Oncologist at Royal Manchester Children's Hospital. In other words his patients were usually extremely sick children. On Monday, 21 July 2003, he went into work and was seen to do so on CCTV. After that he seemed to vanish.

He was reported missing the same day because he had not been seen by his colleagues nor of course did he return home. Because the disappearance appeared to be so out of character and because of his professional status, the media gave the story a very high profile. For a while other CCTV footage was played showing a man on a railway station who looked like Dr Stevens. As events showed it was not.

On 6 January 2004, a group of six people walking and exploring caves on Coniston Old Man noticed a rather unpleasant smell in one of the caves. They assumed initially it was a dead sheep but about 200 yards into the cave the group, which included a doctor, came across the remains of a man behind some rocks. The doctor noticed that there was a canula in the left wrist with a syringe attached which had been pushed all the way down. Another syringe which had not been used was found later. The surrounding items and the clothing soon led to the suspicion that this might be the missing Dr Stevens and this was subsequently proved by comparison with dental records.

The post mortem examination was carried out by Dr Joglekar, and with the help of the forensic science service who analysed body fluids, the cause of death was established. I will not give the name of the two drugs that were used but one was an anaesthetic which can have a side effect of muscle twitching and the other was a muscle relaxant which would combat that side effect. In other words the two drugs were deliberately chosen by someone with intimate knowledge of their effects.

In the course of the investigation it became apparent Dr Stevens's private life was not quite as straightforward as might have been the case. He was having a relationship with another woman, the mother of one of his patients, and in the day or two before he disappeared he had had a row with his wife and had then gone to the hospital where he worked. As I said in the summing up:

that may have been because he had to go to work to see a patient; it may possibly have been to make preparations for what was to happen in the next day or so.

I came to the conclusion that:

He made his way pretty directly to the Lake District area and in particular to the Coniston area, which I think he must have known quite well from outings in the past. It's my very firm belief that he climbed to this shaft; he'd made a throw-away remark that he knew a place where he wouldn't be found and I think he very deliberately went there, having taken the drugs that we have heard led to his death and I believe he almost certainly died the same day, that Monday. I think he went directly there with the firm intention of ending it all and he did end it all in that place where he said he thought he would not be found and indeed he was not found, as we know, for many months until January of 2004.

My verdict was that he committed suicide and I said:

the stress that drove him to it was not the stress of his job, it was the stress of his personal relationship with the other woman that was coming to a head and although he could cope with the work, he could not cope with his own personal difficulties.

I see now from the transcript of my summing up that I did more or less get through it but I do remember cutting it short. Towards the end, Dr Stevens's widow started wailing in a manner that simply could not be ignored.

Dr Stevens had made a remark to a member of his family that he never had anything nice to say to anyone by which I am sure he meant that he was usually, as a doctor, delivering bad news and there is a parallel, though perhaps at a different level, with the daily job of a coroner. Coroners deal with death and bereavement and trauma and extreme emotion. I have been asked how I dealt with this and I found the answer very difficult to give. I know that from time to time in the office, and certainly in private, my staff and I resorted to black humour and although I always knew that I had to remain detached from what I was dealing with in a personal sense, I also had to show sympathy and understanding to those left behind and I think it is simply my natural character that enabled me to do this rather than any particular strategy.

TEN

Ian Jason Allison

On 20 June 1995, Bruce Irving had been fishing on the River Kent. He noticed the sole of a walking boot and then realised that sadly it was attached to a disarticulated human leg. He did what any good citizen should do and rang the police. They conducted systematic searches of the river banks with dogs and the following day the underwater search team from Lancashire searched the river and found the torso of a male person nearby. A Home Office post mortem on the remains was carried out by Dr Edmund Tapp. Although he could not establish a cause of death and thought that the body had been in the water for many months, a surprising amount of information was collected and recorded.

There are tables which help to estimate a person's height based simply on the length of the leg bones and this male was estimated as 6' 7" tall with size twelve feet and probably no older than 25 years. Much of the clothing was present – the collar of a blue cotton shirt, a waistband and pocket of a pair of blue Lee Cooper denim jeans, a pair of blue lightweight 100% nylon shorts, extra-large size with a 40-42" waist with a Campion Sports logo and 'St John's University'. Also a pair of maroon underpants, one size twelve boot (made in China), diamond pattern green socks, a leather braided friendship bracelet and £10.76 in his pockets. The police did not know who he was but made enquiries and discounted any known missing persons.

The river at the point where the body was found is tidal and so he could have gone into the water almost anywhere along the river or in the Irish Sea. Stranraer Police wondered if he was the pilot of a Harrier jump jet which had crashed into the sea off Burrow Head, Dumfries and Galloway (the pilot's body had not been found) but the boot alone discounted that possibility. The police discovered that there are 10 St John's Colleges in the UK but that St John's University is in America. All these institutions were contacted but there was no news of anyone missing. There was much press coverage but simply no leads on who this might be, let alone how he had ended up where he was found.

Cyril Prickett was the coroner for the southern district of Cumbria, previously Westmorland, and having waited for all the enquiries to be completed he held an inquest in April 1996 and recorded that the person's identity was unknown, the cause of death was unascertainable and an Open Verdict which was the only conclusion any coroner could have come to. The remains of the body were buried in Kendal cemetery.

In 2004, on Mr Prickett's retirement, I became coroner for his area as well as my own. Some years later, a circular landed on my desk. It was from Devon and Cornwall Constabulary and had been sent to all coroners along the western side of England and Wales, enquiring if we had any unidentified bodies and that the person they were looking for was very tall at about 6' 8". The only reason I was able to connect the two was that I remembered all the publicity locally in 1995, particularly on Radio Cumbria and in the *Westmorland Gazette* and the crucial factor that the body that was found was tall and the missing Ian Jason Allison was tall. I was still by no means convinced that it was the same person but I told Devon and Cornwall Constabulary and they started to investigate. It was discovered that the laboratory where the post mortem had been carried out had retained some tissue samples and it proved possible to get DNA from there. The DNA matched his mother's DNA. It was she who had reported Ian missing. It was discovered that Ian had been to America in 1992/1993 with Camp America and had spent time in Minnesota which is where St John's University is.

An explanation about registration of death is needed at this point. Following Mr Prickett's inquest in 1996, the Registrar of Births and Deaths was notified of the outcome of the inquest, as is required by law, and so the death of an unknown person was recorded with a date and place of death "Dead body found on 21 June 1995, in River Kent Estuary at Sampool in the Parish of Levens, map reference 487845."

Now that we knew that the body was Ian Jason Allison, the previous inquest had to be quashed before a new inquest could be held and a more specific death certificate issued. This requires a formal application to the High Court explaining why the previous inquest should be quashed. This was done and I was then able to hold a fresh inquest in which I accepted that the DNA evidence showed that the deceased was Ian Jason Allison and that this was corroborated by the evidence in the form of the clothing. As I said at the inquest:

> Ian had been to the area from which the clothing originated – not exactly on the tourist trail in America.

That left me with having to answer the four questions which every inquest has to answer: who was the deceased, how, when and where did that person come by his death. I said that I was completely satisfied that the body buried in the cemetery at Kendal was Ian Jason Allison. There was evidence, which I again accepted, that he had been alive on 25 November 1994 and that his body had been discovered on 20 June 1995. Sadly there was no evidence to explain what had happened between those two dates. There was no known reason why he would have been in Kendal and I said that it was possible that he had gone into the river from upstream of where he was found but just as possible, because the river is tidal, that he had gone into the water in the bay somewhere or in the Irish Sea and by pure chance the body had washed up where he was found.

I therefore had to stick with the cause of death as being unascertainable and an Open Verdict. But as I said:

> the big difference to Mrs Allison, to Ian's mum, is that a) she knows for certain that her son is dead which she didn't know and b) she can now get a death certificate because what is currently registered in relation to Ian's body is – unidentified male. So she could get a death certificate of an unidentified male which is no assistance to her and she will now be able to get a certificate confirming Ian Jason Allison is dead. As I say, no more than that but that in itself, I think, is some kind of closure to Mrs Allison. I hope it is. It is very sad obviously that she has lost her son in circumstances that remain unknown but at least she knows.

Just how Ian's body came to be where it was found and how he died remains entirely unknown. Following the inquest I notified the Registrar of Births and Deaths of the outcome and the death was registered once more but this time with Ian's name on the death certificate.

In some ways I am proudest of the outcome of this case during my 25 years

Figure 9: In Kendal Cemetery.

109

because as a senior police officer said to me, the police have no corporate memory. They rely on an individual remembering specific details and matching them up and on this occasion no police officer had done that but fortunately I was able to make the connection. This also highlights the importance of the coroner being local to the area that he or she serves remembering that where the body was found was not even in my area at the time and it was simply my recollection of what I had seen and heard in the local media.

Obviously it is very sad that Mrs Allison lost her son but it would have been even more difficult for her not to have known for sure if he was alive or dead, always wondering if he might contact her out of the blue.

Devon and Cornwall Police retained responsibility of the investigation from start to finish on the basis that their area was the last known place where Ian had been even though the investigation was initiated by his mother in Glasgow and the body was discovered somewhere between those two extremes in Cumbria.

ELEVEN

President for a Year

1 THE POSITION

The Coroners' Society of England and Wales was founded in 1846 and its membership consists of coroners and assistant (previously deputy) and area coroners. Its principal objective is to promote the usefulness of the office of coroner but it also acts as a contact between coroners and the government and protects the rights and interests of coroners. The society is important because the office of coroner is a lonely one. Since each coroner is responsible for a specific geographical area, there is little contact between coroners on a day to day basis. Different areas of the country form their own local groups and I became the Northern Society's representative.

I also became a member of the Coroners' Society Local Government Committee. One function of this committee was to negotiate with the Local Government Association to try to achieve a consistent level of salary for coroners across the country. There is no legal requirement for this and coroners can agree a salary with their own local council if they both wish. One year we had negotiations in the basement of a hotel near Euston Station in London. We started in separate rooms with a bit of shuttle diplomacy which led nowhere. The chairman of the local government team invited us into their room for the buffet lunch. He was affable pleasant and inclusive. One of his members however made his position clear by taking out his *Guardian*, opening it fully and holding it in front of himself. I think he must have regarded us as a militant trade union rather than a professional body.

In 2007 I was appointed president of the national society. The job of the president is to act as leader of the society for a year and to put on the annual conference, although the society has a conference secretary to carry out the negotiations with the hotel and make other arrangements. I issued a press release about my appointment as president. This was to keep control of the information published. The local paper sent back my words altered and with quotations that I would never utter. I restored the original and the paper then ran the story in my words. This taught me that a lot of what you read is not written by journalists at all but by media departments of organisations. The power of the press was again demonstrated by the fact that at least half a dozen people, many of whom I did not know came up to me in the street with congratulations. I was pleased to give Cumbria a small place on the national stage. I thought I might have been the first Cumbrian coroner to be president but later learned that Tom Strong the Carlisle coroner was president in 1968. Cumbria under that name came into being on county reorganisation in 1974.

During the year I visited all the other regional societies, which I had expected to be pleasant but little more. In fact it was highly stimulating and meant that I met many members of the Coroners' Society for the first time. There is always a central group of people who enjoy attending meetings and conferences and joining in generally. It was these I had met often at previous gatherings. The others were content to go to the local meeting twice a year but still had opinions and suggestions. I also went to many of the sub-committee meetings where topics ranged from pathology to courtroom availability to salaries and far beyond.

2 FINDING HOW GOVERNMENT WORKS

As it happens, my year as president coincided with part of the reform process which I will describe separately. This led to me seeing how government and its officials work and I have to say I was not particularly impressed.

During my year as president there were numerous meetings between a few officials of the Coroners' Society and officials of the Ministry of Justice. The Ministry of Justice produced a Bill which was to go before parliament and deliver reform. The ministry officials were very protective of their Bill which was to bring in the emasculated change. The officials regarded it as their baby and were offended if we pointed out problems with it. For example, the Bill originally included cremated ashes within the definition of the word 'body'. This is important because the coroner's jurisdiction arises when a body is lying in his or her area and we pointed out that it would be impossible to know whose ashes were being put forward or even to know if they were human ashes at all. Ultimately this was changed but it took a lot of persuasion.

At one meeting with the Ministry of Justice officials, the Coroners Society representatives included a professor of law who had a number of legal points to make. The officials, in response to pretty well every comment, said that our views would be 'logged' or 'looked at'. After a little while we worked out that if they were going to be logged then that meant that they would be ignored from the outset and if they were going to be looked at they would be ignored subsequently.

During the regular meetings we had with government a number of things became apparent. Firstly, there is a pecking order for government ministries. The Treasury is firmly at the top. The Ministry of Justice is well towards the bottom and the Department of Health is very important. Secondly, that talented civil servants quickly moved on from one project to another with the result that the project was not seen through from start to finish by the same person. Less able officials stayed in one place, making sure that they did not do anything to rock the boat. Government ministers move on after a couple of years in post and so it seems that just as anyone is beginning to get to grips with a problem they have to leave it behind.

Thirdly, government ministers differ greatly. I lost track of how many ministers had responsibility for coroners, but their styles varied from Paul Boateng who bullied our conference and would not take questions to Paul Goggins who sadly died young, who thanked and encouraged us in what we were doing, to Bridget Prentice who steered the 2009 Bill and who said she thought it was a good Bill. If she truly believed that then she was deluded. It was a compromise that did not deliver what the Luce Report and the Shipman report said was needed. They wanted a truly national service and integration of the services that come into play at the time of a death. This simply did not happen as we will see.

Ministers operate with groups of civil servants around them. A little like a naval destroyer with its attendant service ships. My brief observations showed that the officials were terrified of the minister and had to answer any question even if they did not know the answer. One story I was told but did not witness was The Tale of the Coffee Pot. A minister (Labour, female) had summoned a couple of coroners to talk about something in another Bill which had a tangential bearing on coroners. She treated them from the start like a special interest group there to further their own cause. Coffee had been ordered in and duly arrived. But the minister did not ask for it to be poured. As the meeting went on all eyes turned more and more to the coffee pot till it was the sole but unspoken focus of everyone's attention. When the meeting ended the coffee pot and its contents remained intact. If only someone had had the nerve to say (preferably in a northern accent) "Ooh, I do hate waste. Shall I be mother?"

One curious thing I must record is that the table we often sat around at the Ministry of Justice was long and fairly narrow but wider at one end than the other and every time it seemed to me that we were sitting round a giant coffin lid. Very apt to what we were talking about.

3 Conferences

Each year the Coroners' Society held a conference. The purpose was to meet fellow coroners and deputies and exchange points of view and to learn. Lectures were relevant and designed to widen our knowledge rather than teach us directly how to be a good coroner. That was what training courses were for.

We heard from police firearms officers, from doctors in particular fields of expertise, and from pathologists involved in interesting cases. We also exchanged thoughts and ideas about what we did from day to day. Because coroners are responsible for their own territory we rarely met otherwise. Judges often sit in court centres and can compare notes at lunchtime. Coroners are essentially lonesome animals.

In the early years the conference was at a university or college with single rooms and communal bathrooms. The lack of modern comforts was worth enduring when the venue was Magdalen College Oxford. The star attraction was Lord Denning, Master of the Rolls. When I was a student at University College London I would go down to the Royal Courts of Justice in the Strand with colleagues and though we sat in on other courts the Court of Appeal was the favourite as Lord Denning presided. He spoke with a Hampshire burr and used simple language. When he wrote he used short sentences and his judgements told the story of the people involved in the court case. Later when I was an articled clerk I would occasionally see him and his wife getting out of the official car on High Holborn to walk through Lincoln's Inn Fields to the Royal Courts of Justice in The Strand. The conference was in 1985 and Lord Denning was 86 years old. He parked his walking stick across the lectern and talked to us about decisions on coroners cases. He had no notes and held us spellbound for an hour. He also spoke after dinner and was as funny as he was erudite.

Though most of the content of conferences was in the form of lectures there were occasionally more exciting events. We observed a full scale air-sea rescue exercise from a control room at Falmouth and in a place I will not record we were bussed from point A to a church at point B to attend evensong but with a police escort practising for when they had royalty. Police cars escorted us with blue lights and sirens, side roads were blocked off and we sped through red lights. We went on another occasion to Porton Down, the government research laboratory, but ended walking the corridors with our guide repeatedly saying, "I can't take you in there" so we saw nothing.

Some lectures were admittedly less relevant to the work of coroners. A lecture on police horses was interesting and relaxing but perhaps not essential to what we do. We heard from Dr. Van Velzen, later disgraced for keeping body parts of patients without consent. He was highly intelligent and clearly an expert in his field which was cot death. Perhaps just too expert to worry about mundane things like paperwork and permissions.

At Harrogate we had a lecture from Baroness Hale of Richmond, later to become President of the Supreme Court, the leading judge in the country. She gave us an erudite exposition on European law. To be honest most of it flew clear over my head.

Coroners were originally the responsibility of the Home Office but later came under the Ministry of Justice. Two or three officials would come to our conference each year. Not everyone was comfortable with this especially in the years of uncertainty after the reports recommending reform. We were told that all existing appointments of coroners might be cancelled and we would have to apply for our own jobs. This was a serious threat to many office holders who had given up a partnership in a law firm or practice as a barrister. The response was that we would claim compensation for loss of office but Parliament could have legislated away this possibility. One year we felt we needed the freedom to formulate our response to what the Ministry of Justice might have in store for us and they were not allowed to attend. This caused animosity on their part but we felt under threat from the ministry when they should have been supporting us.

The conference at the end of my year in office was at the Low Wood Hotel on Windermere and was blessed with glorious weather and amazing sunsets. We had good speakers, including Professor Sir Ian Kennedy and Lord Justice Scott Baker. Sir Ian was my tutor at university and had gone on to specialise in the medico-legal field. He virtually invented the discipline of Medical Law and wrote textbooks on the subject. He held various public positions including heading the committee which decides MPs' salaries.

Lord Justice Scott Baker had recently completed the inquests into the deaths of Princess Diana and Dodi al Fayed. I had looked in on the inquest when I was in London and found a kind of annexe outside the court room with space for journalists on one side and public on the other. There were television screens showing the court room and who was speaking and another with an immediate transcription of what was being said.

One speaker at my conference, Dr Alison Armour the local Home Office pathologist, delivered her talk while being harassed on the phone by a barrister saying she should be at Liverpool Crown Court giving evidence and the Judge was going to have her arrested. This did not happen and apparently the Judge was very understanding when she did arrive. Her point of view was that she had promised to give the lecture two years previously and she was not going to let me down. Thank you, Alison.

During the year as president I clocked up well over 10,000 miles. Most meetings were of course in London and I had to travel from Windermere. I also made life rather difficult for myself because completion of my Masters degree in Medical Law at the University of Northumbria overlapped my year as President. I also decided to raise money by walking across my jurisdiction from Alston in the north east to Barrow in the south west. As it happened, I thoroughly enjoyed the walk which was done almost entirely in dry weather and I raised nearly £10,000. Other complications were not my choice – I ended up as a witness in an employment tribunal instituted by the acting coroner for a different part of Cumbria and I was also taken to Judicial Review by the Ahmed family. These stories are told elsewhere in the book.

The main project funded by the money raised was the building of a school in Burma. Once the school was built, the government paid for the teacher. In 2008 a school could be built for £6,000. I am proud of the result. A few hundred children will have received an education they might otherwise have missed.

At the conference the current president hands over to the next one. My successor was Paul Knapman the long-serving and very experienced Coroner for Westminster. A very different president to myself but that was the strength of the society. Different characters, different ideas and different conference venues.

On the Monday after the conference my inbox was unfilled and the telephone seemed to have stopped working apart from deaths being reported. I was now yesterday's man and the Coroners' Society carried on happily without me. In the year I had travelled across England, met dozens of society members for the first time, seen how government works and had a thoroughly enjoyable time. But one year was enough and I was glad to return to what I was paid to do without the added strain of an extra part-time but unpaid job.

I continued to go to conferences and the last one was at Buxton. The Lord Chief Justice, Lord Thomas spoke. He welcomed us to the judicial family. Most of us thought we had been part of it for centuries. In his talk he said that the central role of the family must be recognised and added, "I am sure the overwhelming majority of coroners have always acted in this way." It was good to hear most of us were already doing what he wanted.

He told us we had to modernise and embrace change. Lord Thomas was newly appointed and his own inauguration was pictured in *The Times* the following week, Lord Thomas resplendent in shoulder length horse hair wig, knee breeches and elaborate black and gold gown.

4 EMPLOYMENT TRIBUNAL

In 2005 my county, Cumbria, got into an awful mess by ignoring the basic legal position of a coroner and a deputy coroner. Ian Morton, the coroner for North East Cumbria retired on 30 November 2005. He had a deputy called David Ian Osborne and by operation of provisions in the Coroners Act 1988 he would automatically become acting coroner (and entitled to a coroner's salary) until a permanent coroner was appointed. This provision was meant to cover a short period of up to three months. The county made the mistake of writing to Mr Osborne purporting to appoint him as Acting Coroner, something they had no power to do. In the meantime the county officials were dealing with the Ministry of Justice to reduce the number of coroners districts from three to two. Much more time went by than should have done. Mr Osborne settled in, did his temporary job for well over a year and must have felt permanent and secure.

David Osborne mounted a campaign to keep a coroner in Carlisle, and gained support from the undertakers, Registrar of Births and Deaths, the local MP Eric Martlew and Carlisle City Council. There were many column inches in the press in Carlisle. The argument was that the service would be poorer, slower and less personal if the status quo was changed.

It was not until 1st May 2007 that a statutory instrument came into force with exactly the result that David Osborne had opposed effectively depriving him of his jurisdiction and what he thought was his job. Not surprisingly he was upset and took the county to an employment tribunal. I was called as a witness by Cumbria County Council though I was never clear why. The other remaining Cumbrian coroner John Taylor was not a witness. Neither of us could add anything to the facts of what had been done by the county and I suspect that I was called because I was the current president and might make the council's case look stronger. However if I was called as an expert witness I should have been told so and I never was. At the tribunal hearing in Carlisle I made my independence clear throughout and spent nearly two days in a waiting room at the tribunal venue on my own. The tribunal concluded that coroners are not employees so Mr Osborne was never employed by Cumbria County Council and that he could not therefore be unfairly dismissed by them nor made redundant.

To my mind this was a statement of the obvious and it is and always has been fundamental that the coroner is independent of everyone, even the local authority who pays the coroner's salary and expenses, otherwise the coroner could not act with the true independence that is vital to any judicial office holder. Coroners may well have to consider and criticise roads, care homes or other settings run by the local authority and must not feel inhibited about doing so if it is necessary.

As a follow up to this, towards the end of 2007, Eric Martlew put an entry on his website which was picked up by most of the papers in Cumbria. This was that the time taken to hold an inquest had increased since the reduction to two jurisdictions in May 2007. This was completely inaccurate because the figures that the MP used were those for the year ended 31 December 2006 published by the Ministry of Justice. These showed that the national average time between death and an inquest was 24 weeks. For South Cumbria it was 19 and West Cumbria 22 weeks. Carlisle, under David Osborne was 30. When I pointed out the true facts to Mr Martlew's office the item was removed from his website but I never received a reply let alone an apology.

I took over 29 pending inquest cases and John Taylor took over 64 from the Carlisle area and we both had to make a concerted effort to deal with them. Mr Osborne himself died only a few years later.

5 AN ASIDE

Andrew Walker, a London coroner, had also been Assistant Deputy Coroner for Oxford. The significance is that the bodies of servicemen repatriated from Afghanistan and Iraq were flown first into Brize Norton RAF base which is in the jurisdiction of the Oxford coroner. He therefore became responsible for conducting the inquests. Mr Walker was not shy of criticising government and in particular the Ministry of Defence. He criticised the body armour soldiers were issued with and the vehicles they had available. In one case he said there had been 'serious failings' and the MoD took him to Judicial Review. The application for Judicial Review was not upheld by the Court so the criticism remained.

In April 2008 Andre Rebello the Secretary of the Coroners' Society was summoned to the Public Bill Scrutiny Committee of Parliament to give evidence relating to the Counter Terrorism Bill. This took place in Portcullis House opposite Big Ben and the Houses of Parliament. It was a public hearing though it is not just a question of turning up and walking in. You had to notify your intention to attend and be security cleared in advance. As I was in London I went along to support Andre. The proposal about coroners in the Bill was, in summary that if an inquest had to be held but the subject matter to be aired was sensitive i.e. a threat to national security, then the minister responsible could parachute someone in to conduct the inquest.

This person would be security cleared, but not necessarily a coroner. The court would be closed to public, press and family but they would be represented by a designated cleared barrister. This sounded more like Stalinist Russia than the United Kingdom where the rule of law and public transparency are part of our national psyche. The proposal did not go through. Whether there is any connection between the two previous paragraphs, I do not know.

TWELVE

Other People's Stories

I record here and elsewhere the stories of people who cannot tell their own. Every day in my work I came to know parts of the lives of many people. Some were tragic, some sad, some foolish. Some I would have liked to know and a few I am pleased I never met. None of the following fall into the latter category.

1 THE RUSHTONS

In 2002 I had to deal with the tragic deaths of Stewart Rushton and his son Adam. They had been out on 4 January, 2002 to dig for bait so that they could go fishing the next day and they completed this successfully. On the following day they went to Priory Point which is near Ulverston by the Morecambe Bay sands. The visibility had been bad earlier in the day and was getting worse. Judging by the fact that the fishing gear was left in Mr Rushton's car, it seems that the decision had been made not to go fishing but unfortunately Mr Rushton walked with his son into the mist and onto the sands. This is what I said in the summing up:

> It wasn't a case of being caught out by mist coming down, it wasn't that Mr Rushton and his son went out in relatively clear conditions and the mist overtook them and came down on them while they were out on the sands. I have to say that I think they went out into conditions that were already so bad that it was a bad move to make and to the point of saying that I think Mr Rushton was reckless about his safety and about his son's safety by going out on the sands in those conditions at all.

I recorded verdicts of Misadventure on Mr Rushton and Accident on his son and the press picked up on my use of the word 'reckless'. The awful tragedy was made even worse for Mrs Rushton because her husband had phoned her telling her that he was disorientated on the bay. He asked her to ring the coastguard. After that Mr Rushton also rang the police and was in touch with the control room describing to the call handler how the water was rising and ultimately the call ended when the water overtook him. This must have been desperately difficult for the call handler to deal with. It was difficult enough for me to listen to the recording several weeks later in the comfort of my own office.

Over the centuries hundreds of people have died on the sands overtaken by the incoming tide but of course historically the first anyone would know about this was when a body was washed up. In the age of the mobile phone, people at a distance can be in direct contact as the tragedy is actually happening.

Bay Search and Rescue was one consequence of what happened. They have specialist caterpillar tracked vehicles to go out on to the treacherous sand. Boats are of little use in these conditions until it is too late and the fog meant that helicopters were no help either.

2 Peter Holt Shaw

This gentleman died in 2005 aged 74 years. He had done well over 1,000 parachute jumps. Unfortunately he seemed to develop a tendency to delay opening his parachute. He was stopped from jumping at one club and told them he would not jump again. But he persuaded a different club to let him jump there on condition that he pulled the cord on the parachute by 4,000 feet and had a bleeper in his helmet triggered at the right height to remind him to do so. Over time he 'stole' height and pulled the cord at under 1,000 feet on the day of his death, landed badly and suffered fatal injuries. He was obviously a very active and lively man and I suppose he must have got a thrill out of operating the parachute as late as he dared. I wrote after the inquest to the British Parachute Association because there was apparently no system in place to ground someone permanently across the country if they posed a danger to themselves or others.

3 Michael Kenneth Webb

Mr Webb died in 2007 and at first sight you would assume he had taken his own life. He left a recording on a dictation machine which was transcribed at nearly five pages. He says he planned to asphyxiate himself with the car exhaust but hadn't got enough petrol. He then speaks of garrotting himself but is afraid of waking up having failed to do the job properly. Then he speaks of diabetes control tablets but the post mortem report and the toxicology report showed he had not died from deliberately overdosing on these. The cause of death was actually a heart attack as if the effort and anguish of all he had said on the tape induced enough stress to kill. At the inquest a friend had a large rucksack and said she was going to the Isle of Man to scatter Mr Webb's ashes which were in the rucksack. As far as I know this was the first and only time I actually had the deceased in the inquest with me.

4 THREE WIRELESS TELEGRAPHY TRAINEES

I include this sad tale because of the end of a statement in the file. A relative of one of the trainees who died asked for any information I could pass on otherwise I would never have seen the file about events that had happened half a century earlier. Wray Castle is a National Trust property, an example of a Victorian Gothic residence built like a castle for a Liverpool surgeon and his family. For many years it was a training college for Merchant Navy radio operators. It is now open to the public. I did once conduct an inquest there when I was a deputy coroner. A trainee had fallen from the roof. The precise details were never clear.

The events that I am relating here happened in 1959. Three trainees decided one Friday night to go for a drink. They chose the Low Wood Hotel. This presented a few problems which they solved with the ingenuity of youth and a disregard for safety. It was November, the chosen venue was only a mile away but across Windermere and although they could quietly 'borrow' a boat and oars they could not find any rowlocks. I imagine they looked like a cross between a kayak and a gondola. They got to the venue, had their drinks and set off back never to be seen alive again. Life jackets and oars were found floating the next morning.

I was taken aback by the end of the chief instructor's statement, which is best set out verbatim and left anonymous:

> The three boys had deliberately broken a number of college regulations being
> (a)Visiting the Low Wood Hotel which is out of bounds.
> (b) Taking a boat out in the hours of darkness to visit the Low Wood Hotel.
> (c) Not being in uniform.
> (d) Not wearing life jackets in the approved manner.
> (e) Failin [sic] to sign for the boat.

5 DAVID SHIPLEY

David was twenty years old and a private in the Army. He died on 22 June 2002 after an event at Gutersloh Army Barracks in Germany when he was found unconscious in a makeshift pool of water which had been part of an 'It's a Knockout' course. It was constructed from oil drums and a large tarpaulin and the water was no more than eighteen inches deep. David was said to have been deprived of oxygen at birth and to have developed slowly but he had been accepted by the Army and was apparently a thoroughly nice lad. How he had got into the water and then been there unconscious was never properly explained. This is what I thought about the evidence of the other members of the Army who gave evidence:

This story has all the hallmarks of a concocted story whereby a group of people get together, think up a story, decide they are going to stick to it, agree set facts, remember those facts but when you examine them and you question them and go into other detail that they have not pre-arranged and pre-agreed, the answers you get consistently were "I don't know, I can't remember". So to me the evidence that I got about what happened in and around that pool was not reliable evidence.

This was because certain facts and certain phrases were used in evidence by several witnesses. David had water from a boot poured over his head, which he had taken exception to. Several witnesses referred to him saying "smelly foot water" or "smelly sock water". He then went off for a shower but the witnesses referred to wondering where he had gone to and one witness explained "You look out for your mate's back." I said I didn't see what there was to look out for. I posed various theoretical possibilities as to how David might have ended up in the shallow water unconscious, dismissing them in turn.

The sixth possibility I raised was that he was thrown into the water, left there and the person or persons who did that did not expect it to have any serious consequences.

I have got to say I think that is a very real possibility indeed. He did not want to go in the water and to suggest that he was gently taken hold of and placed gently in the water in the circumstances that we have been hearing about, I think is a little bit unrealistic. I think there is a possibility that he was taken hold of, arms and legs, by different people and thrown in the water and they may have run off and left him just expecting that he would get out in due course in his own time. That would tie in with the concerns that people were expressing as to "well, where has he got to? What's he done? Where is he? What's happened to him?" I have to say there is no evidence to support that. That is speculation. It is a possibility and because there is no evidence to support it I cannot say that is what happened. Evidence in this case is very thin on the ground.

I recorded an open verdict.

This was to my mind one of those inquests when the outcome was inconclusive but I hope that the process itself was helpful to David's parents. At least they had other people who were around David near to the events that led to his death and they could ask them questions. Even if the answers were unsatisfactory, the explanation of what did happen may have become a little clearer to them. I do hope so.

6 GEMMA GILL

Gemma Gill was a twenty year old woman from Kendal. She had a medical problem with her veins. She had surgery to try to improve her condition. Two weeks later she saw her surgeon for post-operative follow up and all appeared to be progressing well. Soon after, however, she felt pain in her leg and very sensibly went to her GP's surgery, where she was seen by a nurse and a doctor who considered whether she had a deep vein thrombosis (DVT) but thought probably not.

A couple of days later Gemma arrived at the A & E department of Westmorland General Hospital by ambulance. This was during the evening of Good Friday. The doctor on duty, a locum was concerned there might be a DVT and ordered a diagnostic test, a 'D Dimer'. The machine at Westmorland General was not working so the sample had to be sent by road to the Hospital Trust's nearest laboratory at Lancaster. Gemma was sent home to await the result and when it came back positive Gemma returned to the hospital more than six hours after her first attendance. She sadly died of a pulmonary embolism caused by the deep vein thrombosis on that day.

The inquest process showed a number of facts. At each step in Gemma's care and treatment there was delay, adding up to several hours. As I said in my summing up, there was no guarantee that the outcome would have been any different even if the delays had been avoided, but the fact was that chances were missed, i.e. administering Clexane or Heparin when Gemma first arrived or even immediately she arrived the second time. These drugs are sometimes called clot-busting drugs.

Though I did not use the phrase in my summing up I thought the facts showed a tendency I christened 'sat nav medicine' – the use and utter reliance of machinery at the expense of old fashioned diagnostic skills. Just as a lorry driver keeps going along a narrow lane and gets stuck because the sat nav is directing him that way even though his eyes can see it must be wrong. I know that modern doctors would disagree. They would say that medical practice and treatment must be evidence based. I accept that DVT is not a simple diagnosis to make, but there seemed to be several clues pointing to it and Gemma might have had the Clexane nine hours earlier. There was also the fact that the first doctor to see Gemma discharged her home because he felt under pressure to come to a decision inside four hours – a time limit imposed by politicians, not doctors.

Ultrasound scans might have confirmed a DVT but they need specialists to work the equipment and interpret the results and these were not available at Westmorland General Hospital at that time on a Good Friday. The facilities the

NHS has, do therefore vary depending on the size of hospital, the time of day and the day of the week.

7 JOHN STRUTHERS

John Struthers was twenty seven years old when he died. He was a strong character because he had many medical problems to deal with and he also gained the Duke of Edinburgh Gold Award. When he was only six a brain tumour was found but successfully removed and followed up with radiotherapy and chemotherapy. Unfortunately these affected John's pituitary gland and the result was that he did not grow as expected. The doctors offered a new treatment of growth hormone injections. The way the substance was obtained is crucial to what happened later and I will come back to it. The treatment was not very successful in that John only grew about an extra inch, and it ended when he was sixteen.

In 1991, with John now in his mid-twenties further problems appeared: tremors, difficulty with balance and slurred speech. In due course the doctors said the problem might be Creutzfeldt-Jakob disease, a debilitating and aggressive form of deterioration of the brain which led to a rapid decline in John's ability to look after himself and to his death in June 1993. This was what I said to explain how the growth hormone was produced:

In 1976 the treatment for lack of normal growth was just becoming available and the way the treatment was given was by injection but more important is the way by which the hormone was collected... All over the country in pathology laboratories, pituitary glands were removed from people who had died, collected and then sent to the centre in Cambridge to be processed and the growth hormone extracted from them... I think that mortuary technicians were asked or told to collect pituitary glands and I think they did that pretty well without much of a thought for where the glands were being collected from, what possible diseases the person may have had and I think the collection was pretty haphazard.

It is quite clear to me that at some point a pituitary gland infected by Creutzfeldt-Jakob disease got into the general collection of glands and affected one particular batch or more likely a whole series of batches. All it would have taken was one infected gland to get in there and the particular batch it was in would clearly have been affected and I have heard evidence that the machinery itself once infected may have remained so and may then have contaminated further batches that were produced on the same machinery.

So there is a batch or a number of batches of the growth hormone infected and it is quite clear that one of those affected was John because he was injected with the growth hormone treatment over a long period of time, about ten years, and I am quite certain that amongst the injections that were given to him at least one and possibly more were infected and that is what in due course led to him developing Creutzfeldt-Jakob disease.

I returned a verdict of misadventure and explained that by saying:

Years ago somebody did something quite deliberately, with good intentions, which ultimately went wrong.

The solicitor who represented John's family did not appear to have a high opinion of coroners. He obviously knew a great deal about CJD and feared I would not have researched the problem adequately. Before the inquest he suggested he could supply a medical expert and did not appear reassured when I told him I already had one from Edinburgh University, Dr (later Professor) James Ironside. In the event I think the solicitor was satisfied with the inquest, the hearing and the outcome.

8 MRS WILLIAMS

This lady's story starts with a simple trip on the pavement. She hardly hurt herself at all but found that it was more comfortable to walk around the house in stockinged feet. This led over time to a blister and some skin rubbing off one foot. The district nurse was called and apart from treating her she provided surgical type slippers. Mrs Williams tripped over these twice and on the second occasion fractured her femur and was admitted to hospital. The family complained that her call bell was removed because she used it too much – the most common complaint I heard over more than three decades was that the call bell was out of reach – but Mrs Williams died of a pulmonary embolism, a blood clot on the lungs. A cautionary tale of such serious consequences from such a small beginning.

In the inquest was one of the most dramatic moments in court in my career because no one expected a certain reply to a question; not even the witness herself. In those days, early in my career, medical witnesses were asked to bring the medical records with them to the inquest. Later on, partly because of what happened in this case records were taken by the coroner's officer so they could be examined at leisure before the hearing.

In Mrs William's inquest a nurse was asked about the drug prescribed to prevent embolisms because these are a recognised complication of trauma, surgery and immobility. The nurse looked at the drug chart and said the drug was prescribed from a certain date, then her confident demeanour changed to horror and she added that it had never actually been given. This changed the story fundamentally. Embolisms can happen despite therapy given to prevent them but are much more likely if the prophylaxis is not given at all.

An inquest that had appeared straightforward had changed in one answer. Instead of a minor accident which led to a more serious accident which led to death we now had a death which might possibly have been prevented. Sometimes inquests do bring surprising facts to light but usually this happens during the investigation phase, not in the courtroom itself.

9 SARAH LOUISE McCLAY

No English or Welsh coroner could reasonably expect to conduct an inquest into the death of a young woman mauled by a tiger. But this did happen at Dalton in May 2013 and I did the inquest. Somehow three doors/gates were all open at the same time allowing the tiger Padang to get from his outside enclosure through the indoor area and into the food preparation area where Sarah was. A jury was required because Sarah was at work and we all visited the animal park where it happened. It is too close in time to go into detail, but the case and the subsequent history of the park generated a huge amount of media interest. There was even a bizarre suggestion that Sarah had engineered her own death. This was clearly untrue. Sarah was dedicated to the animals she worked with and felt she had her dream job.

Site visits can be helpful. If there is no jury the coroner can go quietly either alone or with the coroner's officer. If there is a jury then a site visit has to be carefully managed as it is part of the inquest. You cannot therefore have a free for all discussion and the person taking the group to the scene must not be a witness. Changes that have occurred since must be clearly understood and the visit must remain part of the inquest and not assume a disproportionate importance.

Subsequently there was a successful prosecution of the South Lakes Safari Zoo under Health and Safety legislation but criticism of the zoo persisted and the management changed. Padang was put to sleep about three years later.

THIRTEEN

Shafilea Ahmed

1 FINDING AND IDENTIFICATION

Sometimes being a coroner is like reading a detective novel. You are presented with a body and the police on your behalf have to work back to try to establish what happened. Sometimes the identity of the body is not known at the start. This is very much how it was with Shafilea Ahmed. I have seen her name spelt Shafilea, Shafelia and Shafilia. It seems the first is correct.

On 4 February, 2004, three workmen parked their lorry in a lay-by near to the River Kent at Sedgwick, so that one of them could answer a call of nature. The river had flooded to an unusual extent, stripped out some vegetation and uncovered something that the workmen realised needed further investigation. Human remains should not be disposed of in undergrowth by a river so the police were called.

There was a risk that the river might flood again and wash away the remains so they were removed

Figure 10: Shafilea.

to the mortuary and Dr Alison Armour, a Home Office Pathologist, was called in to carry out a post mortem examination.

The skull was missing but the jaw bone remained and nine days after the discovery, the possibility that this was Shafilea was strongly confirmed by her dentist who said he was 90% certain that the teeth matched his records and ten days after that DNA tests confirmed that the body was indeed Shafilea.

Shafilea was born on 14 July 1986 in Bradford, and when last known to be alive was studying for her A levels and wanting to go on to be a solicitor. She was the eldest of five children. She was reported as missing on Thursday, 18th September 2003, not by her parents but by a former teacher.

The question of how Shafilea had ended where she was found and in that state was of course what the police wanted to know. The investigation was handled by Cheshire Police because that was where Shafilea had lived and they did a very thorough job.

Dr Armour was unable to confirm any specific cause of death due to the advanced state of decomposition. In the bones that were present there were no fractures. Dr Armour gave the opinion that a natural cause of death was unsustainable due to the concealment of the body on the river bank and suggested the most likely cause of death (though this could not be proved) was smothering or strangulation.

Dr Julie Roberts is a forensic anthropologist. She confirmed that the upper part of the body was more decomposed than the lower and suggested one explanation for this was that the lower half of the body might have had longer submersion under water reducing bacterial activity on that part of the body.

Professor Jennifer Miller's expertise is identifying and interpreting the vegetation and insect life on and around the body. One moss stem had grown through the fabric of the trousers and a strand of liverwort was attached tightly to the trouser material indicating the body was likely to have been where it was found since the end of the previous growing season (around October). She recorded that the river bank has a covering of deciduous woodland and that the growth under the canopy of the large trees would have provided good cover for concealment.

Under the body was a depression (the underlying soil had been recovered with the body intact) and she thought that the weight of the body was the cause of the depression not an attempt to dig a shallow grave. She thought that the pattern of growth of the mosses and liverworts attached to the lower leg of the trousers indicated that the body had been covered by something dense enough to exclude light and oxygen but flexible enough to wrap around the body and she suggested that this might have been carpet, plastic or a tarpaulin. She noted that the mosses and the liverworts on the trouser leg tolerate dense shade but not total darkness and had spread from the surrounding vegetation. She concluded that this must have occurred in the late summer to early autumn before the growing season ended.

Dr Brandt is an entomologist and studied what I will call for simplicity, insect eggs laid on the body. He concluded that they must have been deposited at the latest by mid-October 2003. He also said that the type of insects concerned favour rural environments and that this was consistent with death having occurred either in the place where the body was found or that death had occurred not long before the body was put in that place.

From this expert evidence it was therefore possible to be satisfied:-

1. The body was that of Shafilea Ahmed
2. Her death was unnatural
3. The body had been put there shortly after death and then decomposed
4. Death probably occurred before the end of the growing season, quite likely in September the previous year.

With the publicity which inevitably surrounded the finding of the body, a number of witnesses came forward to add to the story. A mother and daughter described a white van being at the scene in September the previous year though the precise date was uncertain. Both noticed a horrible smell at the scene a couple of weeks later. Several more witnesses noticed the smell too but no-one reported it to the police and all must have assumed that it was a decaying animal.

My own position in all of this was that when the body was found I was not coroner of that area. Remembering that Shafilea was found on 4 February 2004, and that it inevitably took time for the dental records to be checked and the DNA results to be obtained, my predecessor, Cyril Prickett was able to open an inquest and confirm identification on 26 March, 2004 and he retired just a few days later on 31 March.

I became coroner on 1st April, 2004. By that time I believe that the Cheshire Police had requested that the jurisdiction in the case be transferred to the Cheshire Coroner but Mr Prickett had declined. I released Shafilea's body on 6 April and she was buried. It seemed much more likely that a criminal trial would take place with Iftikhar and Farzana, Shafilea's father and mother being the defendants rather than an inquest and indeed that remained the case for many months whilst the police investigated and Mr & Mrs Ahmed remained on bail.

It was into 2006 before the police, on legal advice, released Shafilea's extended family from their obligations to answer bail and it then became necessary for me to prepare to hold an inquest.

The police gave me a detailed explanation of the evidence they had available and which I would need in order to be able to hold the inquest. The police were convinced that Shafilea had been murdered and wanted to prosecute somebody. My position was different because the law required me to establish the answer to four questions – who was the deceased, how, when and where did she come by her death. At that point I could certainly not make any assumptions that Shafilea had been murdered.

The logistics of arranging an inquest, spread over nearly a week with approximately 30 witnesses are difficult. In a civil or criminal court all of this is done by staff and the judge listens to the evidence presented. A coroner however has to make the arrangements himself and ensure that witnesses turn up on the right day, that translators are available if necessary, the courtroom is big enough and available without interruption. I did not have my own courtroom and always had to rely on council chambers provided by Barrow Borough Council or Cumbria County Council at Kendal.

Because of the high profile the case was likely to have and the cultural complications, it was suggested that I should bring in media experts which initially I was reluctant to do. In the event I agreed and representatives from the press departments of Cumbria County Council and Cumbria and Cheshire Police worked well together. Their job was to manage the media. This meant sorting out practicalities such as giving the family their own private room, freeing an area of the car park so that TV satellite vans could park in one place and witnesses and lawyers could park somewhere else. The media team issued a circular to the press which spelled out very clearly where the press could film or take photographs (outside the building) and where they could not (inside the building). The circular also made it clear that I would not be making comments to the media direct and the media were allocated their own room which went down very well indeed with them. Two members of the press made a point of thanking me for the luxury of a room to write their report and submit it on line. Not to mention endless cups of coffee provided by the stewards.

The result of all this was that I was left largely untroubled by the media. It is very intrusive to walk into a building and have microphones thrust in your face every time and because of the management this did not happen. The cameras did film me each day when I went into Kendal County Offices and on one occasion I asked why they needed to do this. Apparently the background weather should match the prevailing weather on the day that the filming is broadcast. If you are shown walking into a building on a bright sunny day and in fact it rained then people watching the television may feel they are being shown misleading pictures. Or at least that is what the media themselves think.

Before the hearing, I was contacted by a firm of solicitors acting for the Ahmed family and the exchange of correspondence should be mentioned because it became relevant later. In a letter dated 1st November, 2007, the solicitors wrote:

> ...We would be obliged if you would be kind enough to let us have copies of all information, all documents in your possession prior to the Inquest hearing.

I replied:

I note your blanket request for all information or documents in my possession. I cannot comply with this request but if you can be more specific I will consider it again.

The solicitors did not respond to this until 10 December 2007, when they said:

We would be obliged if you would be kind enough to let us have copies of all information or documents in your possession as soon as possible in order that we may consider the same prior to the Inquest hearing.

When I replied I said:

I dealt with your blanket request for disclosure in my letter dated 7 November, paragraph 3. I repeat that you need to be more specific.

There was potentially a problem with handing over everything that I had because this could have released some information the police regarded as sensitive and which might harm any possible future prosecution. The solicitors never responded specifically to list what they wanted but as we will see later that was not the end of the matter.

Somewhat unusually, the police decided to have a barrister represent them at the inquest. They have a legal right to do this but rarely exercise it. The inquest was scheduled to start on Tuesday, 8 January 2008 and to last four days.

2 THE INQUEST

The twenty or thirty minutes before a long inquest starts are among the most nerve wracking and worrying times that a coroner goes through. At least that was my experience. You have probably 50 or more people in the building and many members of the press poised and at that late hour there is nothing whatsoever that the coroner can do to alter arrangements so if you have forgotten to call a key witness or failed to arrange an interpreter or someone crucial does not turn up then the whole hearing can be scuppered. Fortunately this never happened to me but equally the nervous time before the start of these long hearings never improved. The only strategy that I worked with was to walk out of the building and then about 100 yards to the River Kent which flows through Kendal. Here was peace and quiet and a chance to see wildlife.

The Shafilea Ahmed inquest did not start terribly well. At approximately ten minutes past ten I was sitting in court getting my papers in order when a young woman (as I later discovered she was a trainee solicitor) marched in without any preliminaries and announced that Mrs Ahmed would not accept a male interpreter. Since I had gone to some trouble to get an interpreter and he was certainly male, I simply had to reply that with 20 minutes to go to the start of the inquest, it was not going to be possible in Kendal to get a female interpreter and in the event no more was said on this subject.

At the start of the inquest I always give a brief explanation of what the inquest is for. This happened at the start of every inquest I conducted. It sets the scene, and hopefully puts a stop to any unrealistic expectations the family may have about the scope and purpose of the inquest. This is what I said that morning:

> Good morning to you all. My name is Ian Smith. I am the local coroner and my job today is to conduct an inquest relating to a body found some time ago now by the River Kent at Sedgwick. I just want to explain one or two things principally for the sake of the family before we move on. Which is to say that the purpose of the inquest is to establish as best we can what the facts are relating to someone's death. An inquest is a formal legal hearing in public, it is court and it is dealt with in the way that courts are, a formal way with witnesses giving their evidence on oath. It is not, however – and I stress this very strongly – it is not a trial of anybody or anything, but it is a serious fact finding exercise to try to establish what happened as best we can.

The importance of my introduction in this particular case was to underline the fact that nobody was on trial because there was a danger, especially with the police represented by a barrister, Mr Bassett, that it might appear to become a trial.

What I did next was to call Mr Ahmed to establish the formal details about his daughter, her full name, date of birth and suchlike. I had not warned him that I was going to do this but after a little uncertainty about the year his daughter was born, he told me that she was a bright girl and that he encouraged her to do whatever educational course was right for her. His main evidence would come a couple of days later.

I then began to hear the evidence of the many witnesses I had called to court. Mrs Gibbon told us that she remembered in September 2003 a white van parked in a lay-by near Sedgwick with its back end into the shrubbery and its front end out into the road. A few weeks later when walking her dog she was aware of 'piles of black bin liners' and an atrocious smell.

Anthony Kitchen worked for Cumbria County Council on highway maintenance but he explained when in February 2004, after bad flooding, he and two colleagues had been at the lay-by and come across what they thought at first was a dummy but quickly realised was something more sinister so they did the right thing and immediately called the police.

Detective Chief Inspector Mike Forrester and scenes of crime investigator, John Weighman, attended the scene and between them were able to confirm an initial view that the body was found where it had originally been placed rather than been washed there by the flooded river.

Miss Whitaker was a Forensic Entomologist. She explained how she worked. She said:

> I put a data logger to record the temperature at the scene where the body was found. That was like that for a period of time. We then obtain temperature records from the nearest possible meteorological station. In this case I actually received three different sets of data. The first two sets of data were related, I believe, to highway maintenance and they were fairly local to the area. And I received later on, a few months later, some other data. The reason for putting out a data logger at the scene is that you monitor the temperatures for at least a week if not more and then you do a regression analysis for the same time period with a local meteorological station. From that you can then work backwards and you can try and work out what the temperatures probably would have been at the crime scene.

The importance of the temperature is that the development of insects and specifically blowflies is very dependant upon temperature. Miss Whitaker found blowfly larvae and from her analysis she estimated that the eggs must have been laid on the body by approximately 9 to 12 October 2003. They could have been laid earlier but not later.

Andrew Davidson was a forensic scientist and gave evidence as to how he had obtained a DNA sample relating to Shafilea and that it matched the DNA obtained from the remains found by the riverside.

The final witness on the first day was Superintendent Geraint Jones of Cheshire Police who spent many years of his career working on Shafilea's case. He gave his extensive evidence without notes. He was completely committed to trying to achieve justice for Shafilea and as we will see later he eventually succeeded. Superintendent Jones then went on to explain how police had become aware of Shafilea being missing. They were notified on 18 September by a school teacher named Joanne Code and upon further enquiry at Shafilea's home it became apparent that she had last been seen on the night of the 12/13 September, 2003. The family did not report her missing.

Brian Monaghan gave evidence that he was a former police officer with Mersey Police, had no involvement whatever professionally with the investigation but had viewed the Ahmed family home on 18 September, 2003, as it was very newly on the market and Mr Ahmed said in the course of explaining why they were selling that one of his daughters had been mixing with the wrong people, got into some trouble and brought some shame on the family.

Pauline Moorhall gave evidence of contact with Shafilea in January 2003 at which point Shafilea was not residing at home. Ann-Marie Woods followed this up. She was Senior Homeless Officer for Warrington Borough Council and Shafilea applied to her on 5 February 2003, accompanied by a teacher, Joanne Code, saying that she was fleeing domestic violence and a marriage that her parents had arranged for her. Joanne Code was the person who later reported to the police that Shafelia was missing.

Lorraine Kryziuk gave evidence that she was from the Benefits Agency and she had to get Shafilea to tell her why she was there and why she was claiming benefit and

> she said she had left home because her parents had arranged a marriage for her in Pakistan. She did not want to go to Pakistan. She did not want the arranged marriage and she did not want to leave this country where she had made friends and she was very settled.

Mian Khan gave evidence through an interpreter that he was the father of Iftikhar Ahmed and therefore Shafilea's grandfather. The police did not believe that and there was a clash between their barrister, Mr Bassett, and Mr Khan, who had chosen to affirm that he would tell the truth rather than swear on the Koran. Mr Bassett suggested to him that he had done that because he was not prepared to lie about his relationship with Iftikhar after taking an oath on the Koran. Mr Khan's solicitor interjected at that point and Mr Khan declined to answer the question which was his absolute legal right. Mr Khan could not offer any explanation of events in Pakistan when Shafilea had been there and he clearly did not want to be in court at all. He left as soon as he had given his evidence without so much as a glance at Mr and Mrs Ahmed.

Friends of Shafilea gave evidence and then her tutor, Joanne Code, explained how she had been Shafilea's tutor for several years and she had proved to be a hard working, determined young woman who began to show signs of problems at home. Initially she was kept at home for several days and her parents explained that she had decided to give up studying and was going to burn her books but it seemed she had been subjected to violence at home after contacting boys and this later turned to a fear that she was going to be married off by the family in Pakistan and she would not be able to fulfil her real ambition of becoming a lawyer. It was Joanne Code who rang the Police to say that she was worried about Shafilea's whereabouts in September 2003. Mrs Code confirmed that Mr Ahmed had given notice of absence in respect of the younger children at the school because they were going to Pakistan but they had not given notice in respect of Shafilea.

Shafilea had been to Pakistan and the events there were never made clear. She had certainly drunk bleach and suffered a damaged oesophagus and the family said this was a mistake by Shafilea who had meant to use mouthwash during a power cut. The interpretation that others put on it was that it was a desperate attempt by Shafilea to avoid a marriage she did not want though there was no direct evidence of this.

Iftikhar Ahmed's evidence lasted a considerable time. He explained that at the time when the family were planning to go to Pakistan 'for a holiday' Shafilea ran away. Mr Ahmed came home at 3am after working as a taxi driver and found his wife sitting on the stairs crying. She explained 'the daughter's left again' and so he went driving around to see if he could spot anything in town. They went into Shafilea's school on the Monday and a few days later he came across her and a friend going to school and she got in the car and went home. The friend had given evidence that he forced her into the car but he denied that.

The trip to Pakistan was rearranged and Mr Ahmed said that Shafilea knew a couple of days in advance of the trip that she was going. She had been shopping with some friends at the Trafford Centre on 17 February and not mentioned going to Pakistan.

I asked Mr Ahmed about arranged marriages and he said:

arranged marriages are conducted between two families with the consent from the girl with the consent from the boy. They are actually shown each other. Whether they like each other, if they say yes to it, then the next procedure comes along and if they don't then obviously it stops there.

I asked him if he eventually intended to arrange marriages for his children and he said:

we are talking as a whole community type of thing but when you look at the children who are actually born here now, whether they want to follow into our footstep is a different matter. That's not something I can decide or somebody else can decide it is something for them to decide for themselves.

When asked about a specific suggestion of marriage to someone called Rafakat, who had been mentioned in evidence by Mian Khan, Mr Ahmed confirmed that he was the son of his uncle, that he was somewhere between 26/27 and his mid-30s and at the time resident in Saudi Arabia. He said that the possibility of a marriage between Rafakat and Shafilea had been mentioned by the uncle and he, Mr Ahmed, told the uncle that his daughter was in education and until she was finished with her graduation and decided what she wanted to do with her life it was too early to even think about it. He said that the topic was raised while he and Shafilea were in Pakistan and she simply said 'no way' and so

Iftikhar said to his uncle 'I'm sorry it is not going to happen.'

I asked him if children are allowed to react like that and his answer was:

Yes of course, I mean look it is in the interest of the girl right. If she is not going to be happy with the marriage like then what sort of marriage is that? That's my opinion.

Mr Bassett asked questions and this is how it started:

Q - Mr Ahmed by 18th September 2003 Shafilea had been missing from home for about a week hadn't she?

A - By the 18th yes.

Q - On that date was the sale of your house more important to you than knowing what had happened to your daughter?

A - No

Q - What actions had you taken by 18th September 2003 to discover her whereabouts?

A - When the police actually called on the Tuesday night, then you expect them to continue with their enquiries so what was I supposed to do?

Q - My question was, by 18th September, by which time Shafilea has been missing for a week, what actions had you taken to discover her whereabouts?

A - Well we waited for the workplace, we waited for the hospital and the college to see if they would let us know anything from there, so we didn't hear anything in that time.

Q - Well if you do not hear anything from the college, if you do not hear anything from the hospital and you do not hear anything from the workplace the indication may well be that she has actually attended the hospital appointment, she has been to college, she has been to her workplace?

A - Well we didn't know anything about that.

Q - So when you received no contact from any of those organisations in the first week did you get in touch with the college to ask has Shafilea been attending?

A - Well by that time the police was already involved so

Q - When you heard nothing in the first week from the college did you contact the college and ask yourself has Shafilea been attending her course?

A - No not myself

Q - Did anyone from the family contact the college?

A - No

At the end of the questioning, this was the exchange:

Q - Mr Ahmed, were you involved in Shafilea's disappearance?
A - No
Q - Were you involved in her death?
A - I do not have to answer this question

Mr Ahmed's own Barrister, Mr Flanagan, explored the question of whether Mrs Ahmed was present in Pakistan and whether Rafakat was present in Pakistan and in due course the following exchange took place:

Q - In terms of your culture, I am just trying as shortly and concisely as possible if any marriage were to take place what are the expectations of the parents in the marriage?
A - Like I explained before, if you are actually going to do anything of this sort right, it is the consent between the parents of the girl and the parents of the lad and since it wasn't the case we only discussed the matter a few months back and that was the end of it as far as I concerned.

I think that Mr Ahmed said more in that reply than he realised, having previously said it was the consent of the boy and the girl that mattered rather than what he said here, that it was the consent of their parents.

Mrs Farzana Ahmed gave evidence through an interpreter. She seemed to have got over her difficulty with a male interpreter. She accepted that there had been a discussion within the family about a possible marriage of Shafilea to Rafakat and she accepted that there was a wedding of different family members planned for the time when the family were going to be in Pakistan.

Mr Bassett, the barrister for the police, opened his questioning of Mrs Ahmcd very directly as follows:

Q - Mrs Ahmed do you know who killed Shafilea?
A - I do not know about it. If I know who the murderer was then would I not get a proper punishment for my daughter's murderer?

She played down any conflict between Shafilea and herself and Mr Ahmed and she played down the extent of the apparent damage to Shafilea after drinking bleach in Pakistan. Her own barrister, Mr Flanagan, asked a number of questions to try to clear any involvement with Shafilea's disappearance and death and this ended as follows:

Q - I know you have been asked this before but I just want to be clear. Were you at all involved in the disappearance of your daughter?
A - No, not at all, definitely nothing at all
Q - Did you feel any shame about what your daughter had done?

A - I stated this before that I did not feel any shame at all

Q - Were you involved in her death at all?

A - I had no involvement whatsoever. I personally am not happy with the police. They did not investigate the tragic death of my lovely daughter. I personally want a proper investigation to be taken out to be done. It is now more than four years, what have they been doing? Is it not a police job to find out what happened with my child? Again and again they are blaming myself and my husband. I am not happy at all. They did not co-operate with us at all. Had they co-operated with us there was a possibility that we could have found our daughter alive.

That was the end of Mrs Ahmed's evidence and in light of what the legal process uncovered later it is clear that she was using the old adage that attack is the best form of defence.

Rebecca Hunt was a nurse who looked after Shafilea while she was in hospital after her return from Pakistan. She told us that Shafilea was very withdrawn with her mother and would not make eye contact with her. She said there was no conversation but with another younger visitor she was much more animated and lively.

3 SUMMING UP

I worked on the summing up over night and spent several hours preparing it. I delivered the summing up on Friday, 11 January, 2008.

The first job I had was to confirm whether I accepted the identity of the human remains that had been discovered by the river at Sedgwick. Remembering that the body was incomplete and badly decomposed this was not a foregone conclusion but I had heard from the dentist, Gerald Southern, who compared his records of Shafilea's teeth with the mandible that was discovered at the scene and he said there was a large degree of matching although it was not a complete match and he also recognised his own handiwork. Further, some jewellery belonging to Shafilea was identified but most convincingly DNA samples had been obtained from Shafilea's toothbrush and the scientist who compared the DNA from the toothbrush with the DNA from the remains said that the chances of them being a random match were as high as a billion to one against. I was therefore able to say:

There is the clearest possible evidence that you could wish to indicate that this body on the riverbank was indeed Shafilea matched up by DNA, matched up by dental records. So there is no doubt whatsoever that the body deposited on the riverbank was Shafilea Ahmed.

The next question that I had to consider was whether it was possible to state a cause of death. Doctor Armour, the Home Office Pathologist, had speculated strangulation or smothering or both, but I said:

> I think that is speculation. I think that is conjecture and hypothesis and whilst it may be right there is nothing to support that conjecture or hypothesis and so we are going to have to remain with the cause of death which will be officially recorded by one word which is 'Unascertained'.

Next I dealt with the circumstances of Shafilea's death. I said that in theory she could have died naturally and that she did have a life threatening problem with her oesophagus but the evidence had said that there was no likelihood of a sudden collapse of the oesophagus or a sudden bleed though if it remained untreated for a period of time the oesophagus could have closed and led to her death. I said:

> in theory the possibility existed that there was a problem but I think the possibility is so small that it is not going to detract from my finding when I get to the verdict.

I also discussed the question of suicide and I said that I believed that whilst she was in Pakistan Shafilea did harm herself. I said:

> that has been presented to me as an accident and I will come back to it. I do not think it was an accident. I think it was deliberately inflicted damage but I do not think it was a suicide attempt in the sense of she really wanted to kill herself.

I also dealt with some theoretical possibilities in order to dismiss them but to show that I had given them some thought. This is what I said:

> I also want to deal with the position that Shafilea was in at the time that she disappeared in September 2003 and to deal with the suggestion, if anybody were to make it, that because she had self harmed once she might do again. In September 2003, Shafilea was back in the mainstream of what she had been doing previously. She was back at her education in the new school. She was working again and she was going forward. She was not stuck with any problems at that point that I am aware of and I do not believe that she did self harm and I certainly do not believe that she killed herself. Where I am going to on this is that somebody who finds themselves with a body that has either died naturally or has committed suicide could conceivably be so embarrassed or so confused that they do actually get rid of the body even though the death has been natural or the result of suicide. Anybody doing that would be extremely

foolish but it could conceivably happen. So, as I say, I put these possibilities up simply really in order to knock them down again. I do not believe that Shafilea died from natural causes. I do not believe that she killed herself.

This left me with three questions to answer, being, where, when and how did she die, and this is what I said:

As to where she died, I have absolutely no idea. There is no evidence what-soever of the place of death. I am very confident that she did not die at the place where she was found, on the riverbank, but where she died we do not know.

When did she die?

It is my belief that she died within a few hours of leaving work on 11 September 2003. I cannot say if it was 6 hours later, 12 hours later, 24 hours later. I think probably 24 hours is the maximum period. I think she was probably killed well within that period of 24 hours. I do not believe that she escaped on 11 September. I believe that she was taken and I will come back to that as well.

How did she die?

Well quite simply she was murdered. I am convinced of that by a number of facts. Firstly, the way that her body was disposed of. It was hidden. It was taken many miles from where she lived. I am satisfied beyond all reasonable doubt and, so as I understand it, everybody else is as well, both the family through their lawyer and the police directly and through their lawyer. I think everyone accepts that she was murdered. She was unlawfully killed. I agree.

I said that in one sense that had dealt with all the questions the law required me to answer but the inquest had gone over a fairly lengthy period of time of Shafilea's life leading up to her death and although I had hoped this would throw some light on the circumstances of her death it did not appear to have done so. I did say that because of all the evidence we had heard and the exten-sive comments about it in the media, I felt I had to deal with the evidence. I said that without doubt a central issue for Shafilea was the concept of an ar-ranged marriage. There had been a conversation between Mr Ahmed and an uncle in which the possibility of a match between Shafilea and Rafakat had been raised and although Mr Ahmed had said that it was too early the proposi-tion was not completely dismissed but was perhaps shelved. Mr Ahmed told his wife, who in turn told Shafilea, and I came to the conclusion that this did worry Shafilea. I said this in the summing up:

Mrs Ahmed says that Shafilea was happy throughout this time. Clearly she was not. She was a very frightened young woman. She was frightened of the consequences of an arranged marriage if it happened and those consequences to her were several:

1. She did not want to be married at that point certainly.
2. She did not want to be married to somebody she did not know.
3. She did not want to be married to somebody she might not like.
4. She did not want to stop her studies and she did not want, maybe, to have to live abroad having been brought up in this country, educated in this county and wanted to forge a career in this country.
5. And she feared, whether rightly or wrongly, all of those things might happen.

Shafilea was away from home overnight in November 2002 and I concluded that was a result of a fallout between Shafilea and her parents probably over telephone numbers stored in her mobile phone which indicated that she was in contact with boys and her parents were unhappy about this.

A more significant period of absence was at the end of January/early February 2003 when Shafilea became aware of a proposed trip to Pakistan by the family. In the next few days Shafilea applied for emergency accommodation and income support and her actions indicated that she was expecting to be away from home permanently. People who dealt with her at that point described her as quiet and subdued, withdrawn and very frightened, and she actually said to one witness that she was afraid of being taken to Pakistan and afraid of an arranged marriage.

On 10 February 2003, Mr Ahmed came across Shafilea near the school and she went home with him in the car and, as I said in the summing up:

> There was some kind of mediation between the parents and Shafilea and later that day she went home having apparently been promised that there was no intention to marry her off and that appears to have satisfied Shafilea. I am quite sure that she was torn between her own wish for freedom and a genuine love for the family and in particular for her brothers and sisters and I'm sure that was an agonising thing for her to experience.

Shafilea running away had disrupted the plans for the family to go to Pakistan on 21 February 2003, but new plans were put in place.

On 17 February 2003, Shafilea was at the Trafford Centre with her friends and at no point did Shafilea mention that she might be going to Pakistan or that she was going to Pakistan. As I said in the summing up, this might have been because she did not know she was going but equally that she might have been embarrassed to say so after all the fuss of the previous few days and as a consequence dare not tell her friends that she was going to Pakistan, possibly even going voluntarily.

Remember that Shafilea was totally committed to her studies, to her career path, to go into the law. She is said to be perfectly happy to go to Pakistan at this time, her parents say that she was. I have got to say that I do not think she knew that she was going to Pakistan. I do not think she had any warning of it. She is also said to be happy to stay when the stay was extended. I am not so sure that she had much of a choice. I do not see this girl just abandoning her studies for a few weeks holiday in a country that she had previously been afraid to go to. That just does not sit right with me at all.

But what actually happened we can say to some extent is this. Mr Ahmed, Shafilea and two of the other children did go to Pakistan leaving behind Mrs Ahmed and the other children. School was not informed that Shafilea was going. They were not aware of this and Mr Ahmed says "well when I asked the school where Shafilea was they would not tell me because Shafilea is over 16 so it is not my business to tell the school that Shafilea is going. She can tell them. If she is the responsible person when she has gone missing, she is the responsible person when she is going off on holiday" and you can understand that point of view. Shafilea did not tell the school that she was leaving, temporarily or otherwise, she simply did not turn up. There was no return date specifically arranged and it may be that Shafilea, as I say, did not know that she was going. It may be that she had changed her mind and was willing to go and it may be that she was assured by the fact that her mother was not going with them. It seems likely that if mother was not there then there would be no wedding. So, as I say, perhaps Shafilea was assured by that and was willing to go on that basis.

Mr Ahmed returned to the UK on 18 March 2003 and after his return he cancelled Shafilea's return ticket and received a refund on it. He explained that this ticket was only valid for 30 days whereas the others were open-ended but as I explained in the summing up, this meant that Shafilea was in Pakistan without any arrangement to return and without a valid ticket to return. On 29 March 2003, Mrs Ahmed flew out to Pakistan with the other children so the whole of the family was now there apart from Mr Ahmed.

Which leads us to a very central issue indeed. What happened in Pakistan? I heard evidence from a number of witnesses about what happened in Pakistan. The first witness I heard was Mian Khan. He told me that he knew about the possible proposal of marriage in respect of Shafilea and Rafakat. He said in his evidence that that was not accepted because Shafilea was still studying. Remember that Mian Khan said he did not talk to Iftikhar and Farzana Ahmed.

There was some fall out between them and they were not talking. So how he knew this I am not sure but he did say that in his evidence that he knew the suggestion had been rejected because Shafilea was still studying. He did say in his evidence that arranged marriages are frequent within the family. That does appear to be quite true. He was asked about what had happened in terms of Shafilea not being well or becoming injured, becoming ill, and he said he did not know. He said in response at one point "who would I have asked?" and he gave the explanation that he was not speaking to Farzana and Iftikhar. Well, if Iftikhar was not in the country at the time and he was not speaking to Farzana who would he have asked? Well anyone of the dozens of people who lived in the village related to him. He could have asked anybody. I am quite sure in my own mind that he would have heard the gossip in the village and he would have wanted to know what had happened and there were any number of people that he could have asked but he says that he did not...

We are still dealing with what did or did not happen in Pakistan. I asked Mr Ahmed, remembering of course that he was not in the country at the time, he was back here in the UK, so anything that he knew was second-hand. He just said there was a mistake, there was an accident. He did not really pursue it. He did not really ask in detail what had happened. This is one of his daughters, his eldest daughter. Maybe he does not think she is so badly damaged as she was at that point but he showed what I would categorise as remarkably little interest in what had happened to make his daughter ill and that continues even when she does become very ill back in the UK. He said – "I didn't ask how it happened". He then went on to say "it was something to do with mouthwash. I wasn't there. Accidents are accidents." So we get very little enlightenment from Mr Ahmed but, as I say, fair enough he was not even in Pakistan at the time.

Mrs Ahmed also seemed to minimise the event and its effects upon Shafilea. I said:

We are left with very little information about something that happened in Pakistan and there are things that people know that have not been told to the Court.

On 11 September Shafilea left work about 9pm. Mr Ahmed told me in evidence that everyone went to bed leaving Shafilea up, working at her school work, nothing apparently wrong, nothing apparently out of the ordinary, so he went to bed and left her. The next morning he got up and went downstairs and found the front door keys on the floor and said that he immediately came to the conclusion that that meant that Shafilea had gone again. At this point the family do not do anything. They said "well we went to the police the first time and they more or less dismissed us out of hand, they didn't help, so what is the point of going back to the police just to be disrespected again." So they did not contact the police. They did not contact her friends this time and they say "well what is the point, we went to the friends the previous time and they wouldn't tell us where she was. They wouldn't tell us if they knew where she was. They wouldn't tell us if she was safe. They just covered and lied so what is the point of going to them?" They did not make any phone calls to Shafilea's phone but it is entirely unclear whether she even had one at that point. We know that she had bought a SIM card. The family probably did not know that so again there is a perfectly reasonable explanation as to why the family was not doing the things that they had been doing on previous occasions when Shafilea went missing.

It was on 18 September that Joanne Code notified the police that she feared Shafilea was missing having been alerted by friends of Shafilea.

I then returned to the finding of the body, confirmed that I accepted evidence of the experts in relation to plant growth and development of insects, indicating that the body had been there since approximately September 2003 and this was confirmed by local witnesses observing a terrible smell of decomposition about the same time.

I concluded the inquest as follows:

So what remains? A great deal of speculation, a fair amount of non information but nonetheless what remains is that Shafilea was the victim of a very vile murder. There are no two ways about that. I believe that she was taken from her home on 11th or the early hours of 12th September 2003. She was removed, she was murdered somewhere else, either in a vehicle or at some other premises and she was quickly disposed of. I do not believe she ran away. I do not know who did it. There is no evidence whatever before the court as to who did it. I sincerely hope that further enquiries will be carried out by the police and I hope they will discover one day who did it because this young woman has not had justice. Her ambition was just to live her own life in her own way, to study, to follow a career in the law and this was denied to her. That really is all I want to say and that is the closing of the inquest.

The verdict was "Shafilea Ahmed was unlawfully killed."

The fact that I had arranged facilities for the press and they had been told by the media manager that I would not be making statements, resulted in me being left alone by the press but later I was to see television coverage of Mr and Mrs Ahmed being shepherded to their lawyer's car surrounded by a scrum asking them questions which of course they were not answering and the overall effect was to make them look extremely guilty.

I watched the BBC News at Ten that night and saw that the lead story was the inquest. George Alagiah's headline as the theme music rolled was "the victim of a vile murder".

After nearly four years from the finding of the body, during which the criminal process started but eventually faltered, and after months of preparation at least the inquest was over and the case finished.

Or so I thought.

4 THE APPEAL

They appealed!

In the light of subsequent court proceedings, this is still a decision that I do not understand. Strictly speaking you cannot appeal a coroner's decision but there is a process of applying to the High Court for a Judicial Review to overturn the inquest and this is what the family did. When appealing a previous decision of a court or, as here, applying for a Judicial Review, the applicant cannot simply say they are dissatisfied and want another hearing; they have to state specific grounds for doing so, and show that the coroner has made an error of law.

Being any kind of judicial officer makes you subject to being appealed. At training sessions we were always told not to take it personally when it happens. Every case in the Court of Appeal for example is an appeal from a High Court Judge. I have to say that I found it impossible not to take it personally. I had spent many hours and been very careful with the words I used and I was being told I had got it wrong.

The Ahmed family alleged, firstly, that I was biased against them and that I directly implicated Mr Ahmed in the killing of his daughter. Secondly, I was accused of 'insufficient inquiry' and that I should have called three of Shafilea's siblings as witnesses as well as work colleagues and further medical evidence.

The application to the court refers to "the coroner's finding was that Shafilea's death was an honour killing by members of her family" and it was also stated that I "gave the appearance of bias by spending the time during the adjournments in the inquest in the company of the police and their witnesses. The coroner spent much of his time in the room allocated to the police at the inquest."

Because I had not said that this was an honour killing by Shafilea's family and because the allegation about spending time with the police during adjournments was simply untrue, I had to defend myself as otherwise I was accepting that I had behaved in a completely inappropriate way. This allegation became a matter of specific focus at the hearing as we will see. Incidentally the police had not been allocated a private room. They had simply taken one over without my knowledge.

The procedure for applying for a Judicial Review to overturn a coroner's hearing is not a simple process. Firstly, the High Court has to give permission for the Judicial Review to go ahead. A High Court Judge reads the papers submitted by the applicant (Mr Iftikhar Ahmed in this case) and initially Mr Justice Blake decided that the application should not go ahead. This meant that the applicant had a right to an oral hearing in front of a different High Court Judge to be able to argue that it should go ahead. This took place on Tuesday, 15 July 2008. We were initially allocated to Mr Justice Blair (the former Prime Minister's brother) but he was already hearing a case and we were transferred to Mr Justice Forbes. He had the case papers to read over lunch and in about an hour obtained a thorough and detailed grasp of what the appeal was about. He argued it out with the barrister representing Mr Ahmed and my barrister in great detail and ultimately did not give permission but ordered further statements and evidence to be filed so that another judge could consider the application further. If that judge thought it was right to give permission then he could also hear the substantive case itself at the same time.

I have to say that at no point did I really think I would win the case. It is very easy for a judge to look back at what you said and find fault. I thought it almost inevitable that a new hearing would be ordered though I knew that the specific allegation that I had spent time with the police during adjournments was factually incorrect.

Between July 2008 and the eventual final hearing in June 2009, I had been rather poorly and undergone an operation so I was not feeing terribly well or optimistic when I went to London for the final hearing. My solicitor, Sara Robinson, from Cumbria County Council's legal department and my barrister, Alison Hewitt, managed to keep me going through the two days in front of Mr Justice Irwin. For this hearing Mr Ahmed used a third different barrister. Mr Flanagan had appeared at the Inquest, Mr Downman at the hearing before Mr Justice Forbes and now it was Mr Hartman.

Early in his argument he suggested my 'apparent bias' as a lack of independence and impartiality, proved by the fact that I had used the police's statements as the basis from which I asked questions. The Judge immediately said "Mr Hartman that's rubbish" which is rather more than a broad hint to an advocate that the Judge has a clear view on the matter. Mr Hartman however, said that he wished to try to persuade the Judge and pursued the point as I recall it for about 20 minutes. He argued that I should have somehow obtained an independent investigation into Shafilea's death rather than rely on the police's investigation.

The allegation that I had consorted with the police during adjournments at the inquest was not pursued and the barrister representing the police (once again Mr Bassett) said that the allegation should be specifically withdrawn and an apology given to me because it was after all a serious attack on my professionalism and judgement.

Mr Justice Irwin decided to have Miss Frost, in whose statement the allegation was made, give evidence on oath. She was at the time of the inquest a trainee solicitor and by the time of the appeal hearing a newly qualified solicitor. She explained that there might be a different interpretation to what she had seen though she did not say what she had in fact seen. She also said her statement had been drafted for her by a barrister, she had not been closely supervised in the office and she had no experience of inquests at all. At least an apology of sorts was given. I must say that if when I was a newly qualified solicitor, I had been asked by a High Court Judge to go into the witness box to explain my own statement, I would have been utterly petrified.

At the end of the first day I was still despondent and had little doubt that a new inquest would be ordered but I took myself off to the Coliseum to see *Madame Butterfly*. A tale of betrayal, abandonment and ultimately suicide.

The next morning things somehow seemed a little brighter and around lunchtime Mr Justice Irwin had heard what he wanted to and retired to prepare his judgment which he gave at 3.30 that afternoon.

Firstly, he recorded the facts as he saw them, which were substantially the same sequence of events as evidenced at the inquest.

He dealt with the allegation that I had failed to disclose documentation to Mr and Mrs Ahmed's solicitors and excused me on the grounds that the solicitors had made a blanket request for "all information or documents in your possession" and I had responded indicating that I could not give blanket disclosure but if they were more specific I would consider the request again but the solicitors did not make a more specific request.

Counsel for the family at the inquest made no complaint about the lack of disclosure and participated fully in the hearing and was able to ask meaningful questions. As for the allegation of bias, the Judge excused Miss Frost on the grounds of her inexperience, the fact that she had apparently signed a statement drafted by counsel and overseen by her managing partner or supervising partner and he said:

> It would have been wiser if counsel who had advised her on such a witness statement and her supervising solicitor had examined more closely and thought more carefully about what she was proposing in a witness statement an accu-

sation which amounts to actual bias or indeed the appearance of bias should not be made lightly. It should be made only after real care.

As for the suggestion that I showed apparent bias by relying on statements from the police, Mr Justice Irwin said:

> This was a line which in my judgement was quite without foundation. It is quite inconceivable that inquests could be conducted in the country within our system, other than in many situations relying upon the information provided to coroners from police investigations or indeed from investigations carried our by other public bodies or authorities... There is absolutely nothing wrong with a coroner drawing his information from a source like that.

The Judge accepted that my use of the words 'vile murder' meant nothing more significant than the killing of an innocent seventeen year old girl by whoever did it. The Judge concluded by saying:

> I find there is absolutely no basis in any of the other points advanced to suggest there was any apparent bias, much less any actual bias, to show there was any lack of proper enquiry to show that there was any breach of Rule 42 of the Coroners Rules or any inappropriate incrimination of the claimant or anyone else in the course either of the full remarks or of the verdict or any perversity in the findings of fact as to how the deceased came by her death.

The Judge said that the application failed and permission for Judicial Review was refused.

When a court case is decided the side which wins can ask for the legal expenses – the costs – to be paid by the side that has lost. Both sides have to say how much their bill is. Mr Ahmed's lawyers' costs were about £105,000, Cumbria County Council's about £26,000. Both my barrister on behalf of Cumbria County Council's legal department and the police's barrister asked for costs and the Judge asked Mr Hartman to respond which prompted this exchange:

> Mr Hartman – Your Lordship, I do not resist the application for costs. Of course I do have to ask you for permission for leave to appeal.
> Mr Justice Irwin – Do you? You do not have to ask me for that at all.
> Mr Hartman – Well I am asking.
> Mr Justice Irwin – Well it is refused.

In due course the Judge ordered that the police costs and my legal team's costs should be paid by the defendant but this was not to be enforced without leave of the Court or leave of the Court of Appeal. The point of this was that Mr Ahmed did not have the means to pay. He himself had been on Legal Aid.

I was surprised and delighted that the Judge had not overturned the inquest and I went away feeling that perhaps I had done a decent job. Despite Mr Hart-man's request for leave to appeal, no appeal was ever lodged.

5 AFTER THE APPEAL

This is not to say that the case never came back to court because it certainly did when Mr and Mrs Ahmed were prosecuted for the murder of their daughter.

As coroner, I had no part whatsoever in that hearing so all I can record is what is common knowledge, taken exclusively from the press reporting of the hearing. One of Shafilea's sisters told the police what had happened to her sister and a prosecution went ahead. Mr and Mrs Ahmed were found guilty of mur-dering their daughter. Part way through the trial Mr Ahmed acknowledged that he had killed his daughter in the family home and seemed willing to take ex-clusive responsibility for it but the case continued against Mrs Ahmed and she was found guilty. Apparently she started an appeal but did not pursue it. The judge recommended that they serve 25 years in prison. The judge was Roderick Evans J and his sentencing remarks are reproduced as an appendix to this book. They are a devastating condemnation of the Ahmeds and their behaviour.

Superintendent Geraint Jones had spent years of his career trying to achieve

Figure 11: Superintendent Geraint Jones who gave a large portion of his ca-reer to achieve justice for Shafilea.

justice for Shafilea. He gave evidence at the inquest, sat patiently through the appeal and finally achieved his goal.

The eventual outcome throws a poor light on some earlier events.

After the discovery of Shafilea's body, the police had held a press conference to which the parents were not invited. They did however turn up towards the end together with (according to the *Manchester Evening News* website) three lawyers, one of whom delivered an address and handed out a press release, which includes the following:

First and foremost no-one can possibly overlook the fact that Iftikhar and Farzana Ahmed have lost a beautiful and irreplaceable daughter. Nothing can change that cruel reality – that reality made all the more painful in view of the unsubstantiated allegations against them.

Mr and Mrs Ahmed wish to confirm once more that they strenuously deny any direct or indirect involvement with their daughter's untimely demise. If called upon to do so they shall not hesitate to defend their good and unblemished names in any Court.

The family call upon the Police to now work with them to discover the truth as to how Shafilia met her premature fate and who was responsible for her death.

They specifically appeal to the media and the Police authorities to broaden their investigation so as to consider thoroughly but fairly any possible suspects and to pursue any conceivable leads. That enquiry shall be conducted with transparency rather than being based upon any form of ethnic stereotyping.

Quite obviously Mr and Mrs Ahmed are as anxious as anyone to discover the real truth as to what happened to Shafilia in September 2003 and in the endless months since then. The Police have their total co-operation as all parties must strive to discover the truth about Shafilia's tragic ending.

The family's own lives have been in turmoil ever since their beloved Shafilia disappeared. Now should be the time for them to be left to grieve and for the authorities to go elsewhere to find those truly responsible for any foul play.

I ask you to allow them proper time and space now to grieve for their daughter. Seventeen, beautiful, bright and yet shining no more. A tragic ending to the painful period of waiting.

Shafilea's name is indeed spelt Shafilia throughout. Two years later a different firm of solicitors issued a press release dated 7 February, 2006, stating:

Today eight family members have had their bail cancelled after being held on bail since September 2004. This demonstrates that the Police have from the outset of this investigation targeted Mr and Mrs Ahmed and other family members as being responsible for the unfortunate death of Shafilea.

Mr and Mrs Ahmed yet again strenuously deny any direct or indirect involvement in their daughter's untimely demise.

The family again call upon the Police now to work with them to discover the truth about how Shafilea met her premature fate and who was responsible for her death. The Police authorities are asked to broaden their investigations so as to consider thoroughly but fairly any possible suspects and to pursue all conceivable leads.

The Police must now co-operate fully with the family or risk civil proceedings for breach of duty and care.

In July 2004, Mr and Mrs Ahmed had offered a £5,000 reward for information leading to the killer's conviction. The police told me that at one point of the investigation they had shown the parents CCTV footage from Scotland of someone who might conceivably have been Shafilea. The parents confirmed it was indeed their daughter and said that now they knew she was alive the

Figure 12: Farzana Ahmed and Iftikhar Ahmed.

search could be called off. At all these times they knew better than anyone that Shafilea was dead.

A decade later as I write this I am still annoyed by the lies consistent throughout the Ahmeds' attempts to manipulate the legal system and the media. They have been convicted of their daughter's murder. They lied to the inquest. Amazingly they were not satisfied and tried to have the inquest run again. Just what they thought they could achieve by this is beyond me since they knew what they had done, and in my summing up I said I did not know who had done it. How did they think they could improve on that outcome? The Ahmeds said through their lawyers that I stated this was an honour killing. That concept never featured in the inquest at all and I was very careful to ensure it did not. I am saddened by the waste of public money that financed the appeal and upset that I was wrongly accused of unprofessional behaviour which Mr Hartman was simply intending not to pursue. It was only because Mr Bassett the barrister insisted on following this up and the Judge agreed it had to be explored properly that any kind of apology at all was offered.

Most of all I am outraged at the fact that Shafilea, a hard working student was killed because she had a mind of her own and wanted to choose her own future rather than submit to one imposed on her. I am a strong believer in making your own decisions based on what you know rather than accepting what other people tell you. Shafilea would probably now be a qualified solicitor or barrister but she was not given the chance.

.

FOURTEEN

History

1 A VERY BRIEF HISTORY OF CORONERS

The office of Coroner has existed for at least 800 years and possibly back to the reign of King Alfred. The Articles of Eyre in 1194 recommended the appointment in each county of three knights and a clerk to keep the Pleas of the Crown (*Custos Placitorum Coronae*). This was because the Eyre toured the country collecting fines and other payments on behalf of the Crown, trying cases and reviewing local government. It toured the country approximately every seven years. The official in the local area had to keep records and indeed payments and account to the Eyre when it next visited. The office holder was therefore the Crown's man, the crowner or coroner, but elected by the local freemen.

The office therefore started as a kind of tax collector. If someone should accidentally catch a royal fish, and be honest enough to declare it, it was sensible to take a payment from that person rather than keep the fish till the Eyre next visited. Convicted felons forfeited their property to the Crown and suspected criminals might take sanctuary in a church, abjure the realm and leave the country after 40 days subject again to forfeiture of all their property. This was abolished in 1624. The coroner's job was to escort the suspect to the port and to ensure that the property seized was accounted for when the Eyre next visited. Coroners also had the task of supervising trial by ordeal. If a suspect could pick up a red hot iron bar and not suffer burns then he was innocent – God had protected him. The coroner's position was therefore always at the centre of the administration of justice in the various forms that justice adopted over the centuries and even in the twentieth century the local coroner would be expected to be present at any judicial hanging. The death penalty was not abolished until 1965, well within my lifetime.

Other duties of the coroner in the Middle Ages included collecting deodands. These were items which had caused someone's death and any such item was automatically forfeit to the Crown, presumably on the grounds that the Crown represented God on Earth. The meaning of deodand is something which is to be given to God. Death is an irresistible opportunity for the state to take money from its late citizens and so the connection between death and coroners was established early.

In the industrialisation of Victorian times, deodands became problematic when people were killed on the railway. Should the whole train be forfeit or just the engine, and if so what on earth was the Crown going to do with it? Should the value of the deodand be given to the deceased's family? Coroners' juries probably declared trains to be deodand in an attempt to compensate them indirectly, as otherwise they were unlikely to receive any payment. Deodand was finally abolished in 1846.

The Births and Deaths Registration Act 1836 introduced a requirement to register the first and last events of life and the coroner now had to report the outcome of inquests to the registrar. In 1888 the election of coroners was abolished and instead they were appointed by local authorities. It was not until 1980 that the requirement for the coroner to view the body came to an end. The number of coroners' jurisdictions diminished slowly but steadily from about 300 in the 1930s to about 100 when I retired in 2014, as districts merged. This process still continues.

In the twentieth century there were periodic reviews of the role and work of coroners approximately every thirty years but government had little appetite to change things until Harold Shipman was uncovered as the country's most prolific murderer and then the reform was not as far-reaching as proposed. There is a separate section on the recent reform process and a short note on Harold Shipman.

2 Verdicts and a Little Local History

I have in front of me copies of three inquisitions from 1768 which would now be called the Record of an Inquest. They were unearthed from the Barrow archives by the librarian Aidan Jones. The documents state the dates of death and of the hearing and the names of the coroner and all the jurors (exclusively male). The details of the cases are as follows:

1. William Park late of Hawkshead Hill, Husbandman (Inquest 23 July 1768)
   The Deceased has for some time past been in a desponding, despairing melancholy state of mind and on Thursday last 21st July early in the morning in fit of Lunacy and Despair he forsook his family and in that state of mind travelled to a certain Tarn or Pond of Water about half a mile from his own house and therein drowned himself.

2. Robert Mole late of Kirkby Ireleth, Slategetter (Inquest 28 August 1768)
   Yesterday about six of the clock in the afternoon as the deceased was working at the bottom of a slate quarry at Croglin (a pit near 25 yards deep) from which the men at the top were drawing up a large block of stone which was fastened

in the usual manner with a Chain and drawn up by a Winch; the stone unfortunately slipped out of the chain and fell upon a Rock from which it rebounded
and pitched directly upon the deceased and killed him instantly dead upon the
place.

3. Robert Mellross late of Roosecoat, Labourer (Inquest 14 September 1768)
   Yesterday 13th September 1768 the deceased alone and of himself was burning
   of whins (gorse) in a field called Horsemoor in Roosecoat was then and there
   suddenly seized with an Apoplexy or some other fit of sickness of which falling
   among the whins which he was burning he either thereof presently died or was
   before his recovery suffocated and smothered in the smoke of the whins and
   so and not otherwise the Jurors say the Deceased came to his Death by an Act
   of God.

A number of comments can be made from these inquisitions. Firstly, they are
all narrative verdicts two and a half centuries before my generation of coroners
thought we had invented them. Secondly the inquests were concluded within
hours of the death rather than the weeks, months or even years of today. Thirdly
the jurors would have been required by law to view the body. They may even
have carried out the whole inquest in the presence of the body.

The coroner in each case was Thomas Petty and in one a juror was named
John Pool. This is quite a co-incidence since the Coroner for Furness in the
1960s was John Poole.

The verdict 'Act of God' reminds me of a telephone call I had some years
ago from the Registrar of Births and Deaths. He had come across a death of a
baby in the records from 1895, hardly the Dark Ages, giving the cause as 'Visitation of God'. What did I think that meant? My answer was cot death, sometimes given the spurious medical name 'Sudden Infant Death Syndrome'. All
come to the same thing – the tragic sudden, unexpected death of a baby for no
obvious reason known to medical science.

Another document unearthed by the Librarian at Barrow was the claim for
payment put in by the coroner in 1828. At that time coroners were paid on the
authority of the local magistrates, a source of endless complaint and recrimi-
nations between the two office holders. From 1854 coroners were paid a salary
instead of the fee per inquest for which this document was drawn up. I think it
is worth listing the relatively few inquests, for which the coroner was paid one
pound each plus travel (by horse I imagine) of 123 miles in total for which he
received an extra £4.12s.3d. After the date is the place where the inquest was
held, the name of the deceased and the outcome of the inquest.

3 March: Farr End in Church Coniston.

Samuel Williams. Killed in the Copper Mines accidentally.

20 March: The Workhouse in Kirkby Ireleth.

William Lishman a Pauper who was found dead in bed by the
Visitation of God.

8 April: Outgate Hawkshead.

Thomas Atkinson found drowned in Coniston Lake.

11 June: Dalton.

George Poole. accidentally killed in a sawpit.

19 June: High in Newland.

Richard Robinson. Accidentally killed in Gawthwaite Slate Quarries.

11 July: Ulverston.

John Allen. Accidentally rode over by a Horse.

12 August: Sparkbridge.

George Septimus Helme age three. Accidentally drowned in River Crake.

20 August: Baskel.

Thomas Dixon. Died of Apoplexy

25 September: Henry Bradley. Drowned on Lancaster Sands

27 September: Hugh Iddon drowned in Ulverston Canal

20 October: Dixon Ground Church Coniston.

George Graves. Died by Visitation of God

10 November: Ulverston.

William Atkinson. Died of typhus Fever.

26 November: Ireleth.

James Benson. Suffocated in an Iron Ore Pit.

William Brockbanks. Suffocated in an Iron Ore Pit.

3 THOMAS WAKLEY

Dr. Wakley was born in 1795 and died in 1862. He was one of those people
who straddled many areas of life and left his mark wherever he went. He was
a doctor, a member of parliament and a true radical. He founded the medical
journal, *The Lancet.* He wanted to be a coroner and in those days coroners were
elected. This only ended in 1888.

He described the coroner as the people's judge, but to say that coroners
were instituted for the protection of the public is inaccurate as we have seen.
The office was instituted for the Crown's benefit. The very name – the crowner
– confirms that. But the institution had been ignored and left to its own devices
and Wakley saw the chance to re-invent the position as a champion of the
downtrodden and abused masses. He highlighted the abuse of the poor in work-
houses and prisons.

It has been recorded in two academic papers I have read that he spent £7,000 on one election for coroner, in 1830. If that is accurate it was an enormous sum, perhaps equivalent to half a million pounds today and I suggest it is not really credible. He believed all coroners should be doctors and so would not have approved of the recent reform by which all coroners must be legally qualified.

4 S INGLEBY ODDIE

Mr Oddie was coroner for Central London until 1939, and as I have mentioned he published his autobiography which gives us some insight into life and death between the wars and contains a few comments which show the differences of thought between then and now. His views on judicial hanging would probably lead today to disciplinary proceedings and removal from office of any judge, however lowly, holding them. I quote what he says:

> Contrary to the usual idea, the modern condemned cell is far from depressing. It is large, light and airy with, in winter, a bright fire, and large windows and a cheerful view of a large stretch of sky.
>
> The modern execution in this country is wonderfully efficient and merciful… the reports one reads in the press that the sound of the trap falling can be heard by the other prisoners with a consequent demoralizing effect is just pure rubbish.
>
> The condemned man has only to walk across a corridor into what looks like and indeed is another cell. The floor in this room is really the scaffold and the man finds himself standing on the trap without knowing it. Indeed before he has time to realize where he is, he is dead.
>
> The average Englishman is a decent sort of fellow who does not like homicide and looks on secret poisoning as a low-down dirty game, as indeed it is. Nothing could be less brutal or more merciful than the modern method of carrying out the dread death sentence. (S Ingleby Oddie; Inquest 1941)

He had views on reform which are not so far removed from the wishes of many coroners today.

> If the example set in London were only adopted in the country our system would be perfectly adapted for ensuring that justice shall be done to the relatives of people killed in the streets or whilst at work, and that secret murderers shall be deterred or detected.
>
> The country should be divided up by counties into areas sufficiently large to justify the appointment of whole-time coroners with both medical and legal knowledge and experience. They should be provided with expert pathologists and with modern mortuaries fitted with refrigerating plant and suitable courts.

Here we have the government's wish to put the family at the heart of the inquest process, the desire for full-time professional coroners and the plea for proper resources and facilities. As we will see all of these are echoed seventy years later in the reform of the system. Unfortunately government did not provide any money to pay for the facilities identified by Mr Oddie.

Other stories in Mr Oddie's book also have modern day resonances. A terrorist murder by Irishmen in 1922 and deaths from flooding of the river Thames in 1928. In Cumbria a number of devastating floods have happened in recent years though the death toll has been mercifully low.

Also in the book is a comparison of murder statistics from across the world-USA 10,000pa, Germany 1,000pa, England 120pa. Nearly eighty years later the figures are – USA 12,253, Germany 716, UK 602. If you are basing your holiday plans purely on numbers of murders then it might be best to avoid South Africa with 17,805, Nigeria 17,059 and Brazil 50,674. The country with the worst murder rate was Honduras, 84.6 murders per 100,000 population. The figure for the United Kingdom is 0.9.

5 TREASURE

By the late twentieth century the one part of the jurisdiction that remained from the tax collecting role was treasure trove, renamed simply treasure in the 1996 Treasure Act. A brief definition of treasure trove is an object substantially of gold or silver deliberately hidden rather than lost. The Treasure Act 1997 redefined treasure as an object or at least two coins at least ten per cent gold or silver and over 300 years old. Alternatively at least ten coins over 300 years old. Treasure trove and treasure belong to the Crown but if they are not then the objects belong to the landowner or finder. Even where the Crown is the owner a reward is usually given to the landowner and/or finder equivalent to the value of the find.

The reform of the coroners' system made provision for a Coroner for Treasure to be appointed. In fact this has never happened and probably never will. Coroners local to the find are therefore still able to take a brief and welcome respite from a constant diet of death when a find is notified. Putting yourself into the mind of an unknown Roman or Viking to decide if they accidentally lost something or deliberately hid it sounds like an impossible challenge but solving this interesting mental puzzle was actually easier than it sounds because the help of experts at the British Museum was available.

I had for many years only done one such inquest but then a local museum employee Dot Bruns later Dot Boughton made contact with the local metal detectorists clubs. A detectorist is a person who uses a detector, and a detector is a piece of equipment, not a person. Dot ensured that finds were reported and in the last few years in post I had a steady supply of treasure inquests. The most important was a Viking find in the Furness area of dozens of coins and artefacts. I was visited by a local councillor and a different museum employee asking me to hold the inquest as quickly as I could. I assured them that I always did and explained that any delay was invariably caused by waiting for a report from the British Museum which could often take several months. If they had any influence there then progress might be faster. I duly held the inquest confirming the obvious, that the objects were treasure and they duly went on display at a local museum. There was a grand opening and the great and the good were invited. I in turn invite you to guess if I was sent an invitation.

A potentially greater find turned out rather differently. An elderly gentleman from a village near Barrow was convinced that the Holy Grail along with King John's lost Crown Jewels were secreted in a tomb in a church nearby. He based this on a very imaginative interpretation of unconnected facts and by drawing lines on maps between churches on the continent and in the UK.

My approach was that a coroner has to make legal findings about objects which have been found rather than go out looking for them which is what this gentleman wanted me to do. The episode was played out in the local paper, the *Evening Mail* to whom the story was gold dust in all senses. They ran the lovely headline 'Coroner won't Trail the Grail' but inevitably the story fizzled out. The press had kept asking me for quotes and explanations about my decision as if it was a serious issue and I remember once being pressed by a reporter on what I thought about this man I simply asked: "What do you think?" and received the reply "The man's a complete nutter". I say this not to disparage him but to illustrate how much respect we should give the press, always willing to do anything for a story, or at least a quote. I suppose by recording this I have got my own back in some small way.

FIFTEEN

Disasters

All coroners live in fear of a major disaster resulting in massive loss of life occurring on their territory. Plans are put in place by police, fire and ambulance services, the local NHS Trust and local authority after discussions with the coroner, in the fervent hope that those plans will never have to be put into practice. A major disaster with multiple loss of life can overwhelm even a full-time coroner's jurisdiction. In the course of many meetings and discussions over the years, many facts and comments emerged some of which were surprising and disturbing.

A police officer told me that the plane in the Lockerbie disaster actually exploded over Cumbria but its forward momentum took it into Scotland. Just a few minutes difference and my colleague, the late Ian Morton, from Carlisle would have been dealing with an inquest involving nearly 300 people, with each family entitled to be represented in person or by a lawyer. The logistics of holding such an inquest, and even finding a venue suitable, would have been very difficult to resolve. In Scotland Fatal Accident Inquiries are held but not as commonly as inquests in England.

At Lockerbie, bodies were stored at a local ice rink and no-one afterwards wanted to use it so when we in Cumbria were looking for potential sites for temporary mortuaries to house multiple bodies, there was a reluctance to agree. At one point we had various military bases lined up to house temporary facilities. This is what happened in London after the 7/7 bombings when the Honourable Artillery Company was used to construct temporary facilities for storing bodies, carrying out post mortems and identifying victims. The temporary structures were built across one of the oldest cricket pitches in the country. A major factor in the choice was the ability to screen off activities from television and press cameras. If they can film or photograph anything, they will. The cricket ground was well screened by buildings.

I visited the site when it was still in use but scaling down. Coroners were invited to see what could be achieved in a short time. A mortuary, a viewing suite and laboratories were in place. There was a bereavement suite elsewhere in London which several of us visited first. The taxi driver who ferried us between the two sites thanked me and my fellow passengers profusely for what we were doing – not that we were doing anything really – in redressing the desecration that had been inflicted on his city.

Two disasters occurred very close to my area but in the event did not affect me directly.

On 2 June 2010 I had been working at home and just missed the start of the one o'clock local news as I set off to Barrow. The first words I heard as I switched on the radio were "The exclusion zone now extends to Coniston" and I thought that Sellafield must have a major problem and that a nuclear cloud was heading my way. However it soon became apparent that there was a gunman on a rampage with a dozen people murdered. This was Derrick Bird who had a grudge against a couple of people. One was his own twin brother, the other was the family solicitor Kevin Commons who had appeared in an inquest I conducted. Bird shot them and then randomly shot others he did not even know.

When I arrived at my office the police station yard was empty of vehicles for the one and only time – every available hand had headed to the Whitehaven/Workington area where there was quite literally carnage. Dead and injured spread over a wide area, multiple crime scenes to protect and a gunman still for a time on the loose threatening anyone he came across. Bird shot himself and at least the hunt for him and the fear of more deaths was over.

In the next few days I was telephoned by pathologists who wanted to help me and a number of fellow coroners (from the cities) offering to help me deal with a case of multiple deaths. They were a bit deflated when I said it was nothing to do with me as it all happened on my neighbour's patch not mine. I found it a little disheartening that though some were genuinely offering help, other people clearly wanted to become associated with the case because of its notoriety. There was an implied suggestion from some that remote Cumbria would not be able to cope. One pressman asked this directly to an Assistant Chief Constable. I found this a patronising attitude, exemplified by *The Times* headline 'Hardy Cumbrians Mourn...' as if we all lived in barns on the fellside.

David Roberts had been a deputy coroner for years but HM Coroner for North and West Cumbria for only a few months. He had a very difficult start as he had to deal with not only Bird but also the Keswick bus crash where three people died. It should be recorded that David Roberts ensured that all post mortems were carried out very speedily and bodies released to the families within a few days. On 23 June 2010 there was a parliamentary debate in Westminster Hall in which all Cumbrian MPs took part and in which they rightly paid tribute to the West Cumbrian community and the emergency services for their response to Bird's rampage. Not one mentioned the contribution of the coroner ensuring that funerals were not delayed.

The inquests themselves were completed by March 2011 after a four week long hearing. To complete the inquests in this time was a remarkable achievement given the amount of evidence to put in order and the physical separation of the shootings meaning that each death had to be dealt with as a discrete event.

Bird's body was always kept separate from the bodies of the victims, in fact at the mortuary in Barrow with my complete agreement. This mirrored something from the 7/7 bombings in London. Because the killings were by bombs there were many small fragments of human tissue which were identified by DNA. The relatives of the victims did not object to the disposal of these small fragments together but were very insistent that they must not be mixed with any remains from the bombers.

For some reason the national impact of what Derrick Bird did is far less than Raoul Moat's killings, also in 2010. Moat killed his former girlfriend's partner, shot her and blinded a police officer. Moat later shot himself. It was not uncommon to have a conversation with someone and refer to 'The Derrick Bird shootings' and for the response to be 'Oh yes, Raoul Moat…'

The other disaster was the Morecambe Bay cockle pickers. Morecambe Bay is a wild and beautiful place, home to many thousands of birds. The tide comes in fast and relentlessly, along channels which can snake around you and cut you off. There is quicksand too. I have twice walked across the bay with hundreds of others led by Cedric Robinson the Queen's Guide to the Sands. Both times in summer in daylight.

Around the turn of the century the sands were being exploited by the harvesting of cockles to an industrial level by illegal operations using smuggled Chinese labour. This threatened the livelihood of a few local fishermen who had made a meagre living from fishing the sands in a way which sustained the shellfish and the flatfish called flukes. Some fishermen lived in and worked out of the village of Flookburgh. The local population largely supported the local fishermen and decried the fact that the commercial exploitation would ruin the natural balance of the bay for years to come.

So-called gangmasters were exploiting the foreign labourers by having them out on the sands at all times of day and night raking for cockles. On 5 February 2004 more than 20 Chinese workers were swept away by the incoming tide and perished. It must have been a fearful death for each of them. The thought of being on the sands at all in the dark is frightening and to realise that the tide is coming in must be truly terrifying. Hearing on the news that a search was under way for people missing on the sands and realising that at 10pm on a

February night this was a forlorn endeavour I prepared for bodies being washed ashore on the Cumbrian side of the bay. In fact they did not and the deaths were dealt with by the Lancaster coroner. As there was a criminal trial full inquests were not held.

Two disasters did affect me. One is the story in the next chapter, and only one person died. The other was unusual because for quite some time no-one realised that a disaster was happening at all. I will tell this story too.

SIXTEEN

Mrs. Margaret Masson
The Grayrigg Train Crash

I was watching television on 23 February, 2007 and saw a news report of a train crash north of Oxenholme which set me on high alert though it was not until 11.30pm that the police rang me direct and it was 12.40am when I was told that someone had died.

I continued to watch as further information became available through to about 3.00am, by which time I had had various telephone conversations with the police and had been informed that one person had definitely died and others were likely to do so. No-one else did. Knowing what happened and seeing photographs of where the train ended up (Figure 16), it is almost incredible that only one person died. She was Margaret Jane Cree Masson, who was born in 1922.

The train was the 5.15pm from Euston to Glasgow on the West Coast main line, a class 390 Pendolino of nine coaches. I often use the service between London and Oxenholme but this particular train did not stop there. About five miles north of Oxenholme, at a point where the line is actually orientated more or less west to east, a set of points had disintegrated to the extent that one side of the rail in the points had come up against the main line rail meaning that the space between the two rails was less than the standard gauge. When the wheels of the train came up against this obstruction, the train was forced up out of the track and derailed. It was travelling at approximately 95 miles an hour.

The photograph opposite (Figure 13) shows what the points looked like before the accident. The flanged wheels of the train pass along the main track, marked 'Normal route'. If the points were engaged to divert the train to the other track ('Reverse route') the points would move both rails together because they are attached to each other by three stretcher bars making the points a rigid structure. This is shown on the diagram that follows on page 166 (Figure 14). In each case the direction of travel is from the bottom of the picture to the top.

After the accident the points were as shown in the next photograph on page 167 (Figure15). The stretcher bars had disintegrated, the two rails of the points could move independently of each other and the left hand switch rail had moved against the fixed left hand rail thus reducing the overall width of the track.

Figure 13: The points before the accident.

The result is shown in the next photograph (Figure16) on page 169. Each time I see this I marvel that only one person died in the crash

☙ ☙ ☙ ☙ ☙ ☙ ☙ ☙

In the following few days I asked if I could go to see the scene to get a better idea of what had happened and the general lie of the land but those involved obviously did not want anybody present to interfere with the recovery of the train and the investigation by the experts and so I never did go to Grayrigg which is where it happened. In the early days after the crash I saw a BBC reporter describing the location as very remote and that a few miles behind him were services on the M6. "Some of you may even have driven past them" he said, implying that no-one sensible enough to be watching the BBC would make the mistake of stopping there. A patronising slander on Cumbria and Cumbrians.

Railway accidents are investigated by the Rail Accident Investigation Branch. They are not a branch of anything else and are a government agency. They work closely with the Department for Transport and their website is part of the government website. Their investigations are however independent. My first impressions of them were strange. They gave a presentation to the

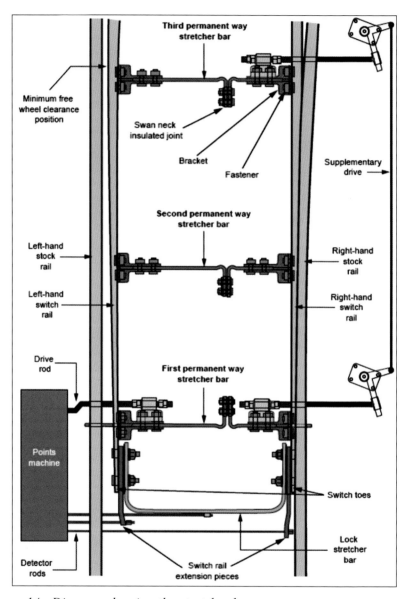

Figure 14: Diagram showing the stretcher bars.

Labels on figure:
- Swan neck from third stretcher bar
- Lock stretcher bar and left-hand detector rod disconnected from switch rail
- Fractured third stretcher bar
- Three bolts missing
- Second stretcher bar missing
- Fractured ligaments on first stretcher bar

Figure 15: The points after the accident.

Coroners' Society conference in 2007 and to my amazement it was a detailed explanation of how the Grayrigg crash had happened. There was far more information than I had at that stage and I felt like standing up in the middle of the talk and asking them to stop. Their philosophy is however to make information public as quickly as possible in order to prevent a problem from happening again. Once I accepted this and once it became clear that there would have to be an inquest rather than a public enquiry I began a very fruitful relationship with them and discovered that they are highly professional and expert and they had the personnel to cover various aspects of the crash and several witnesses at the inquest were Rail Accident Investigation Branch staff.

One of the consequences of the crash was that the High Court Judge who was conducting the Potters Bar inquest promptly adjourned it. The Potters Bar crash happened on 10 May 2002 and the focus of investigation was also points failure as it was at Grayrigg. Seven people died in the Potters Bar crash. The Judge thought there might be similarities between the two accidents. He was subsequently promoted to the Court of Appeal and so another judge, His Honour Judge Baker was appointed instead. Apparently he is the brother of Lord Justice Scott Baker who conducted the inquests into the deaths of Princess Diana and Dodi al Fayed.

For some time there was a possibility that the two inquests would be adjourned and instead there would be a public enquiry but after several months, the Minister for Transport decided not to adopt this course leaving the inquests to proceed. He did however say that the Department for Transport would "make funds available to the coroner to assist him in carrying out a full investigation". I never really did discover why he promised to do this because there was no obligation to do so, but Cumbria County Council was grateful to be relieved of a large financial burden.

In his announcement the Minister for Transport, Lord Adonis, said that he was satisfied that separate inquests would allow for the bereaved and injured to participate in a transparent forum open to public scrutiny. This is actually inaccurate because only certain persons have a right to participate in an inquest and that does not include survivors of the same incident. I wrote to ask the Department for Transport what he had meant by this and his response was that he thought that they could participate as witnesses. I found the way the Department for Transport communicated was strange. Though the Minister did respond directly to letters his officials would send me copies of correspondence with third parties without a covering letter or even a compliments slip. It was not clear if I was meant to respond or not.

I visited His Honour Judge Baker on 21 May 2010 to compare notes and learn what I could from the way he and his team were organising the inquest. Among the team available was a solicitor from the Department for Transport together with her assistant and leading counsel, i.e. a QC, James Dingemans and Junior Counsel to the Inquest, Jonathan Hough.

Although the Department for Transport had promised to pay the costs of the Grayrigg inquest as well as the Potters Bar inquest, they were more generous in the latter than in the inquest I had to conduct. In the event we did not have a solicitor or indeed anyone seconded from the Department for Transport nor did we have Leading Counsel to the Inquest. I was able to form a small team to help me consisting of a local recently retired solicitor, John Siddle, and a recently retired police officer, whose speciality was investigating road traffic accidents, Tony Foy. In the event, this team proved more than adequate for the job and I did have the benefit of working with Jonathan Hough who acted as the sole Counsel to the Inquest, a role I will explain later.

Although the accident at Grayrigg occurred in February 2007, a number of matters had to unfold before I could fix the actual inquest and these included the decision by the Minister for Transport on whether or not a public enquiry should be held and also the possibility of a criminal prosecution for the death of Mrs Masson.

When it became clear that the inquest would go ahead I convened a

Figure 16.

pre-inquest hearing. This was to set the parameters for the full hearing and it took place at Kendal on 6 May 2011. It was a happy gathering as several of those present had worked on the Potters Bar inquest in the summer of 2010. It had the atmosphere of a class reunion and it set the tone for the inquest to come. Representatives of all interested persons were invited. They all agreed that it would be appropriate for me to take up an invitation to visit Rail Accident Investigation Branch's premises at Derby. The potential complication was that coroners can only use evidence given in court and a seminar at Rail Accident Investigation Branch was certainly not in court, but the lawyers were very sensible and agreed there was much to gain from a clear initial understanding of what had happened. This would save much time at the inquest and it would be for a jury to decide the facts not me as coroner.

I visited Rail Accident Investigation Branch's premises at Derby on 13 July 2011 with my two assistants for the inquest, John Siddle and Tony Foy. This was also where I met Jonathan Hough for the first time. The seminar was very professional and it was far easier to assimilate what had happened in and before the accident in this way than it had been by reading the report and of course you can ask questions of the person presenting the lecture. The seminar was repeated later for the lawyers. I did not attend this but my two assistants did, to ensure that it was not turned into any kind of pseudo-court by over enthusiastic solicitors or barristers. This did not happen.

The preparation for the inquest was a huge undertaking stretching over many months. We needed a venue that was big enough for a full size court room and attached to it several offices for the use of those taking part, including somewhere quiet for the family. We managed this by booking County Offices,

Kendal, for several weeks in the hope that we would only need it for two, which is what happened. The inquest took place between 24 October and 4 November 2011. The offices belong to Cumbria County Council and they were entitled to charge a fee to the Department for Transport for the hire of the rooms in line with Lord Adonis's promise.

My room housed obviously myself, Jonathan Hough, John Siddle with a computer to keep all the administration ticking over and Colin Dickenson, my coroner's officer. Pete Gardiner, a police officer and later my coroner's officer, was there to take charge of the jury. Tony Foy was also there but his main job was in the court room ensuring that the correct pictures and documents were on the large screen for everyone to see as and when they were referred to. This was by far the largest team I had at any inquest.

There was a separate room for a transcription team, who produced each day's full transcript by the following morning and the press were also given a room. Previous experience showed that this was very well received by them. They normally do not have such facilities and they were extremely grateful that they could write their pieces somewhere in the dry and have facilities to email them to their newspaper or news desk.

Food was brought in for the coroner's team and separately for the jury each day to avoid having to go out into town and find somewhere to eat where you might anyway be bumping into witnesses and jury members. If I needed a bit of a breathing space then I had only a short walk of 100 yards or so to the back of the building where the River Kent runs and here I have seen all kinds of wildlife such as dippers and goosanders but I only saw the elusive otter after I retired.

The documentation for the lawyers ended up filling seven lever arch files, approximately three thousand pages. In order to make things more understandable and manageable for the jury we had a separate jury bundle of key photographs and documents which was much smaller. This smaller bundle was adequate in itself in my view. I am no fan of having reams of paper because in my experience it is hardly ever referred to and it is better to listen to people telling their story plainly and directly.

There were many legal representatives and these did vary from day to day and they included two QCs. They were Prashant Popat who represented Network Rail and Nicholas Hilliard on behalf of the Office of Rail Regulation, responsible for regulating Network Rail's activities and ensuring that railway operators comply with health and safety requirements. Anne Methera, solicitor, acted for Virgin Trains. The rail union was represented by John Sleightholme a barrister.

The family was also represented in the shape of Mrs Langley, the daughter, who had a solicitor, Soyub Patel; George Masson, the son and William Devlin the brother of Mrs Masson.

Jonathan Hough was counsel to the inquest. In effect he was my barrister. His job included help with the preparation of the case generally and the reduction of the paperwork to a manageable quantity. He asked the witnesses questions before the other lawyers just as I would do normally. This enabled me to concentrate on the answers and write down what I needed and to watch the body language of the witness more closely. It is difficult to do all of these things at once though in most inquests you have to. He also gave me advice and acted as a courier between the other lawyers and myself. It was in this role that he brought news of a legal googly that Mr Popat bowled at the end of the first week.

This needs a little legal explanation. Article 2 of the European Convention on Human Rights and Fundamental Freedoms gives people a right to life. This has been developed by the European Court to include a wide ranging investigation when someone dies while in the custody of the State. The Potters Bar inquest was conducted on the assumption that Article 2 applied. This was because everyone involved tacitly accepted that it did. Mr Popat suggested to Jonathan that in law it did not. The consequence would be that the questions posed to the jury at the end would not be so expansive. Mr Popat quoted a legal precedent that being on the railway did not put you in the hands of the State. Over the weekend we researched and called in help on the law from fellow coroners. I hope I do not offend anyone by missing them out but Professor Paul Matthews, Coroner for the City of London was very helpful. So was Chris Dorries, Coroner for Yorkshire South (West), in effect Sheffield and District, who was emailing as I recall it from a cruise ship in the Mediterranean, and Nicholas Rheinberg, Coroner for Cheshire. They all responded in their spare time at the weekend. This was the close-knit family of coroners in action. Every coroner knew every other coroner and we formed friendships from meeting at training weekends, conferences and Coroners' Society meetings.

We all came to the conclusion that Mr Popat was legally correct but that it made little difference. The witnesses were the same, the questions to them were not limited and the jury still had a number of questions to answer though perhaps not as wide ranging as we had anticipated. The representative of the Department for Transport who had liaised with me throughout was unimpressed and raced north by train from London to find out why they were financing what had suddenly become, in his mind, a second class inquest. Jonathan Hough soon mollified him, reminded him that the inquest into the deaths of Princess

Diana and Dodi Al-Fayed had not been under Article 2 and we were all able to get on with our task. I will never know if the Department for Transport would have paid the bill had they realised in advance that Article 2 did not apply.

A jury is a legal requirement when a death occurs on the railway and this added its own complications. In advance the jury had to be screened to ensure that we did not have anybody who worked on the railway or was a close relative of someone who did and it was also important to have people who could be taken away from their work for a lengthy period of time. Once the jury was picked, during the inquest, they had to remain entirely separate from the witnesses so they did not have private conversations. It was also necessary to ensure they had regular breaks and that they did not go off at a tangent and try to investigate events themselves by researching on the internet. Any court case is an artificial environment and decisions can only be reached on the strength of evidence heard in court by everyone. It was incumbent on me to ensure they were reminded about this regularly. As it happens the jury was extremely engaged from the start and asked many sensible and pertinent questions. A coroner's jury must consist of between seven and eleven people, not the dozen required in the Crown Court.

The points which had disintegrated were between the up and down mainline tracks. They had been found to be defective on previous occasions and put right. Ironically the points had become superfluous and were removed after the crash.

David Lewis was central to what happened at Grayrigg. He had spent his working life on railway track maintenance starting in 1978 and worked up through the ranks to a management position. He had then deliberately gone down a couple of rungs on the management structure in order to have more direct involvement with the track and management of the men who patrolled it. He was recruited to Carnforth early in 2006, as Track Section Manager, with responsibility for over 170 miles of track, of which between 40 and 45 were on the West Coast mainline. By the time he gave his evidence on 1st November, two of his superiors had already given us an idea of his approach to work. One was Paul Kingham who was Track Maintenance Engineer for Carnforth and Barrow, and therefore David Lewis' superior. He said of Mr Lewis:

he was pedantic, he was exceptionally considered and at times, some of the comments he made were over the top, but he was worried about the interests of the railway and the safety of his staff and his supervisors, so he was a very diligent person, he did not do things by half.

David Eyley was Maintenance Delivery Unit Manager and therefore responsible to see that track maintenance was properly carried out. He described David Lewis as:

hard working, dedicated, diligent and highly competent... [a man] who carried out his duties with enthusiasm and great professionalism.

Early in Mr Lewis' own evidence he was asked by Jonathan Hough what was the effect of enhanced permitted speeds on his job and he answered:

It meant that for West Coast mainline, working on it seven days a week went down to one day a week. So it limited everything that I wanted to do to only being done on Saturday night/Sunday.

This was because the increased line speeds following the upgrade of the West Coast mainline meant that maintenance staff could not go on the track whilst trains were running because it was simply too dangerous.

Mr Lewis highlighted this in an email, dated 17 February 2006, only a few weeks after he had taken up his post and this contained the following:

Ensuring the infrastructure is safe and fit for purpose is now becoming virtually impossible due to the restrictions and current methods in use in which we must carry out the most basic but important task, patrolling.

Part of Mr Lewis's responsibility was to carry out a periodic patrol of the track himself, and although this was different from the regular weekly patrols, he decided that he could carry out both functions at the same time. The important point was however that the supervisors' inspection that he was carrying out did not cover the same exact length of track as the normal weekly patrol and crucially it fell short of the points at Grayrigg/Lambrigg. The reason that Mr Lewis chose to combine the two roles was simply shortage of staff.

On Sunday, 18 February 2007, Mr Lewis left home at 5.00am and went to Oxenholme. He was driven to Paddy's Lane, 23 miles and 660 yards from Lancaster, looked at a specific problem he was aware of on a curve and then headed south. In other words he started the patrol south of the Grayrigg points, overlooking the fact that the standard patrol H, that he had agreed to do, started further north and would have included the points. A total distance of 1,520 yards was omitted from the inspection.

In the week between agreeing to do the basic patrol (Monday) and the day it was to be carried out (the following Sunday), Mr Lewis had had to deal with specific problems further north on the line, where speed restrictions had been imposed and when asked if there was any reason why he had forgotten that he had agreed to do the basic patrol as well as the supervisors patrol, he said it was simply that there were so many things going on at the same time that he remembered that he was going to start at Paddy's Lane and did not remember that he had agreed to cover the whole patrol which would have started slightly further north.

On Friday, 23 February, the day of the derailment, Mr Lewis was notified and went to the scene arriving at around 10.00pm but it was the following morning on the telephone when he was asked about patrol H having not been done that he immediately realised that he had agreed to do that and had not done it and he accepted responsibility at once.

In questions from Mr Popat, he was asked if his failure to carry out the inspection on 18 February was a tragic mistake and he answered: "yes it is a bit ironic that the guy who... flagged everything up was the guy who did not do the patrol."

As with many accidents or events, the immediate cause can be worked out but the more thought one gives the more apparent it is that other more distant events have had unexpected consequences.

The upgrade of the West Coast mainline around the turn of the millennium meant that the trains could run at higher speeds and because of the geography of the track it became impossible to patrol and inspect the track whilst trains were running even if a guard was posted. This meant that maintenance, including inspection, was carried out in the brief period when trains were not scheduled to run which was from about 11pm on a Saturday night until about 10am on a Sunday morning. In the winter this meant that there was only a short period of time to look at the state of the track and it became clear that there were tensions between the maintenance team on the one hand and the people who ran the trains and who wanted 'possession' of the line back as early as possible with the result that track walkers were being pressured to complete their inspections.

It is perhaps surprising that the track can fall apart so quickly but trains weigh several hundred tons and can travel at 140 mph so the forces must be immense. The speed limit for the line where the accident happened was 95 mph. The track including the points was last inspected on 11 February 2007 and should have been looked at again on 18 February, the day Mr Lewis carried out the inspection, but started too far south. By 23 February various nuts and bolts had come loose and the three stretcher bars which connect the switch rails in the points were broken or missing. This meant that the two rails could move independently of each other and the left hand switch rail came up against the fixed rail which reduced the clearance for the train to pass to such an extent that it was forced upwards and came off the tracks at 95 mph.

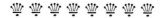

It is not often that you can have a bit of fun in an inquest because of the inherent seriousness of what you are talking about but we did manage one bit of levity when Mr McCormick, Acting Track Chargeman, was giving evidence. He was being asked questions by Mr Hough about nuts missing from the stretcher bar in the points set-up and this is how it went:

Question: Were they greasy?

Answer: Yes, kind of clarty you might describe them.

Question: Was the thread clean or did it have anything on it from the elements?

Answer: They were not clean, no. As I say in general, a clarty condition you might describe them.

At this point the assembled galaxy of legal talent was looking a little confused, and in particular Mr Popat was shrugging his shoulders and mouthing 'what?' at me. So I chipped in.

Coroner: Clarty is dirty. We all know what it means but…

Mr Hough: Yes, the fancy lawyers from London may not.

☙ ☙ ☙ ☙ ☙ ☙ ☙ ☙

Jonathan Hough suggested a move towards the end of my summing up to the jury, the point of which was to try to ensure there would be no appeal. He suggested that I send the jury out just before I had finished the summing up and ask the lawyers directly:

"Is there anything that any of you wish to draw to my attention? Is there anything that any of you want me to correct, add to or say in some kind of different manner? Can I just check through each of you in turn?"

None of them had anything to say and fortunately nobody did appeal but if they had they would have had some explaining to do as to why they had not taken this opportunity to put things right.

☙ ☙ ☙ ☙ ☙ ☙ ☙ ☙

An inquest has a function limited by law to discovering who the deceased was, how, when and where she died and completing the necessary documentation to enable the death to be registered. It is not meant to be a mediation or some kind of truth and reconciliation commission but sometimes these things can come about and when they do it is incredibly rewarding to all concerned and it did happen in the Grayrigg inquest.

Mr George Masson, who had started with intense feelings against David Lewis, ended by saying this:

In relation to this inspection and Mr Lewis, what this man did was a genuine mistake and he has my utmost respect. He will suffer from this for the rest of his life; the same as we are.

Mr Devlin agreed with what Mr Masson said.

It is also strictly not part of the remit of an inquest to exonerate anybody but everybody agreed that the driver of the train, Mr Black, needed some kind of reassurance that there was nothing different he could have done and it was agreed that rather than put a question to the jury I should deal with this which I did after the inquest was legally complete. I was able to tell him, with everybody's consent and approval that there was absolutely nothing that he could have done differently and I recorded the fact that he had been injured but still contacted his girlfriend Jan, who he had subsequently married, asking her "where am I, what am I supposed to be doing" and Jan was able to contact the railway authorities and ensure that there was no second crash and I described him as a man of extreme courage and character.

I was also able to tell the jury some of the understanding that had resulted from the Inquest. This is what I said:

> The day that Mr Lewis gave evidence, Mr Black went up to him. They shook hands. They acknowledged each others position. They parted on extremely good terms. They had never met before. That is of enormous benefit to both of them. Mr Lewis also talked to Mr Devlin and Mr Masson. That was on one of the days when Mrs Langley was not present so he did not speak to her. Again that went very well, it ended with no animosity. It was a spontaneous gesture. I hope it was helpful to Mr Lewis. It was certainly helpful to the family. That is not planned. It is something that happened and it is a huge benefit out of this process.

I also said words that I hoped would benefit Mr Lewis:

> I thought that Mr Lewis himself, when speaking publicly did so with enormous dignity, with a great deal of emotion and I do hope that he has gained some benefit from the process and come to some measure of peace with himself. I thought that he did again show a great deal of courage in the way he gave his evidence with no fudging and no trying to say anything different happened to what really has happened. I hope that was good for him.

I had noticed during the evidence of one witness, Andrew Jones, Head of Track Engineering at Network Rail, that he was clearly affected by some of the things that he had heard from the men who walked the track inspecting them. His role included maintaining and developing the standards that govern track engineering within the company, developing the policy for management of track assets to give the board assurance that the standards were sufficient and to act as professional leadership for professional engineers and track engineers within the company. He was the most senior engineer on track discipline at Network Rail. This is what I was able to say about my observations of Mr Jones:

> The other thing that I have observed in court is communication between different levels of staff on the railways who I do not think ever used to talk to each other. They managed each other top to bottom but I do not think they ever actually talked to each other. I think there were signs in several of the other witnesses that they were beginning to understand the point of view of the other people involved and to understand the realities of walking five miles up Shap on a Sunday morning when the rain is in your face. I think that was beneficial. Specifically Mr Andrew Jones – he was the Network Rail Track Engineer – I thought that he was visibly affected by what he had heard. We heard from him a couple of days ago. He pretty well said as much that he had begun to understand the true conditions that his men, as it were, were working in. I think that will stay with him for the rest of his working life. I certainly hope it will. But he, I think, had developed an understanding here that he had never had previously. I thought that he gave his evidence very impressively and with a great deal of humility. He was accepting that there were things that he had not known and he did now know and he would act accordingly in the future.

As the law stood at the time of the inquest, if a coroner believed that action should be taken to prevent similar deaths occurring in the future then he could report this to the person or authority who might have power to take that action. The point is obviously to learn lessons from what has happened once and try to stop it happening again. The coroner was not supposed to make recommendations and had no power to force anyone to take action, but could insist on a reply. This was the only aspect of coroners' law that had been strengthened in the few years before the inquest (though it has changed considerably since).

While the jury was out considering its verdict in relation to Mrs Masson and the answers to the questions posed to them the inquest was able to deal with the question of whether I ought to write such a letter or not. This was because the rule 43 question was for the coroner alone and the right of a jury to add a rider to its verdict was abolished years before. Potential recipients of a rule 43 letter seem to regard it as a slap on the wrist which it most certainly is not. As a consequence the practice was that lawyers and family could offer a point of view to the coroner about whether the letter should be written and if so what it should contain. I accepted that since my colleagues across the country followed this practice then I should too, though the rule put the onus on the coroner and his belief that action should be taken.

There were divided opinions, and in particular Network Rail did not want a letter written and even suggested at one point it might divert their staff from doing other work. Unfortunately, I was not quick enough to ask how many staff Network Rail employed, nor what their annual turn-over was. They employed well over thirty thousand and their turnover can be measured in billions of pounds. In the event I decided that it was appropriate to send a so-called Rule 43 letter. I wrote a single letter and circulated it as widely as possible. I wanted all the separate companies and agencies to see what I had to say and hoped that they would communicate with each other after reflection. The alternative was to write separate and different letters to Network Rail and to the train companies. The way I chose also allowed me to introduce a comment which was not made under rule 43 at all. This was the question of whether drivers of trains should wear seat belts. I highlighted the problem of lighting panels coming loose and potentially causing head injuries. This is best understood from the picture of the inside of the carriage after the crash (Figure 17). The panels are level with the tops of the seats and able to swing freely. They should be firmly attached to the carriage structure above the level of the windows, but had come loose.

Figure 17

As for the rule 43 letter, it is reproduced in full as Appendix II. The acronym on page 2, SIN stands for Special Inspection Notice which is a notice issued to people within the company to inspect specific parts of the railway infrastructure or carry out particular work.

Network Rail responded very constructively and at length and had clearly given much thought to the accident, the evidence given at the inquest and the rule 43 letter. The train companies were rather more defensive of their own position but they had clearly heard the evidence at the inquest and taken it on board.

☙ ☙ ☙ ☙ ☙ ☙ ☙ ☙

After the end of the inquest which was before lunchtime on Friday of the second week we were all able to relax and enjoy the lunch that had been sent in for the jury. They went out for a drink together and the foreman politely invited me to join them. I had to refuse because inevitably the talk would have come round to the inquest itself and that would have been improper.

During the buffet I said to the solicitor Anne Methera acting for Virgin Trains, that we had finished the inquest ahead of schedule and well within the budget. She said it was obviously good that I had satisfied these KPIs. I asked what on earth she was talking about and was informed it was Key Performance Indicators. I explained that coroners did not work with such matters but obviously we had in fact done a decent job. Coroners did return statistics to the Ministry of Justice and some of these were published but they were for information only and enabled one coroner to compare with another the average time it took to complete an inquest and similar facts but they were not meant to be used for criticism or disciplinary purposes.

☙ ☙ ☙ ☙ ☙ ☙ ☙ ☙

In April, 2012, Network Rail were fined £4 million for their breach of Health and Safety Regulations.

Looking back on the inquest now, ten years later I realise how successful it was and how enjoyable. For the only time in my career I had a team working around me to cover the administration I was used to doing for myself. They ensured the efficient management of the witnesses, the court room, the presentation of the evidence and the pictures for the jury the press and everyone else in court. Back at my office Alan Sharp was dealing with all the deaths being reported each day and he was so reliable I did not need to give this a second thought.

The inquest did bring out the facts, it did enable a degree of reconciliation between the family of Mrs Masson and the rail workers and it did change the perceptions and attitude of some managers.

SEVENTEEN

Babies

About ten years before I retired there was a series of deaths of babies at or shortly after birth in the maternity unit at Barrow. It is perhaps black humour to say that the day you are born is the second most dangerous day of your life (the most dangerous is the day you die) but the serious point is that birth is a complicated and risky process. Early in the twentieth century parents had larger families and perhaps expected to lose one or two children. By 2000 society expected childbirth to be a rewarding and uplifting experience with no danger attached. That was unrealistic but advances in medical science meant that the vast majority of mothers and babies did survive the trauma of childbirth.

It began to appear that there might be a problem at Barrow. I do not relate all the cases here. Families will hopefully have moved on emotionally and will not want to be reminded of tragedy, but I will record a few. One has nothing to do with maternity and problems at or just before birth and another has nothing to do with medical intervention.

1 JOSHUA TITCOMBE

Joshua Titcombe's life was very short and must have been very unpleasant for him. What happened certainly traumatised his family and had ramifications for many people which continue even now more than ten years later.

Joshua was born on 27 October 2008 at Furness General Hospital. He died at the Freeman Hospital in Newcastle eight days later and his father James approached me to investigate. I had to explain that the Newcastle coroner had legal jurisdiction. In fact the doctors in Newcastle and the coroner there had discussed Joshua's death, concluded it was natural and it had been registered. This highlighted a defect in the system of reporting deaths and how they are investigated which I will come back to later.

Mr Titcombe did not fully accept what I had told him and waited several months before asking me again to investigate. Eventually he did persuade the Newcastle coroner that an investigation was required and he immediately (with my approval) transferred jurisdiction to me.

In his book *Joshua's Story* Mr Titcombe takes exception to a letter I sent him at that point setting out the limits of an inquest and the way in which I would keep him informed of progress. He says this contact was negative. The reason I wrote to him in the way I did was that otherwise I feared daily or more frequent calls from Mr Titcombe. He had already displayed a habit of dropping a letter into the front desk of the police station late in the afternoon then ringing the same afternoon to ask what my response was. I could not cope with the level of contact I thought he expected and also I could not have James referring back possibly in the inquest itself to a comment I might have made months earlier.

An inquest has to be an objective investigation on behalf of the Crown. It is not the family's investigation and all witnesses have to be dealt with fairly and this means you have to retain a distance. Becoming too close to James might have led the Morecambe Bay Trust to saying I was prejudiced against them. I am sorry that James felt hurt and upset but at least the ground rules were clearly laid out in black and white.

In the event Mr Titcombe got his thorough and objective investigation and a public hearing lasting three days. His lawyer, Paula Sparks, a very capable barrister, was able to ask questions of the witnesses and between us we uncovered a number of problems and failures that led to Joshua's death. In an inquest questions are asked first by the coroner and then by lawyers for the other interested persons. This phase of course includes the family but also for example the Health Trust. In most court hearings the function of the judge is to adjudicate between competing parties – the two or more sides involved in a civil claim, or the prosecution and defence in a criminal case. A judge in these proceedings could in theory sit and listen without ever intervening or saying a word until both sides have put their cases. It is very different in an inquest where the coroner is at the hub of the case. This is because there are no competing parties to an inquest. The hearing is an enquiry to establish the facts, the truth. It has been said, perhaps maliciously, that civil and criminal cases are about winning and the truth is incidental, whereas in an inquest no-one wins or loses and establishing the truth is all that matters.

The hearing was of course necessary and was what James wanted, but it must have been very uncomfortable for him and his wife Hoa and his extended family and friends to sit through. The transcript of my summing up is thirty four pages long and it must have taken well over an hour to deliver. The following account is taken from my summing up.

I acknowledged to Mr and Mrs Titcombe the tragedy of the loss of their son Joshua. I noted that two doctors Dr Taufik and Dr Kumar acknowledged their loss, but that no other medical person did acknowledge that loss during the course of the inquest.

The cause of Joshua's death was bleeding in his left lung but the underlying cause was *pneumococcal sepsis* (infection). My verdict was that "Joshua died from natural causes following a number of missed opportunities to identify that he was ill and to provide him with appropriate treatment."

As I often said in inquests the verdict has a place in the process but it is a categorisation partly for statistical purposes and is not the central purpose of the inquest. The important part is the process itself – witnesses giving evidence in public on oath and available for questioning by those with a proper interest in the death.

Mrs Titcombe attended all her appointments during her pregnancy. Close to her due time her daughter picked up an infection at nursery and both parents were affected. This is central to what happened to Joshua. When Mrs Titcombe's waters broke she and her husband went to Furness General Hospital. They told medical staff about their infection (sore throat, headaches etc.) but that was not recorded in the notes and in essence that complication was ignored. It was nearly thirty six hours from rupture of membranes to Joshua's birth and the longer that period lasts the higher is the risk of infection being passed to the baby.

After the birth Mrs Titcombe became so unwell that she needed intravenous antibiotics, but no one considered whether that problem might have any bearing on Joshua and his wellbeing. An obstetrician treated Mrs Titcombe but no doctor ever looked at Joshua until after he had become extremely poorly. This was symptomatic of a deep rooted problem I saw and which was confirmed in a subsequent report. The midwives and the doctors were two separate teams and not integrated into one. I said: "I get the impression that doctors did not step on midwives' toes, did not come and look unless they were invited to do so by the midwives."

The midwives in question were referred to as the musketeers with an agenda of natural childbirth and involving doctors, who were in the main male, only as a last resort.

There was a hospital protocol which said that if a baby was born at less than full term (defined in the protocol as 37 weeks) the baby would be given antibiotics. Joshua was delivered at around 37 weeks but this cannot be a rigid date. The menstrual date would have made it 36 weeks (approximately) but the scan said 37 and that was taken as accurate so the protocol was not invoked and antibiotics were not given. One independent doctor from another hospital in evidence said she regarded full term as 38 weeks anyway.

I said that the protocol should have been used as a guide line but was applied as if it were a tramline. No one applied thought to what happened – Mrs Titcombe's collapse twenty minutes after Joshua's birth and the need for antibiotics; the lengthy time between rupture of membranes and birth; the illness suffered by the Titcombe family.

Joshua clearly had problems maintaining his temperature. A heater was brought in at one stage, he was put in a heated cot, but no midwife realised this meant Joshua might have an infection. In adults an infection increases temperature but in a new born child a low temperature is a warning sign for infection. This is part of basic midwifery training and knowledge, yet every midwife who was asked denied knowing that basic fact. This is what I said in summing up:

> I have got to say that the evidence given by the midwives on that specific point was so consistent and so clear, not one of them had any suspicion that a low temperature in a baby could indicate sepsis. I have to say, I think they got together at some point earlier and the discussion went something like this; well, some of them had forgotten that or never knew it, and some of them did, and I honestly believe that they collaborated and decided that they are going to stick together on that point, and say that, no, none of them knew that this was the case, a low temperature in a baby could be a sign of sepsis. I think some of them did know that. I find it absolutely inconceivable that nobody on the department knew that simple basic fact, which is in the textbooks, and which they ought to have learned in basic training, and it is all very well saying, "We never had training on that issue." No, they probably never did have specific training in-service to say low temperature equals suspicion of sepsis, but as Mr Halsall said this morning, "Well, you would not really need that, it is so obvious, it is basic that everybody should know that." A newborn baby cannot maintain temperature in a way that an adult can, is susceptible and as I say, I find it inconceivable that every single midwife on that unit did not know that as a basic fact.
>
> Moving on to Dr Olabi, he gave evidence that there is no national standard for a protocol on pre-labour spontaneous rupture of membranes. There are no NICE guidelines apparently, and he said a very interesting and a very telling remark, he said, "If we had been told that baby Joshua was not feeding well, was not maintaining his temperature, he was bubbling around the mouth, if all that had been documented" and these are his words, "We would have thrown the guidelines out of the window and treated the baby." Now, in one sense that says it all. The baby should be treated by the application of observation, expertise, and to an extent common sense, but unfortunately the guidelines were used rigidly and that had the effect that we all know.

Tony Halsall was Chief Executive of University Hospitals Morecambe Bay

NHS Trust and Dr Olabi a consultant paediatrician.

Once Joshua collapsed and doctors at last saw him he was transferred, very ill, to Manchester and then the following day to Newcastle where a technique unavailable at Manchester was tried. Sadly despite all their attempts to help Joshua, including surgery, he died on 5 November 2008.

At the end of my summing up I listed the problems which caused or contributed to Joshua's death:

> Firstly, there was a failure to listen to and understand what the family said, what their concerns were about their own illness and whether that might pass on to Joshua.
>
> There was a failure to record fully, or indeed on some occasions, to record at all many of the factors which, if they had been considered together, might have led to a greater degree of suspicion amongst the midwives and a referral to a paediatrician.
>
> There was a failure to understand the basic medical facts that a low temperature and/or failure to maintain a temperature can be a sign of infection in a neonate.
>
> There was a failure to notice and act on signs in Joshua, which should have prompted suspicion of infection.
>
> There was an absence of continuity of care pretty well throughout the whole period that Joshua was being seen by anybody from Furness General, and I include that before birth, when his Mum went in.
>
> Very relevant is the treatment of this protocol on pre-labour rupture of membranes, treatment of it as a rigid formula to follow and not as a tool to assist in reaching a considered diagnosis or at least to prompt a reference to have a doctor attend and assess calmly and fully.
>
> I think that Mrs Titcombe and Joshua were treated as two unrelated individuals, and thought was not given to the fact that if something was affecting Mrs Titcombe it might have a bearing on how Joshua was.
>
> There was a failure to think laterally, a failure to think holistically, not just for each of them, but for the two as mother and baby.
>
> There is a failure even now to acknowledge by some members of staff that the record keeping was inadequate.
>
> There is a failure by pretty well the whole of the staff to acknowledge that midwives acted as one team and doctors acted as a separate team, when to an outside observer they should act as a single integrated team.

Because Joshua's death was not the only one of a newborn baby around that period the Care Quality Commission and the Nursing and Midwifery Council became involved. Several midwives were disciplined and some struck off the register. Each time the press reported and said the family had finally learned what happened to Joshua, ignoring the fact that the tragic events had been gone over in detail in the inquest.

An inquiry was set up to look at provision of maternity services at Furness General Hospital. This was known as the Kirkup Inquiry. Initially they wrote to me demanding information on a large number of cases. I told them I would co-operate with their enquiry but asked them what their legal status was. It quickly became apparent that they had no powers to force me to do anything, but I did co-operate and supplied the information they wanted. I was also anxious to make a point, namely that coroners are independent judicial officers, not paid servants of central or local government.

When a baby at a non-specialist unit is very poorly he/she is transferred to a specialist centre. This could have been Manchester, Leeds, Newcastle, Liverpool, Burnley among others. So there was no particular centre receiving all the babies from Barrow and therefore no pattern was noted by anyone. Joshua's death had been certified and registered as natural. No-one had asked why he was in the state of health in which he arrived at Newcastle. That delayed the investigation by months. The Kirkup report includes a chapter on this point as if they had come to the conclusion by their own efforts. They do not acknowledge that they are simply regurgitating the information I supplied them.

In fact the report hardly acknowledges that inquests were held into many of the deaths which the Kirkup enquiry investigated and came to similar conclusions to theirs. They do say the inquest into Joshua's death should have been a wake-up call for the Trust but otherwise do not refer to the inquests. It is true to say that an inquest looks into a single death and a coroner has no power to link facts in one case to those in another. This may be a fault of the system and it has not been addressed in the reform process. Common themes did emerge from the series of inquests into the deaths of babies and I did refer my findings to the Trust and to the Department of Health. The inquests and their attendant publicity are what prompted the calls for a public enquiry. Once the deaths were known about and the inquests reported in the press the Trust had little choice but to acknowledge problems and to try to show they were dealing with them. The inquests were fundamental to uncovering what had happened and led to the Kirkup investigation and report.

2 ELLEANOR HOPE LOUISE BENNETT

In 2004 when Elleanor died her mother was told by a doctor that it was "just one of those things". She accepted that in the way that people did because they trusted the medical profession. Eight or nine years later the police were investigating Furness General Hospital following the revelations in the case of Joshua and others. When facts emerged Mrs Bennett wanted an inquest and she got one. It was clear from the notes that the baby's heart rate had not been monitored for 43 minutes during labour, which is an unacceptable delay. A memo was found from the head of midwifery saying that if she did not know that X was a competent midwife she would conclude negligence by omission. This midwife had been involved in other cases I had handled and was one of the 'musketeers' who wanted to keep doctors out of the delivery room. She was later disciplined and struck off. It took nearly ten years for Mrs Bennett to learn the truth.

James Titcombe attended at least part of the inquest and I was aware at one time that he was vigorously nodding his head but a little later shaking it. It is not always easy responding to the body language of the next of kin when you are summing up and to have this mute appraisal of what I was saying as I went along was worse. I made sure I did not look in Mr Titcombe's direction again during the hearing.

After the inquest I wrote an official letter of my findings to the Health Trust and the Department of Health. These letters are to alert the recipient of my findings and to indicate they can and should take action to avoid a repetition and possibly another death. They are not a slap on the wrist. You could describe them as official constructive feedback. Health Authorities however hated receiving them and always asked me at the inquest not to send such a letter usually saying that any shortcoming was recognised and had been dealt with.

After some reflection I wrote such a letter to the Chief Coroner himself. I wanted him to circulate other coroners, particularly those in major centres to the fact that babies were coming to them from smaller units like Barrow and no one was questioning why the baby was so poorly. This meant that no one picked up a pattern or realised there was a problem. The Chief Coroner has to be given a copy of any rule 43/rule 28 letter but he told me I could not actually make him the recipient of one. I wish in hindsight that I had not accepted this. I think it would have been constructive to alert coroners in centres where poorly babies are sent to the fact that more thought should be given by clinicians about the reasons for the state in which the babies arrived and coroners should ask more questions along these lines when deaths were reported.

The connected but still unresolved problem is that of stillbirth. If a baby never draws breath or shows other signs of life after delivery it is classed as stillborn. The difficulty is that this is not always totally clear. The importance of the distinction is that a baby who lives a short time and then dies attracts all the legal processes that an adult would. A baby stillborn does not warrant, in law, any investigation by a coroner. In fact the coroner has no legal power to investigate a stillbirth. The decision on whether the baby was or was not stillborn is taken by the medical staff in attendance and they may not be unbiased. I did hold inquests on babies when it was unclear whether they had breathed or not and on at least one occasion in the period for which Furness General was under scrutiny I returned a verdict that the baby was indeed stillborn. But by that time we had had a thorough investigation in court and unearthed shortcomings. The investigation was therefore meaningful and I think it helped the parents.

In 2017 and 2018 this topic has been in the national press as there is a move to have stillbirths investigated properly. This will require a change in the law and it is obviously a change which I would welcome. At the time of writing it looks as if the change may happen.

A consequence of the various deaths including the two I have related above was the building of a new unit at Furness General Hospital called South Lakes Birth Centre at a cost of £12million. This is a very modern building separate from the main hospital unlike the previous maternity unit, where it might be necessary to rush a mother in labour along a public corridor to an operating theatre even though the building was only 25 years old.

I hope that the new centre and a fresh attitude will enable trust to be rebuilt between the staff and the public. Several midwives were struck off and those who were not responsible for what happened must have been traumatised by the events around them and the negative publicity which went on for a decade. When things go right there is no publicity and recognition of the sterling work midwives do. I hope the new Birth Centre is a fitting memorial to those who died and some comfort to those who suffered deep hurt and loss.

3 Poppi

Very shortly before I retired I completed an inquest into the death of a baby called Poppi. This was to give me much grief in the first year of my retirement and result in the only successful appeal against a decision I had made. Somewhat ironically the appeal was made by my successor, David Roberts, who became coroner for the whole of Cumbria. Poppi died on 12 December 2012.

Family proceedings had taken place and in the course of those a hearing lasting something like thirteen days had taken place, enquiring into the circumstances of Poppi's death. The High Court Judge had come to a certain conclusion, on the balance of probabilities, and he also concluded that the cause of death was "unascertained".

If I were to come to the same conclusion as the High Court Judge as to how Poppi had come by her death, I would have had to be satisfied beyond reasonable doubt, a much higher level of proof.

Because of the various other legal proceedings and the police investigation, a long period had elapsed since Poppi's death and I thought it made sense to draw matters to a conclusion in order that the family could obtain a death certificate. The family proceedings were covered by a detailed and rather complicated court order, protecting some people from being identified but not everyone in the case. Throughout, I was concerned that I myself might breach this court order. A High Court order very clearly out-ranks a coroner.

The first step I took was to hold a pre-inquest review, which is a discussion about the process to be employed. Everyone involved with the case had a legal representative at this hearing – mother, father, police and local authority. I had the right to exclude the press, and I did, so that we could discuss things without fear of breaching the High Court order. One of the representatives was a QC and the other lawyers deferred to her seniority though they all agreed on the course of action that was proposed. This was that we would have a very short hearing, I would adopt the findings of the High Court Judge, which meant that the baby's cause of death would be recorded on the death certificate as 'Unascertained' and the only sensible verdict that I could record would be an Open Verdict. This hearing lasted about an hour.

I was helped by the fact that the Chief Coroner had issued his official guidance on inquests once family proceedings had taken place. The guidance said that the findings could be adopted to avoid duplication. The guidance was agreed by the President of the Family Division of the High Court, Mr Justice Mumby. I also corresponded with the High Court Judge who conducted the family proceedings on two occasions, receiving a response to my first letter but unfortunately none to my second which was the one in which I outlined what my proposals were once I had held the pre-inquest review.

In due course the forthcoming inquest was listed on the Cumbria County Council website but without using the baby's name. Many members of the press rang my office to check and clearly knew exactly who we were referring to. In due course several members of the national print and broadcast media turned up for the actual inquest which lasted only a few minutes and I did indeed record an Open Verdict and subsequently registered the death.

After my retirement, the media, particularly the *Times* and the *Guardian*, approached my successor, threatening to apply for Judicial Review and he, after taking advice, decided that the easiest thing for him to do was to apply for a new inquest, which he did, unopposed by anyone.

A few months after the order for a new inquest, the High Court Judge himself had a further hearing into the facts. It was made public that the father Paul Worthington had been found, on the balance of probabilities, to have assaulted his daughter sexually before she died. He denies this.

The result troubles me. In English law a person is innocent of a crime unless and until found guilty of it beyond reasonable doubt by a jury of his peers. Paul Worthington has been found guilty on the balance of probabilities by a single Judge and the whole world has been told so.

The press was annoyed I think at being unable to report the family proceedings and exerted pressure to get the information out via the inquest process instead. They claimed a public interest, a public right to know but I think they just saw a story which would run and run, as indeed it has.

The protection given to others in the family proceedings is largely illusory. Since the father's name was not protected, nor Poppi's, then in a small community many people would know the identity of everyone involved. As for the public right to know, if the press mean this then they should be reporting every inquest but in fact the national press report a tiny fraction of inquests and the local press do not always send a reporter. What the national press really want is a right to report any inquest they feel is interesting or prurient or salacious enough to sell papers. As you will have worked out I am extremely cynical about the motives of the national press.

After I retired I was tracked down at my own home by Ed Hanson, a BBC producer – literally doorstepped. It went against my nature but I did not invite him in and of course I did not comment about the case. He subsequently wrote to me inviting me to record an on camera interview about the Poppi Worthington case. He said "We want to ask you about the first inquest... some of the actions and the decisions you took and subsequent criticisms of the way the case was handled." This was nearly two years after I retired. The press has such power in our country. They bully people into making comments and they can then report part of the comment. I declined to go onto television to justify myself. I was answerable to the High Court, not to the media.

After three years the inquest was conducted by my successor, David Roberts. It lasted about eleven days. The press got their story. Paul Worthington was again said on the balance of probabilities to have sexually assaulted his daughter before she died in the unsafe sleeping arrangement of a bed. The cause of death was 'Asphyxiation' and a narrative verdict was recorded. "The deceased died as a result of her ability to breathe being compromised by an unsafe sleeping arrangement." There were calls for a public enquiry and a prosecution.

I received my second doorstepping by an independent journalist who drove up from Lancashire to ask if I regretted what I had done three years earlier. I responded in the only I could which was a dignified "No comment". Paul Worthington appealed David Roberts' decision but the appeal was unsuccessful.

4 ANONYMOUS

Many years ago I was told by the head of the maternity department at Barrow about a baby who had been born but died within a few hours. The story was that the parents, both seventeen, had been play fighting and the boy had accidentally kicked the girl, the placenta had separated and this was the cause of the baby suffering loss of blood supply in the womb leading in due course to his death. The doctor obviously believed the story and said they were just children and gave me a picture of the girl in bed, the dead baby next to her and the boy exhausted and asleep in the chair.

I took a much more cynical view, called in the police and insisted on a Home Office pathologist. The local pathologist did not want to do the post mortem anyway as the death involved some degree of violence. The police thought I was over-reacting, but they did their job professionally and came to a different opinion. First the pathologist confirmed that considerable force would have been necessary to rupture the placenta, then the mother accepted she had been out for the day and come back to find her partner had had his mates in, made a mess and been drinking and she told him what she thought. He reacted badly and in the course of the row kicked her in the stomach. The boy was charged with manslaughter and given two years probation.

I was left with a clear impression that some people thought I made a lot of fuss about not very much because "it's only a baby". I still think many years later that it was a lot of fuss about something very important. There was a lot of concern for the very young parents but I felt my obligation was to the baby. One of the reasons for the existence of the coroner is, to use the archaic language of one of the textbooks, "the prevention of clandestine murders" and this was one case where events that most people involved thought were innocent proved to be anything but.

EIGHTEEN

Legionnaires' Disease

Any building which emits potentially lethal fumes over the public is a source of great embarrassment to the organisation running the building. When that organisation is a local council it is even worse.

In the first week of August 2002, I was on holiday in China. At breakfast in the city of Wuhan, having recently disembarked from a Yangtze River cruiser, two people told me that they had seen on the BBC World News that there was an outbreak of Legionnaires' Disease at Barrow. There was no mention of any death at that point but a few days later my wife and I arrived back to Windermere railway station and in the taxi between there and home we heard the news confirming that a second death had by this time been announced.

That seemed to bring the holiday to an end before we had even arrived home and I spent the same afternoon finding out what was going on at the office. My deputy, Alan Sharp, and my assistant Charlie Johnson, had spent hours in the previous few days going through records, looking for deaths that might in retrospect have been caused by Legionnaires' Disease and the health authority must have gone through the same exercise in relation to deaths that had never been reported to the coroner at all, on the grounds that they appeared to be completely natural. Because criminal proceedings might follow the police were involved and post mortems were being sent as a routine to the Home Office pathologist Dr Alison Armour. Eventually she had to plead "No more" as she was being overwhelmed by post mortems on almost anyone who might have developed a chest infection whether or not there was any immediate connection with the place where the infection originated.

The source of the outbreak had been quickly tracked down and was Forum 28, a venue for shows with a café and directly opposite Barrow Town Hall. The building was run by Barrow Borough Council. There is a fairly narrow access way by the side of Forum 28 into Barrow's modern shopping area, and it was into this alleyway that I now remembered walking through musty smelling steam. I had thought it was pretty unpleasant and somehow or other thought it must be coming from the kitchens but in fact the kitchens are not on that side of the building at all and the fug was coming from an air-conditioning unit, about which I was to learn a great deal in the following months. Dozens of people became ill as a consequence of contact with the bacterium and seven people became the subjects of inquests.

Their names should be remembered and they were:

> Harriet Sarah Mary Low
> Wendy Anne Millburn
> Georgina Somerville
> Richard Gerred Macaulay
> June Miles
> Christine Margaret Merewood
> Elizabeth Dixon

Three of the victims were well over pensionable age but the other four were in their mid fifties. Just a year or two older than myself at the time.

It seems that most interesting stories cover a period of many years and Legionnaires' Disease certainly had its roots back in 1991 when the Civic Centre in Barrow was upgraded and refurbished and turned into Forum 28. Air conditioning was installed. This required the building of two cooling towers. This caused the factory inspector, Mr Yeo, to write to Barrow Borough Council on 18 July 1991, which included the following:

> I understand that the air conditioning system of the building incorporates a wet cooling system. It appears that a suitable package of measures for the control and treatment of any bacteria, such as *Legionella Typhi*, which could build up in the wet cooling tower had not been implemented. I understand that arrangements have been made for Norscot Cooling Services Ltd of Manchester to visit on 8 and 9 July to undertake the necessary remedial work, clean and disinfect the system, and to instigate a dosing regime.
>
> During my meeting of 4 July, I did express serious concern that the air conditioning system was being used without there being apparently any procedure for dosing the water. A decision was therefore taken to close the system forthwith and keep the units turned off until after the specialists have visited.
>
> I would draw your attention to the Health & Safety Executive Guidance note EH48 concerning Legionnaires' Disease risk and the guidance given to prevent the building up of any bacteria which could give rise to a *Legionella* risk. I understand that in the longer term you are considering the provision of an automatic dosing system. I would strongly recommend that this provision be made. I understand that automatic dosing systems, providing they are properly maintained, offer the best control against this risk.

Right at the start, therefore, it was foreseen what could go wrong and Barrow Borough Council was told but unfortunately the letter in question was not widely circulated within the council and the existence of the letter and the fact that the system had been closed down by the factory inspector was soon forgotten. As someone said to me, in a different context, "we have no corporate memory" and that certainly seems to have applied to the council.

As I said in my summing up at the inquest:

> The letter was the clearest possible warning to Barrow Borough Council of what could go wrong. It summarises a number of things that could go wrong. It uses the words "Legionella" and "Legionnaires" on three occasions. He (Mr Yeo) voices serious concerns and closes down the system in 1991. So, well done Mr Yeo. He did a good job at that point. He had got his points across, clearly, forcefully with no room for any misunderstanding on anybody's part and that should, to my mind, have set the scene for Forum 28 for the system air conditioning and the way it needed to be treated for all time to come.
>
> That letter went to Forum 28 and disappeared somewhere into a file, onto a shelf, we do not know where. We do not know really who read it at the time. I am sure somebody did. But what would have been extremely helpful I think is if somebody had had the foresight and imagination to say "That is quite important. This looks quite serious. They have shut the system down and maybe I ought to send a copy of this around to a few people who it might be interesting to" – maybe even the Chief Executive or the Town Clerk at that time or whoever it might have been. But circulation of that simple, forceful letter would have been extremely helpful in terms of what happened ten years later. As I say, Mr Yeo summarises what might go wrong and ten years later it all did just as he had predicted if the systems were not maintained properly. So he got it right and nobody really took on board what he was saying. So that is the first step and that is why I think it is important to go right back to 1991.

The second warning bell came from Kathleen Rae who worked for Norscot, the company to whom Barrow Borough Council contracted. This is what I said in the summing up:

> Kathleen Rae told Kevin Borthwick what was required in general terms. She did specifically tell him about Legionnaires' Disease testing which she said that he confused Legionnaires' testing with the dip slides which were the more regular testing for infection generally. I suspect that he never did make a differential between those two sets of testing and I think that others confused it as well and I think that had some bearing on what ultimately happened.
>
> Kathleen Rae also told Kevin Borthwick about registering the tower and so the company Norscot was leading, was telling the person that they were

dealing with at Forum 28, what to do and it was getting done at that point.

So, this was the second warning if you like. It is not as big a banner as Mr Yeo's letter but we have got a lady from a reputable company giving sensible advise to Mr Borthwick, which should, you would hope, have been reinforcing the message that had been got over in that letter from Mr Yeo. Sadly, the attempt to get that information across was not as successful as it might have been.

In 1994, the contract with Norscot was cancelled and replaced with one by George S Hall (this company had nothing whatsoever to do with the similarly named George Hall & Son Funeral Directors in Barrow-in-Furness). They employed another company called Streamline to carry out the work and this was successfully done until their contract ended on 31 December 2000. They did accept call-outs for a further period up to the 31 May 2001.

The next contract started on 1st September 2001 with a company called Interserve, but their responsibility was for a six monthly clean and chlorination and did not include water treatment. There was a suggestion that this could be done 'in house' but the Local Authority Environmental Health Department, which was asked to do it, immediately said that this was not something that they could get involved with but unfortunately the problem from that point was left in mid air.

Formal contracts were not drawn up. No-one checked that what Interserve were asked to do, covered all matters that the previous contractors had been doing and in the event Interserve did not carry-out the clean and chlorination which had therefore not been carried out for at least eleven months.

As I said in the summing up:

The overall picture is utter and total confusion between Barrow Borough Council on the one hand and Interserve on the other, resulting in inactivity. The supervision of the contract itself and the negotiation of it was Gill Beckingham's and the putting into place of the contract was extremely sloppy and was not followed up by a formal exchange of contracts. And as regards the supervision of the operation, the contract, once it came in, that was less than sloppy, it was just non-existent. Nobody was supervising the operation of the contract once it had come into force. As it happens, Interserve were not carrying it out very well anyway, so the lack of supervision was important.

So we have got a careless customer and a careless contractor with the possibility of a very bad outcome indeed. I have to say, I think in the event the outcome was worse than anybody involved at the time, could conceivably have imagined although imagination is not a faculty that any of them either had or used to any extent at all. They seemed to be working down tram lines. They were not opening their minds to the possibility of consequences to what they were doing or were not doing.

The engineer from Interserve, Andy MacDonald, first went to Forum 28 in December 2001 and in his evidence he described what he observed at Forum 28 in relation to the air conditioning system as "Beirut". He went on to explain that the electronics, the electrics were inadequate, they had not been maintained and the air conditioning chillers, the towers and boilers, were all in very poor condition. They were dangerous. There was some equipment without guards. He returned in January 2002 and was still deeply concerned by the state of the equipment he was supposed to maintain and he emailed to someone in his own company and to Gill Beckingham at Barrow Borough Council and took photographs of what he saw. Nobody responded to that first warning and later he also went to see Gill Beckingham in person and asked her "who is doing the water treatment" and she told him "we have our own chemists, environmental health will do it" though this was in fact not the case. He went back to Interserve, told them about the drums of chemicals not just being empty but covered in dust.

On a subsequent visit, Mr MacDonald noticed water running down the wall in the alleyway opposite Wilkinsons shop and again went to see Gill Beckingham to ask if the water was being treated and she asked him if he could give her a price for doing the work. Clearly nobody was treating the water and had not been doing for several months but no alarm bells went off in Barrow Borough Council about the possibility of serious consequences.

Again from my summing up:

> When Andy MacDonald went to Gill Beckingham in April/May 2002 and said "is the water being treated" and got the answer "No" we have effectively got precisely the same position as we had in 1991 before there was a dosing system. So if the imagination, memory, etc, etc, had come into force somebody – and specifically Gill Beckingham – might have thought "well in 1991 when we did not have a dosing system, the Health & Safety closed us down, closed that system down" but as I say they got precisely back to 1991 the system was there but the system was totally inoperative. But as I say, nobody thought this might be an immediate source of danger right now.

Somewhere around the turn of the millennium, Kevin Borthwick was informed that he was now the Health & Safety person at Forum 28 but he said in evidence to the inquest that he did absolutely nothing different after he was told he was Health & Safety compared to what he had done before.

On Monday, 29 July 2002, Dr Sue Partridge at Furness General Hospital noticed that there had been increased admissions to Furness General Hospital with pneumonia and that a larger than normal number of community patients were being tested for pneumonia. She did apply lateral thinking and by the following day the strain of the infection, *Legionella,* had been identified and very quickly the source of it was also identified thanks to Mr Philip Newton on Barrow Borough Council who had experienced the vapour cloud and received a phone call from Dr Partridge and he made a connection between the two which of course proved to be a correct connection.

Criminal court proceedings were instituted against Barrow Borough Council and Gill Beckingham individually. At the first trial in February 2005, the Judge dismissed a charge of manslaughter against Barrow Borough Council as a matter of law. Barrow Borough Council pleaded guilty to Health & Safety offences. The jury could not decide whether Gill Beckingham was guilty of manslaughter but did convict her of the Health & Safety offences and Miss Beckingham appealed successfully but there was a second trial in which she was acquitted of manslaughter but again found guilty of the Health & Safety offence and fined £15,000. Barrow Borough Council was fined £125,000 plus £90,000 costs and the judge said that he was aware of the paradox that fining a local authority effectively fined the rate payers and council tax payers and that if it had been a commercial company he would have fined them much more.

Only after all the criminal proceedings had ended could I carry on with an inquest. I gathered the families together to ask if they wanted me to go ahead with an inquest because the coroner has a discretion after a criminal trial whether to resume the inquest or not. They told me very strongly indeed that they did want to continue with an inquest and by doing so there was a formal legal process in which they could actually participate unlike the criminal trial in which they might have been witnesses and certainly could observe but could not for example ask questions or make comments.

The normal venue for inquests is Barrow Town Hall and clearly I could not hold the inquest there because it is the local authority's building and it is directly opposite Forum 28 so the inquest was held in the Magistrates' Court in Barrow over several days in June 2007.

Because of the medical conditions and complications in some of the deaths, the verdicts were not identical in all seven cases.

For Harriet Low, Wendy Millburn, Georgina Somerville, Christine Merewood and Richard Macaulay the verdict was "died as a direct consequence of an outbreak of Legionnaires' Disease".

For June Miles it was "Natural Causes contributed to by Legionnaires'

Disease". For Elizabeth Dixon it was "Natural Causes, the treatment of which was compromised in part by Legionnaires' Disease".

Tom Campbell, the Chief Executive of Barrow Borough Council, came under great pressure to resign but did not do so though he retired subsequently in 2012.

This was indeed a sorry episode in the history of Barrow-in-Furness. I hope that my part in the legal process helped some of the families. Towards the end of the summing up I said this:

> I was urged yesterday to ensure that the families have something positive out of this. What I can do is limited. The purpose of an inquest is to enquire into and establish the facts leading up to someone's death and I have no powers to sort out what has or has not happened since someone's death but I will say this: I hope and trust that things have changed at Barrow Borough Council in terms of the Health & Safety approach, culture, philosophy, call it what you will and that it is now going right through all of their activities. I hope that Barrow Borough Council will make public what strides they have taken over the past five years. As I understand it the Health & Safety Executive involved themselves in a re-engagement programme with Barrow Borough Council so there will be dialogue between them. So however the Council make that public is up to them. They have a website. They have no doubt the possibility of using the local paper. But I hope and expect that the Council will make public what strides they have made, if any, what strides they intend to make for the future and I hope they will keep that updated and I hope that that will be a further impetus to them to realise just how serious this issue is and that it will permeate all levels of the Council.
>
> Health & Safety is not just one of those troublesome things that we have to deal with and tick the right boxes. It is important and it has to go right through the Council.

As regards my final closing remarks, these were addressed very specifically to each of the families:

> I recognise and acknowledge the stress and disruption to your lives, the hurt that you have gone through over the judicial process by which I mean not just this judicial process but the criminal trials (because there were two of them) that had lasted in total very nearly five years. I recognise and acknowledge the dignity that you have conducted yourselves with here, throughout these stressful last few days. I acknowledge the patience that you have shown throughout. And I am going to say something at the very end: I suspect that if someone, anyone, had ever come to you and said "sorry" you would have been able to bear this a great deal easier than you have had to bear it. But as I understand

it, nobody has ever come to you and said "we are sorry" and I leave that in the air. I sincerely thank you all for your attendance – the families, the witnesses. That is the end of the inquest. Thank you all very much indeed.

This business of acknowledging and apologising is important. Lawyers and insurance companies tell clients not to say anything because they may be admitting legal liability and will therefore have to pay compensation. This applies to road accidents between individuals and medical mistakes as well. Politicians and others who make stupid remarks are adept at voicing regret if any offence has been caused. They are not good at accepting that they said something crass and using the word "sorry".

Sometimes it would in my view be far preferable for an organisation or individual to accept at an early stage that they have made a mistake and apologise directly and sincerely for it. The alternative fosters suspicion that the organisation is still hiding something. The victim or their family become frustrated at not being told the truth and feel disrespected. They go to their lawyers and any direct communication between the two sides is cut off. This is not a problem for the lawyers and their fees, but it prolongs the period of suffering and hostility. We saw in the Grayrigg inquest that when David Lewis acknowledged his mistake without prevarication or excuses that he earned the respect of Mrs Masson's family. James Titcombe's anger was fuelled not only by what had happened to his son, but also by the lies he was told and the closing of ranks at the hospital.

I think there is a lesson here for large organisations including health authorities and lawyers. I am not sniping at the legal profession. Remember that I was a solicitor for twenty years.

NINETEEN

Reform

1 TIME FOR CHANGE

The reform process started with Harold Shipman. He was a doctor but I deliberately decline to give him that title. He practised as a GP in Hyde Cheshire. He used his position to murder his patients. He was convicted at Preston Crown Court of fifteen murders. The enquiry carried out by Dame Janet Smith concluded he had murdered over two hundred and some suggestions put the figure at over six hundred. This is not meant to be a full account of Shipman and his activities, which have been recounted elsewhere and would fill several volumes, but a few words about his activities are needed.

Shipman did not usually report deaths to the coroner and wrote up medical certificates with a natural cause, which he justified retrospectively by going back to the patient's medical records on the computer and changing them so that they showed the patient complaining of symptoms that matched the cause of death which Shipman invented for them. In the very few cases he did report to the coroner he persuaded the coroner or his office staff that it was a matter of routine and there was no reason to investigate further. In some cases he stated on the medical certificate that the cause of death was "Natural Causes", an unacceptable cause but one not queried by the registrar. Those patients who were cremated were subject to a theoretical vetting by an independent doctor but in reality this was little more than a form filling exercise with no meaningful enquiry carried out.

The various regulatory officials that come into action when there is a death do by and large talk to each other but they are not integrated. A doctor was under no legal obligation ever to report a death to a coroner though of course most were happy to do so. The crematorium referee, a doctor, authorised cremations unless the coroner had been brought in, when it was the coroner who gave authority. The Registrar of Births and Deaths could authorise a burial but not a cremation. The coroner could issue authority for a burial but only if there was an inquest. Much of this nonsense originates at the start of the twentieth century when cremation first became available and stems from the fear that burning a body might allow a murderer to escape for lack of evidence. Cremation was therefore more strictly regulated than burial but all the systems in place worked independently of each other and the chance to integrate them all early in this century was lost.

The system of death registration should help to prevent undetected murders but it had failed to do so and when the activities of Shipman did come to light it was incumbent on government to take some action.

Government responded in the time honoured way by appointing not just one but two enquiries. One was to look at the Shipman case in detail (Dame Janet Smith) and she enquired into and made recommendations about the investigation and registration of death and concluded that there should be far reaching changes. The second enquiry under Tom Luce was specifically into the registration and coroners system and he came to the conclusion that the system was not fit for purpose in modern society.

He listed a number of critical defects in the system which I summarise below:

a) The systems of registration and the coroner are internally fragmented and separate from each other.
b) They deal with individual deaths not patterns or trends.
c) The coroner has no knowledge of deaths that are not reported.
d) There is no mechanism for checking that the death certification process is being carried out properly.
e) The coroner service is not subject to supervision, leadership, accountability or quality assurance.
f) There is no connection with other public health services for example in connection with deaths caused by drug abuse or adverse drug reactions.
g) There is a lack of clear participation rights for bereaved families and standards for their treatment and support.
h) Minority community wishes, traditions and religious beliefs have not always been acknowledged appropriately.
i) There is a lack of appropriate medical supervision over the death certification process.
j) There is inadequate training for coroner's officers.
k) Most coroners are part-time and often work as solicitors in private practice.
l) There is a lack of resources to deal with complex inquests including the absence of premises to house them.
m) There is no clear modern legal base for the conduct of death investigation, no process to encourage systems to adapt and develop and no agreed objectives and priorities.

The report recommended six major changes, as follows:

a) Coroners should be full-time legally qualified professionals and the number of coroner districts reduced to about 60.
b) Consistency of service to families underpinned by a family charter.
c) Each coroner's district should have a doctor acting as statutory medical assessor to oversee death certification, support the coroner and create links with public health and other public safety networks.
d) The procedure for disposal of a body should be the same for cremation or burial.
e) There should be more informative outcomes for coroners' investigations.
f) There should be proper recognition of the work and position of coroners' officers.

The report also recommended the appointment of a Chief Coroner, a rules committee to keep the system up to date, a link with other public interest agencies and a small inspectorate and compulsory training.

Dame Janet Smith in her report summarised what the new service's aims should be as follows:

> The aim of the new coroners' service should be to provide an independent cohesive system of death investigation and certification, readily accessible to and understood by the public. It should seek to establish the cause of every death and to record the formal details accurately for the purposes of registration and the collection of mortality statistics. It should seek to meet the needs and expectations of the bereaved. Its procedures should be designed to detect cases of homicide, medical error and neglect. It should provide a thorough and open investigation of all deaths giving rise to public concern. It should ensure that the knowledge gained from death investigation is applied for the prevention of avoidable death and injury in the future.

To achieve this Dame Janet proposed a national service with medical, legal and investigative expertise under national leadership to achieve some degree of consistency. She suggested the country be divided into ten regions each with three to seven districts, each with a medical coroner and a legal coroner. Every death would have to be reported to this service and procedures for cremation and burial would be the same. The service would have power to carry out random and targeted investigations. There would be fewer inquests but many would end with a written report. The cost implications were not addressed, presumably as Dame Janet was looking at what was wrong with the existing system and how this could be remedied. It would be a political decision what was actually to be done.

REFORM

Government responded to the two reports it had initiated with a Position Paper in March 2004 in which the Home Secretary of the day, David Blunkett, confirmed commitment to providing a world class death investigation and certification service with scrutiny of all death certificates by a medical examiner in the coroner's office. Then the paper undermines itself with this paragraph:

> 86. Our proposals have however been devised on the basis that a reformed system will be funded from existing resources in the coroner and death certification services. We will have to re-visit the proposals if the funds are not realisable or if the plans are too costly. Our final decisions will have regard to both affordability and value for money.

My summary of this is, yes we will do what Dame Janet and Tom Luce suggest provided it doesn't cost us any money. Inevitably it would cost money so the proposals were as good as thrown out.

By 2006 Harriet Harman was the minister responsible at the newly formed Department for Constitutional Affairs. She told parliament there would be reform, and started from the premise that "families frequently get overlooked during the inquest process" and there is no complaints system. This was an unpromising starting point if you were a coroner trying to make the system work with limited resources. Ms Harman said coroners would be full-time, there would be a Chief Coroner and inspection and training. The department issued a briefing which may be summarised as follows:

a) Bereaved to have better access to coroners and a coroners charter.
b) National leadership, a Chief Coroner accountable to government [may I comment that this should surely have been accountable to parliament?]
c) Coroners still to be appointed by local authorities.
d) All full-time coroners with new boundaries.
e) Modernised investigation process.
f) In a limited number of cases a discretion to complete the investigation in private.
g) Coroners to have better medical advice and support at a local and national level.

At this point it was clear that government had lost sight of the reason for reform. Although the appointment of a central overall figure, the Chief Coroner, would lead to guidance being issued and thus encourage consistency, the service itself was to remain locally based and locally funded and coroners officers were to remain police or local authority employees, rather than being brought into a new national stand-alone service. Whilst any improvement in the treatment of anyone involved in a death is to be welcomed the prime purpose of a death investigation system is to discover when death is avoidable or deliberate and learn lessons to prevent further similar deaths rather than to act as a bereavement counselling service.

A draft Bill was published in June 2006 which was subjected to pre-legislative scrutiny by the Constitutional Affairs Select Committee. It was critical of the Bill in a number of respects, including the failure to create a national service, the failure to reform death registration at the same time and what it regarded as the government trying to reform the system on the cheap. The Bill included no medical support for coroners. Government reflected on the scrutiny, altered its stance on some points but not on the main points of its proposed reform.

About this time, September 2006, a survey of recently bereaved people, carried out by IPSOS MORI was published. It found that 77% of those surveyed were either satisfied or very satisfied with the coroners service. This is a very high level of satisfaction especially in the circumstances of their involvement. Those surveyed were particularly happy with information given about the need for a post mortem, the outcome of post mortems and information about inquests, but less so about the fact they were not told they could obtain a copy of the post mortem report, and about delay. This was good for the morale of coroners who had felt unfairly criticised by Harriet Harman.

The first draft Bill faded into the background, but the legislative programme included a Coroners Bill which would be confirmed in the Queen's Speech in 2007. The Coroners' Society prepared a press release welcoming the Bill. This had been the subject of debate within the Coroners' Society. Some of us felt that an effusive endorsement would have left us hostages to fortune. We would have had to make sure the reform worked even if we were given no more resources, support or finance. We therefore gave a watered down welcome "subject to resources" and "within the framework available" etc.

In the event there was no mention whatever of the Bill in the Queen's Speech. It appeared to have been pulled at the very last minute. The excuse was lack of parliamentary time and subsequently there was an announcement that the government was still committed to reform.

The ministry continued to work on the proposed legislation and took feedback into account and further draft legislation emerged with coroners reform and criminal justice measures bundled together in the same Bill.

Ultimately an Act was passed – the Coroners and Justice Act 2009 – in circumstances which coroners had feared, i.e. it was passed through more or less on the nod as one of the numerous Acts that went through parliament just before it was dissolved, so very little discussion took place. The Act did not make the far-reaching changes the two enquiries had said were needed, in particular a national service, but it did bring into being the office of Chief Coroner.

The election resulted in a change of government, with a coalition of Conservative and Liberal Democrats. Very quickly after the election the Lord Chancellor was considering whether the Coroners and Justice Act should be implemented at all and by September 2010 a Ministry of Justice official said there would not be any appointment of a Chief Coroner and a few weeks after that the Ministry of Justice announced that the office of Chief Coroner would be abolished.

At a training course for coroners that I attended in June 2010 the Ministry of Justice official said over lunch to a few of us that although the Chief Coroner would not come into being some of the powers that were given to that office in the 2009 Act could still be used as the Justice Minister could exercise them. To a lawyer this is anathema. The unwritten constitution of our country is based on the separation of powers. Government must not interfere with the judiciary which must remain independent. Coroners may not be high in the judicial rankings but the principle had to be honoured. The same official in her formal address to the delegates took 35 minutes to tell us nothing and told us we must "work collaboratively in these challenging times".

In the event there was opposition to the abolition of the Chief Coroner before he even existed. This was led by Baroness Finlay in the House of Lords and the post was kept and in due course an appointment was made of His Honour Judge Peter Thornton. An appeals process that had been part of the Act was however scrapped. The Act was finally implemented on 25 July 2013 but really this was no way to carry out reform.

Terminology was changed, and coroners were now overseen by the Chief Coroner, but their appointment and payment remained in the hands of local councils. There was a move towards fewer coroners' areas so that coroners became full time rather than fit the job around a legal practice. Investigations could now be opened without opening an inquest so that if the cause of death was shown to be natural the investigation could be closed without having to go through a meaningless inquest.

In my view the outcome could have been so much better. A national service paid for by central government including the employment of investigators i.e. coroners' officers. Properly designed court centres with mortuaries attached. All of that would cost money which central government did not want to spend and so the reform was a series of compromises, rejecting the recommendations of the two reports commissioned by government. I fear that government works like this all the time. Compromise and negotiation with pressure groups rather than carrying out what is really in the best interests of the country. With the change in law I witnessed there was an element of farce as well because the changes passed through parliament before the election were partly scrapped afterwards without ever having been brought into force. The position of the Chief Coroner, created, then to be left dormant on the statute book but the position not filled, then to be abolished, then saved by a campaign waged by one vociferous Peeress. This is not in my view an efficient way to run the country.

2 HAROLD SHIPMAN, A FOOTNOTE

The purpose of this short note is to make a comment that I have not seen made elsewhere. Shipman was finally caught because he murdered Kathleen Grundy. She was 81 and Shipman recorded the cause of death as 'Old Age' which was quite inappropriate because she was a woman who was still very active in her local community. She also had a daughter who was a solicitor and when a home-made will came to light leaving a substantial sum of money (over £380,000) to Shipman and excluding her family, questions were inevitable. It was then discovered that Shipman had a typewriter which matched the one used to type the will.

My comment is that I wonder if the tiny part of Shipman which was still in the real world was deliberately sending out a message that said "Come and get me. Stop this from carrying on." I am not a psychologist but it seems to me that the forged will in that particular case with the daughter a solicitor, the money so considerable and the forgery so amateurish it may have been a deliberate white flag. His motivation for killing was not usually money but control and he seemed to enjoy the game he played of evading the rules. He was adored by many of his patients some of whom apparently still refuse to believe what he did.

I attended one day of his trial at Preston when the judge was summing up to the jury. As the public came out at one break I nearly said to those around me "He's as guilty as sin." Fortunately I stopped myself as I would have been addressing his loyal wife Primrose who did not accept his guilt. I learned something from the way the judge behaved. Mr Justice Forbes did not come in to court after everyone else and expect the assembly to rise in his honour. He came in to court and last of all brought the jury in thus showing their importance in the process and demonstrating his humility. I adopted the same order in the Grayrigg inquest. It was the same judge who sat on the preliminary hearing for judicial review in the Shafelia Ahmed case. As for Shipman he hanged himself in Wakefield Prison in 2004 the day before his fifty-eighth birthday.

3 THE CHIEF CORONER

The tortured genesis of the office of Chief Coroner is mentioned elsewhere. First created by statute; then to be discontinued then abolished and finally saved from an early demise by Baroness Finlay. The first Chief was the only one I worked under; His Honour Judge Peter Thornton QC. He was an Old Bailey judge and he devoted two or three days a week to his new appointment. He was already an Assistant Deputy Coroner in order to carry out an inquest into the death of Ian Tomlinson who died at the time of protests at the G7 meeting in London. The Coroners' Society therefore made him a member against the wishes of the Northern Coroners' Society. This made him privy to our website where we had always been able to vent steam about anything and everything in private. This was no longer possible and discussion of anything controversial ceased.

The Chief also decreed that coroners should not wear robes in court. Practice had varied: Manchester coroners wore robes from tradition, some London coroners wore robes and a wig. I wore robes on a total of four separate half days in the whole of my 25 years as coroner. At the start of two long inquests and on two other occasions, one the inquest into the death of a policeman. Apart from that I wore them on a few ceremonial occasions. As it happens the robes are probably the smartest of the judicial kind, being dark blue watered silk with a black collar. Perhaps we should take heart from the fact that the Judges in the highest court in the land, the Supreme Court, do not wear robes.

Although the Chief did thank us for our work when he had us all together he never in my experience managed to do so without a 'but' to take the edge off anything positive. His guidance on law and practice were clear and helpful apart from the bother I got into over Poppi by following his guidance on inquests following care proceedings.

The Chief published an article in the *Times* on 19 September 2013 listing the various changes and reforms in the 2009 Act. He ended it saying "with a fair wind these reforms will bring back public pride in their work." He repeated the words at a conference for local authority personnel which I attended with two officers of Cumbria County Council and at their request. I found his words negative and discouraging. Cumbria and specifically Kendal had considerable pride in their coroner already. Kendal always invited my wife and me to the ceremony where the outgoing Mayor hands over to the newly appointed Mayor. We also went to the annual parade along the main streets of Kendal from the Town Hall to the Parish Church. As I wore robes for this the vicar could be excused for asking where I was Mayor of.

Cumbria County Council wanted the Chief to visit the county, which he did. We wanted him to appreciate the size of the county and the fact it takes two hours to get from one end to the other, so I met him off the train at Oxenholme near Kendal, drove him to Barrow to meet my team and then on to Cockermouth. As we walked across to my car I had a very revealing exchange. I said "We don't know what your job is. Coroners' champion…" and he completed my sentence "…or government enforcer". After the visit he emailed to thank me but unfortunately sent it to the Stoke Coroner who also happens to be called Ian Smith. Peter Thornton retired in 2016 and was awarded a knighthood in 2017.

TWENTY

Conclusion

The office of coroner was unique in the judicial family. Right from the start the position was cut off from the main stream of the establishment, being an appointment to a district where the office holder lived. Because he was the exclusive custodian of that district and owed his position to local electors he would quickly develop a sense of having to protect it and its citizens. The isolation from other coroners would foster a spirit of independence. As society developed and became centralised in London the power of the coroner waned and he was left to reinvent himself. Some did so by doing nothing useful and others like Dr Wakley became champions of the under privileged and denouncers of injustice. The guardian of the King's income from the shires of the Middle Ages could announce himself as the people's judge. Those in power in London must have thought they were doing no harm and largely left them alone. Reference to the coroner as 'he' is accurate. Female coroners did not exist until the middle of the twentieth century and remained a small minority until the twenty-first when there was rapid movement to equality.

The inquest gave people a forum to air grievances if someone had died. Again its effectiveness varied with the character of the coroner. Some coroners kept questions to a minimum or disallowed them completely, but for many families it was their only chance to have a voice in a public hearing. The process of the inquest was a useful exercise regardless of the outcome and the verdict. Families have often told me the inquest gives them closure. This can be in the confirmation of the facts of someone's death or just because someone in an official position has taken the trouble to listen to what the family has to say and acknowledge their concerns. Remarkably often in relation to a death in hospital the family was not saying that the staff had caused the death, but that their loved one had not been fully respected at the time. How many times I heard that the patient had not been able to call for help because the call bell had been put out of reach.

The reform of coroners' law in the early twenty-first century was an opportunity to make the system fit for the present day by taking it away from local authority funding, and making it into a national service. This would have led to consistency across the country. Death registration should have been integrated with the coroners' service and medical referees introduced to check all deaths not dealt with by the coroner. They could also have looked for worrying trends and clusters of deaths. Medical referees are being introduced but only gradually and on a non-statutory basis. It remains to be seen whether the public regard them as independent of the local health authority.

The start of the process of reform was the uncovering of the most prolific mass murderer in British history. When Harriet Harman announced the first Bill the main elements of it were a charter for the bereaved, an easier appeals process to challenge coroners' rulings, a better mechanism to deal with complaints and a commitment to "put families at the centre". All this was laudable in its way but ignored the problem which started the reform process, namely the possibility of another Shipman coming along in the future and the need to introduce a robust, integrated and effective system to catch him or her.

As for myself, I was one of Her Majesty's Coroners for quarter of a century – thirty six years if you include my time as a deputy. During that time almost all of my colleagues did their best to uphold the oath they swore on taking office – to well and faithfully serve the Queen and the people of the district – but a few fell short. One or two solicitors stole money from their clients. One or two drank too much. Overall most tried to put the coroner's role ahead of everything else and were honoured to have a position in society they might not have expected. When I left private practice in 1995 I found I could give a better service because I could concentrate entirely on being coroner. Conversely it seemed to be the full time coroners especially in London who generated the most dissatisfaction. One was taken to the High Court well over a dozen times. Another, as it happens the first female coroner, who served Croydon was described in the superior court as "a mistress of discourtesy."

What I learned was to listen to what people had to say, and if the law allowed it then to give them what they wanted. I also learned to enjoy life as best you can, for it can be taken away by natural illness or by an external event often when least expected. Every time I climb a ladder I think of those who fell off. Every time I drive along the A590 I think of those who died in the many accidents along its way. There are some things I will never do. I will never travel on a motorcycle; the consequences can be so severe even in a low speed crash. I will never jump out of an aeroplane whether strapped to a parachute or to another person; it just is not worth the risk in my book. But I do drive and I fly abroad, putting my life in the hands of total strangers. I walk in the hills, but never rock climb.

On 23 October 2014 I retired.

The advent of the Chief Coroner was one factor in my decision to retire. I thrive on being trusted and allowed to get on with a job and I found the qualified thanks a great de-motivation.

Around the same time pathologists stopped performing post mortems at Barrow in favour of Lancaster. This meant that bodies had to be transported to Lancaster which is outside the county and was a round trip of about 100 miles. Several pathologists opted out of doing post mortems at all around this time. They felt the fee for doing the work was too low considering the responsibility involved and decided to concentrate on their NHS work.

Barrow Police Station was due to close and be replaced by a modern glass fronted building on the edge of town. I was not going to be allocated any space in it. Local government pensions were based on the best year's pay within the last three years, measured day to day, not on a financial year basis. On 24 October the payment I received for the Grayrigg inquest would fall out of the calculation forever and reduce my pension by several thousand pounds.

It was time to move on. Time to tend my garden. Time to travel. Time to watch more cricket.

But these are other stories.

MORE DEATHS THAN ONE

Appendices

I

Included with the consent of the Honorary Recorder of Chester and Resident Judge at Chester Crown Court

3 August 2012
Sentencing Remarks of Mr. Justice Roderick Evans
R -v-Iftikhar Ahmed and Farzana Ahmed

NOTE: there is an s.39 Order restricting reporting details relating to the youngest child, identified in these remarks as X.

The jury has found you both guilty of the murder of your daughter Shafilea. She was 17 years of age when you killed her. What was it that brought you two – her parents, the people who had given her life – to the point of killing her?

You, Iftikhar Ahmed, came to the United Kingdom when you were 10 years of age and you are fully familiar with western culture. Indeed, you married a Danish woman and had a son by her and lived, for some time, in Denmark. Then, in 1985, you returned to Pakistan and, while you were there, you married Farzana Ahmed, your first cousin. She lived in your home village in rural Pakistan. She had no experience of western culture but in 1986 you both came to England and settled here. You have lived here for the last 25 years. When you arrived here you, Farzana Ahmed, were pregnant with Shafilea. In due course, you had four other children, three daughters, Alesha, Mevish and X and a son, Junyad.

You chose to bring up your family in Warrington but, although you lived in Warrington, your social and cultural attitudes were those of rural Pakistan and it was those which you imposed upon your children.

Shafilea was a determined, able and ambitous girl who wanted to live a life which was normal in the country and in the town in which you had chosen to live and bring up your children. However, you could not tolerate the life that Shafilea wanted to live. You wanted your family to live in Pakistan in Warrington. Although she went to local schools, you objected to her socialising with girls from what has been referred to as "the white community". You objected to her wearing western clothes and you objected to her having contact with boys.

She was being squeezed between two cultures, the culture and way of life that she saw around her and wanted to embrace and the culture and way of life you wanted to impose upon her. A desire that she understood and appreciated the cultural heritage from which she came is perfectly understandable but an expectation that she live in a sealed cultural environment separate from the culture of the country in which she lived was unrealistic, destructive and cruel. The conflict between you and her increased in the last year of her life and you tried to impose your cultural values and attitudes on her by intimidation, bullying and the use of physical violence. She tried to escape and she was determined to do so because she knew what lay in store for her at your hands – being taken to Pakistan to be "sorted out" i.e. having her westernised ideas removed – and to be married off.

She ran away in February 2003 but you recaptured her, dragged her off the street and forced her into your car and, a week later, she was drugged and taken to Pakistan. I have no doubt that your intention was that she should remain in Pakistan and be married there. There came a time in Pakistan when she realised what her immediate future was going to be; she self-harmed by drinking bleach in order to frustrate your plans. She seriously injured herself and her condition deteriorated to such an extent after she had been left in Pakistan that she was no longer wanted as a bride. She was brought back to the United Kingdom where she received prolonged hospital treatment. On her discharge from hospital, even in her weakened condition, she continued to want freedom and to live the life she wanted for herself.

On the evening of 11 September 2003, you berated her for her behaviour and, in temper and frustration, you two suffocated her. It was you, Farzana Ahmed, who said to your husband "finish it here". While I accept that there was no pre-existing plan to kill Shafilea that night, that remark together with the evidence relating to whether or not Shafilea survived the drinking of bleach drives me to the conclusion that you two had previously discussed the way that you might ultimately resolve the problem which Shafilea presented for you.

Your problem was that, in what you referred to as your "community", Shafilea's conduct was bringing shame upon you and your concern about being shamed in your community was greater than your love of you child. In order to rid yourselves of that problem, you killed Shafilea by suffocating her in the presence of your other four children.

I express no concluded view on whether Junyad played any part in the killing of his sister but I have no doubt that, as the result of the distorted upbringing and values to which you subjected him, he told his surviving sisters, within minutes of them seeing Shafilea murdered by you, that Shafilea deserved it. Thereafter, you got rid of her body by dumping it or having it dumped in undergrowth on a riverbank in Cumbria and you told your children what to tell anybody who asked about the disappearance of Shafilea.

You killed one daughter, but you have blighted the lives of your remaining children. Alesha escaped but she is unlikely to be able to avoid the legacy of her upbringing. Mevish, after a period of trying to live independently, was recaptured and brought home and has since become compliant with your wishes. She came to court and was placed in the sad position of having to deny her own words in order to try to help the parents whom she, and no doubt all your surviving children, still care for. X was seven when she saw Shafilea killed and it is difficult to say what effect that has had upon her or will have upon her in the future. However, there is no difficulty in seeing the life which would have lain ahead of her, had she returned to live with you. That future is graphically set out in the Social Services notes of contact sessions between you and her in which you are recorded making clear your views of X's attitudes and what you expected in the future.

As to Junyad, he remains supportive, especially of you Iftikhar Ahmed. Whether that is simply out of filial affection or the result of the warped values you instilled in him, is impossible to tell.

There is only one sentence that I can impose upon you and that is a sentence of imprisonment for life.

However, I have to set the minimum period that you must spend in custody before you can be considered for parole. That has to be done in accordance with the sentencing regime which applied at the time you murdered Shafilea, that is, that which applied after 31 May 2002 and before 18 December 2003.

My first task is to identify the starting point for setting the minimum term. In my judgment, your culpability can, because of the circumstances of the murder, properly be described as exceptionally high and, therefore, I take the higher starting point.

I then have to consider the aggravating and mitigating features of the case to adjust that starting point appropriately ensuring, as I do, that the features which led me to adopt the higher starting point, are not considered again as aggravating features, in a way which would unfairly inflate the minimum term I set.

The first point to note is, of course, that your intention was to kill Shafilea. That is not an aggravating feature but it means that there can be no mitigation which a lesser intent would attract.

Mitigating Features

I accept, subject to what I have said, that there was no pre-existing plan to kill Shafilea that night.

The only other mitigating feature I can identify is the absence of previous convictions and that, while not wholly irrelevant, can in the circumstances of this case, have but little influence on the term I have to set.

Aggravating Features

I identify the following aggravating features in this case:

1. You were the people to whom Shafilea should have been able to look for protection and kindness. Your treatment of her and your killing her was as fundamental a breach of trust as can be imagined.

2. You acted together as a team to kill her.

3. In the year before you killed Shafilea, you subjected her to repeated violence; you abducted her from the street on 10 February, you drugged her to take her to Pakistan and you tried to arrange a marriage for her which was against her will.

4. Shafilea was in a vulnerable condition when you killed her. She was still weak from the effects of the ingestion of bleach which she had taken to try to avoid what you had planned for her in Pakistan.

5. A truly horrifying feature of this case is that you killed Shafilea in the presence of your other four children.

6. The killing was motivated by the cultural issues to which I have already referred.

7. After the killing, you concealed her body.

8. After the killing, not only did you lie and mislead people to cover up what you did, including lying on oath before the Coroner, but you also made your surviving children put forward an account which was intended to hide what you had done.

I have considered the impact of Paragraph 10 of Schedule 22 to the Criminal Justice Act 2003.

There is no basis upon which I should differentiate between you. The minimum term which in my judgment adequately reflects the seriousness of this case in respect of each of you, is 25 years.

You will not be eligible to be considered for parole until you have served those 25 years in prison. When you have done so, you will not be released automatically. You will be released only when the Parole Board is satisfied that you no longer present a danger.

The sentence, therefore, in respect of each of you is life imprisonment with a minimum term of 25 years from which will be deducted the number of days which you have served in custody during this case. In the case of each of you, I am told that you have been in custody for 66 days. If that figure proves inaccurate, it will be amended administratively.

H M CORONER

SOUTH & EAST CUMBRIA

Ian Smith LLB

Central Police Station, Market Street, Barrow in Furness, Cumbria LA14 2LE

Tel: 01229 818966   Fax: 01229 848953

Email: grayrigg.inquest@cumbriacc.gov.uk

GRAYRIGG INQUEST

Your Ref:
Our Ref: 171-2007/JW

10 November 2011

Network Rail, Virgin Trains, and Angel Trains

Dear Sirs

Re: **Derailment at Grayrigg – 23 February 2007**
Inquest: **October 24- November 4 2011 at Kendal**
Deceased: **Mrs Margaret Jane Cree Masson**

At the conclusion of the Inquest into Mrs Masson's death, I said that I proposed to write a letter under Rule 43 Coroners Rules 1984 (as amended). The Rule provides that where the evidence at an Inquest gives rise to a concern that circumstances creating a risk of other deaths will occur, or will continue to exist in the future, and in the Coroner's opinion action should be taken to prevent the occurrence or continuation of such circumstances, or to eliminate or reduce the risk of death created by such circumstances, the Coroner may report the circumstances to a person who the Coroner believes may have power to take such action.

Since I think it is appropriate that as many of the key parties as possible know what my concerns are, I am writing a single letter and in it I will mention the matters that are specifically giving me concern in the circumstances anticipated by Rule 43. I am also going to mention one matter which is not being referred under Rule 43 but which I think should be given some thought by the industry.

In making the points which follow, I should make clear that I do not intend to make any criticism of the Rail Accident Investigation Branch, which made detailed recommendations in its comprehensive report, or the Office of Rail Regulation, which has been carefully monitoring the progress of those recommendations.

Network Rail

The matters I wish to refer to Network Rail are track access, data capture and training/guidance. These issues can be listed separately but are in my view linked together, as I explain later.

Track Access

My main concern arising out of the evidence consistently given through the Inquest was that, on the West Coast Main Line, the access to the track to inspect it properly became severely limited upon the introduction of high speed trains, so that in effect the only track patrols that could be carried out in very many areas had to be done on a Sunday morning before the track was handed back at the end of a possession.

Although I was told that things had improved, in that there are now electronic warning systems that might be used in certain areas and there is some work being done on checking the track by train mounted surveillance in conjunction with a computer, it is obviously still the case that the track does need to be inspected by patrollers on a weekly basis. That inspection regime is a key element of the system for detecting and remedying safety critical faults, including defects in points. The time available for this in many areas is very limited, especially in winter, when true daylight can begin very late, especially in cloudy conditions, and patrollers may have only a couple of hours to do their job. I accept that there has been some change in the length of the patrols since 2007, which would reduce pressure of time. Nonetheless, the thought of a patroller, who might have been working during the previous night, carrying out a patrol in adverse weather conditions in winter gives me cause for concern, especially if he feels pressure of time.

I am aware that some work has been done on ensuring that future line improvement works are accompanied by reviews of the effects on track maintenance. However, I have no doubt that you will agree on the importance of ensuring that the time and conditions allowed for inspections generally are adequate to allow the mandated inspections to be carried out properly.

It is not for me to make recommendations, or to tell Network Rail how to run their operations, but it is appropriate for me to draw your attention to this and to say that the evidence of Mr Andrew Jones led me to think that he now had a thorough understanding of the conditions that his men on the ground had to work in, and I was heartened by his attitude.

Data Capture

One feature of this case which did cause some concern was that, before the derailment, Network Rail had limited data on the condition of points and other infrastructure assets. If inspections are performed properly and information about faults is recorded and captured in a structured way, it is possible for senior managers and engineers to identify trends and matters requiring attention. It is notable that the results of the SIN inspections on large numbers of points across the network after the derailment caused Mr Jones some surprise.

It is important that the exercise in data capture, which has begun, should be continued. I appreciate that this requires a very major effort. It also relies upon the co-operation of the staff on the ground fully reporting what they see, so that superiors will have a proper idea of the state of the track and the problems that do occur and will be able, on the strength of adequate data, to analyse problems and then deal with them.

Training / Guidance
This in turn requires my third concern to be addressed, namely the training of the men responsible for track inspection to an appropriate level and ensuring that the worksheets/job cards they work to are adequate for their needs in the real conditions that they experience through the year.

The evidence at the inquest indicated that, in early 2007, many of the relevant maintenance staff did not have training up to date. It also indicated that the materials they were using for inspections were not satisfactory.

I acknowledge once again that the evidence showed that progress had been made on these issues, which I do think are related, but I thought that re-enforcement of the problems was required.

Summary
I also consider it important to understand that the three matters which I have referred do link together, in that the men on the track need to understand fully the importance of information being fed back up the chain of command and for this training, and appropriate lengths of time on the track, are required. The three matters are not separate but are linked.

Virgin Trains/Angel Trains

Overhead Light Panels
As everyone knows, all of the panels in the front carriage of the derailed train at Grayrigg became detached to a greater or lesser extent and the panels further back in the train did not.

I have to say that the report carried out to assess this was based on very shaky mathematical foundations. Firstly, a claim was made that 8.1% of the panels in the train had detached, which is probably strictly speaking accurate but does not reflect the fact that every panel became detached in the front carriage. The report also made a massive assumption based on no particular data at all, that one serious and two minor head injuries had occurred/might occur as a consequence of panels detaching. There is, in fact, no evidence as to the number or severity of head injuries occurring in the Grayrigg derailment as a consequence of the panels detaching. In the report, there are figures quoted putting a notional cost on the injuries supposed and measuring this against the cost of refitting the whole fleet with better standard locks.

My first comment is that this looks at head injuries in purely financial terms and does not include any ethical dimension in the equation. Also, if the front carriage of a train is at particular risk of forces greater than the carriages further back in a derailment, then it might, for example, be appropriate to strengthen the locks in the front carriages of trains when they are taken out of service for regular maintenance. Once again, I am not making a recommendation. I am simply drawing to the attention of the industry my concerns in relation to this particular aspect of the derailment.

I acknowledge, of course, that in every other respect the train performed admirably. Indeed, its high crashworthiness standards were covered in detail at the inquest. I also acknowledge that the light panel locks complied with industry standards in force at the time (and indeed with standards now prevailing).

F.)int for Consideration – not Referred under Rule 43

Evidence was given that the train driver immediately after the derailment was forced into an upright position and very quickly was thrown around the cab and was unable to apply any emergency braking. I do not know any more than the driver himself, or the expert from the Rail Accident Investigation Branch, whether being in a position to apply the emergency brakes would have brought the train to a halt more quickly, nor do I know if that would have been a good thing or a bad thing.

However, I do wonder whether the industry should give consideration to whether drivers of trains should wear seat belts. The driver (Mr Black) himself was ambivalent about whether a seat belt would have been good or bad but I think it should be considered. I am not aware whether it has not been considered in any detail or whether (like passenger seatbelts) it has been reviewed extensively and rejected as an option.

With some diffidence, I wonder if the appropriate body to consider this is the Rail Safety and Standards Board – if they respond to the effect that it is not their concern then I would appreciate a suggestion from them as to where the suggestion should be referred.

Rule 43 Procedure

A copy of this letter will be sent to The Lord Chancellor, as required by law, and to all persons on the attached circulation list.

A response is required by law from Network Rail and Virgin Trains/Angel Trains within 8 weeks and a copy of those responses will be circulated to everyone on the circulation list. The Lord Chancellor's Department publishes from time to time summaries of Rule 43 Letters and the response to them.

I would also direct your attention to Rules 43 and 43A regarding the procedures associated with Rule 43 Letters.

I thank you for giving this letter your attention.

Yours faithfully

Ian Smith
H M Coroner

Acknowledgements

In the twenty years I worked in Barrow Police Station I had very few staff, and we always shared one room. Initially Charlie Johnson was my right hand man who kept the records meticulously as befits a solicitor's accounts clerk/book-keeper. He was my friend rather than an employee. We never had a cross word, though we did many crosswords.

Helen Towers, by nature and upbringing a farmer, became my secretary and later was part of a three way job share with Julie Watkin and Debbie Prescott. Julie died far too young. Helen and Debbie remain good friends of mine.

Alan Sharp was my deputy coroner and completed some long and difficult inquests for me and covered the office when I was away. I never had a moment's hesitation in leaving him to get on with what I had asked him to do. He always did it without fuss. I could not have wished for a better deputy.

John Siddle supported me with administration starting with the Grayrigg inquest. Collating hundreds of pages of potential evidence is not my forté, but he spared me this with good humour and also organised witness lists, and ensured they arrived on the correct day, were welcomed and had somewhere to stay if necessary. He loves cricket as much as I do.

Dick Binstead shared with me his experience of writing and publishing. He loves cricket too.

David Roberts allowed me access to my own files. When he became Coroner for Cumbria he became custodian of all records current and historic. He also allowed me use of his office space and shared his lunch time with me.

Will Bell from Cumbria County Council Records and Archives found all historic files I asked to see.

Caroline Summeray, Chris Dorries, Andre Rebello and Jean Harkins, all coroners, each identified the source of pieces of information or quotations I knew but could not pin down. Professor Paul Matthews did the same, and has since retired as coroner but become a judge. I have borrowed quotations from his book and Chris Dorries'.

Colin Dickenson was the coroner's officer in post when I retired. He stood alongside through some difficult inquests and kept calm with his dry sense of humour. He remains a friend. Likewise Pete Gardiner, always ready to step into the breach when an officer was needed.

Dr Adam Padel helped by talking to me about the pathologist's world.

Lisa Gartland and her colleagues at the Cockermouth office of the coroner welcomed me as I read files there, and supplied cups of coffee.

Retired police officers Doug Marshall and Mike Forrester helped me confirm information and Mike spent considerable time with me confirming where precisely Shafilea's body was left.

Ken McClurg, South Lakeland District Council made sure I could find Ian Allison's grave.

The staff at Chester Crown Court and the Honorary Recorder of Chester were helpful in confirming that I could reproduce the sentencing remarks in the Ahmed trial.

The Ballad of Reading Gaol by Oscar Wilde provided the title for the book though the poem has little to do with the world of coroners:

> *Yet each man kills the thing he loves,*
> *By each let this be heard,*
> *Some do it with a bitter look,*
> *Some with a flattering word.*
> *The coward does it with a kiss,*
> *The brave man with a sword!*
> *And the wild regrets, and the bloody sweats,*
> *None know so well as I,*
> *For he who lives more lives than one*
> *More deaths than one must die*

I give my sincere thanks to Dawn Robertson of Hayloft Publishing for turning my efforts into a real book.

I wish to place on record my thanks and profound debt to my parents Gladys and Don Smith. They never put pressure on me, always supported me and took quiet pride in anything I achieved. Thank you both.

To Aunty Hazel and Uncle Bill who took me and my brother David and their daughter Josephine to the Lake District in 1962, thank you. That trip helped set the course of my life, insofar as you can ever decide for yourself what that course will be.

Picture credits

The pictures of Farzana and Iftikhar Ahmed and DS Geraint Jones in the chapter on Shafilea Ahmed and of Gordon Park are all copyright of the Press Association. The picture of Carol Park was supplied by the Press Association but they do not claim copyright.

The picture of Shafilea is widely used on the internet and in the press and I do not know who owns the copyright.

The pictures and diagrams in the chapter on the Grayrigg train crash are all Crown copyright and are produced with permission of the Rail Accident Investigation Branch. They are taken from Rail Accident Investigation Branch Report 20/2008 "Derailment at Grayrigg 23 February 2007". I thank them sincerely for allowing me free use of this material.

The picture of me and Charlie Johnson is reproduced from a copy in my possession but the copyright belongs to the *North Western Evening Mail.*

The Campbell pictures were provided by Gina Campbell from her own albums and her support of my book has been well beyond what I could have expected. I thank you most sincerely.

Last and most certainly not least, Marian is my wife, my friend. She has encouraged and supported me. Her sleep was interrupted when the phone rang. She was upset when the media were difficult. I doubt I would have written this without her. Thank you for all you have done and for 30 years together. This book is dedicated to you for many good reasons.